Building Wealth in Israel

A Guide to
International Investments
and
Financial Planning

Douglas Goldstein, CFP®

southern hills PRESS

Published by Southern Hills Press, Pittsburgh, PA, USA.
Distributed by Devora Publishing, Jerusalem • New York

Goldstein, Douglas

Building Wealth in Israel: A Guide to International Investments and Financial Planning / Douglas Goldstein, with guest chapter by Leon Harris (printed with permission).

Includes index.

ISBN 1-932687-84-X

1. Financial planning   2. Investments   3. Israel

Special sales
Companies, professional groups, clubs, and other organizations may qualify for special terms for bulk purchases. Special editions, including personalized covers, excerpts of existing books, and corporate imprints, can be created in large quantities for special needs. For more information, e-mail: sales@southernhillspress.com.

Printed and bound in the United States.

Typeset by Raphaël Freeman, Jerusalem Typesetting, www.jerusalemtype.com
Cover design by Yitz Wolfe, Israel
Cover photo by Yehoshua Halevi
Index by Marc I. Sherman

*In memory of my grandparents who were great
grandparents and great stock pickers*

❦

*For BatSheva and our growing dividends,
Ayala, Chana, Efraim, and Yosef*

Contents

ployee Stock Options · Stop and Think · Review of American Plans · More About IRAS · Roth IRAS · Contributing to Your IRA from Abroad · U.S. Social Security · Working for an American Company in Israel · Working for Yourself · Summary

Chapter 8 Creating a Budget 145

Are You Making Ends Meet? · Building a Budget · Money Coming In · Money Going Out · Helpful Hints for a Successful Budget · Will Your Budget Work? · Can Your Budget Keep up with Inflation? · The Need to Save · Overdraft · Where Does Your Money Go? · Summary

Chapter 9 Planning for Your Future 163

Who Should Have a Financial Plan? · Begin with a Financial "Snapshot" · Set Your Goals · Take Time to Determine Your Risk Tolerance · Be Aware of Potential Problems · Let Someone Else Share Your Risks · Set up an Asset Allocation Model · Rule of 72: Are We There Yet? · Different Strokes for Different Folks · Let Your Financial Plan Be Your Guide · Follow Your Plan · Summary

Chapter 10 The Importance of Estate Planning 179

You Can't Take it with You · Will Your Heirs Have Problems? · Estate Tax Exclusions · Unlimited Marital Deduction · Before You Think of the Hereafter · Why Do People Need Wills and Trusts? · Begin with Your Will · Who Will Love Your Children? · Who Should Be the Executor? · Review and Update Documents Regularly · Will or Trust? · Keeping Your Assets in a Trust · Revocable vs. Irrevocable · Should You Set up a Trust? · Common Trust Concepts · Not All Trusts Are Suitable · Do You Need Expert Advice? · Who Will Be on Your Advisory Team? · Summary

Chapter 11 Dealing with Financial Success (Part I) 199

Who Will Help You? · What Is a "Managed Money" Account? · Are Managed Accounts for You? · Fees · For Now and for the Future

Dealing with *Serious* Financial Success (Part II) 207

Who are the Very Wealthy? · The Team Approach · The Family Office · Family Offices Make Philanthropy More Efficient · The Multi-Family Office: A Sharing Solution · Summary

Chapter 12 An Overview: Two Countries – Two Tax Codes 215

The U.S.-Israel Tax Treaty · Israeli Income Tax · Filing Your U.S. Tax Return from Overseas · Foreign Earned Income · Change Your Address on File with the IRS · Extensions · Foreign Currency and Tax Returns · Non-resident Alien

Acknowledgements

Some authors hesitate to list the names of those who helped them complete their books. The fear stems from the concern that someone's name might inadvertently fail to appear. Lightening that apprehension, I can only apologize to all those friends, missing from this list of "thank yous," who have assisted me along the way and take a few precious lines to thank…

The Profile Investment team – Sandy Ohana, Aaron Katsman, Henry Valier, Gavriella Gobrin, Yoram Ohana, Shmuel Bowman, Yechiel Leiter, Rachel Jacobs, and Naomi Grossman; my professional advisors and friends, Michael Sacofsky, Allan Jerichower, Alan Deutsch, Ira Hauser, Stuart Schnee, Devorah and Stuart Bensusan, Errol Melman, Carl Sherer, Leon Harris (whose help included writing a chapter of the book), Phyllis Singer, and Zev Stub; Tony Camejo and his highly professional and talented team at Portfolio Resources Group; my creative friend, Shmuel Lhungdim, who drew the phenomenal cartoons in these pages; my clients, who have helped Profile develop into a resource for all people looking to understand and handle their international investments; my readers from the *Jerusalem Post* whose questions and comments over the years have been an inspiration to write this book; my parents for their ongoing support – and my mother in particular who, after retiring as an Associate Vice President with Dean Witter, agreed to review and edit this text; and my wonderful wife, whose tireless efforts behind the scenes, constant encouragement, endless patience, and kind words of support led to the creation of this book.

About the Author

Douglas Goldstein, a Certified Financial Planner™ (CFP®) and licensed investment professional both in the United States and Israel, is the owner and director of Profile Investment Services, Ltd. (est. 1997). Through its Jerusalem and Tel Aviv offices, Profile offers high-level planning, investment strategies, and services for an international clientele. Also, as the managing director and senior board member of America Israel Investment Associates, LLC, a Miami-based money management firm, Goldstein provides additional financial opportunities for investors around the world. His career began on Wall Street in 1992 at Dean Witter. After developing a successful practice in New York, he moved with his wife and family (now four children) to Israel. Accredited by the Israel Securities Authority and by the NASD, he has qualified as a registered investment advisor, is a member of the Financial Planning Association, holds a TEP designation as a member of the Society of Trust and Estate Practitioners, and is an associate of Portfolio Resources Group, Inc. (member NASD, SIPC, SIA), an international financial services company. Mr. Goldstein is frequently invited to give lectures on investing, to comment on financial affairs on the radio, TV, and in local and international newspapers, and to serve as a trainer and consultant to banks in Israel. His weekly financial advice, which has appeared in *The Jerusalem Post* for over seven years, provides important and timely guidance to his readers.

Introduction

Should You Read This Book?

If you feel that your existing investments don't quite have the growth potential you've been hoping for, or if you suspect that your current financial situation lacks the structure necessary to help you achieve your financial goals, this book is for you.

After many years of working in financial services both in the U.S. and here in Israel, I decided to write a book that would specifically focus on the unique financial requirements of those people who have moved to Israel, or who are considering making such a move. Dealing with multiple currencies, international tax codes, a dizzying array of investment products, and numerous other issues, *olim* (immigrants to Israel), and long-time residents alike, often need professional help in managing their affairs. Hopefully this book will provide some of the answers.

As a financial planner, I often serve in the role of Chief Financial Officer for my clients. In that position, I help them organize their overall financial situations. That means I coordinate with clients' advisors on wills and trusts, and various tax and insurance issues to develop a total financial picture. As you read these chapters, you may find some important questions about your own circumstances that you certainly should raise with your advisors.

After you've completed the book, if you'd like additional financial ideas, take a look at the "Education" tab of the Profile Investments website, www.profile-financial.com. There's a lot of free and useful information designed to help people with their international investment questions.

Thanks for investing your time in reading this book.

Doug

Douglas Goldstein, CFP®
doug@profile-financial.com
Jerusalem, Israel

Prologue

You are a contestant in a new game show. It's called, "Let's Make *Aliya*." You've made it to the final round, and now you have to choose between two closed doors. The host tells you that behind **Door Number One** is a secure economic future in the land of your birth. Behind **Door Number Two** lies a destiny filled with idealism and Zionism. Which do you choose?

The big **Blue and White Door** to Israel, of course!

You made the right choice. Luckily for the weak-hearted among us, the days of draining swamps and swatting mosquitoes are long gone. Israelis today can visit Biblical sites in the morning and enjoy the convenience and luxury of air-conditioned malls in the afternoon. *Makolet* (mini-market) shelves overflow with both essentials and delicacies, and we no longer need to entreat relatives coming to visit to bring over some Nescafé or Cheerios. We can get those on our own. Schools abound, and medical facilities compete with one another to offer better services. Yet, not everyone is upbeat. For many Americans about to make *aliya*, there is still a feeling of uncertainty. What economic situation lies ahead? What will be encountered beyond the tarmac of Ben Gurion airport?

Material comforts have certainly made immigration simpler and more pleasant over the last few decades. But each new arrival still faces a number of personal hurdles: "Where will I live? Where will I work? What will the future hold for me?" Think back to the time just after you made *aliya*. Did you occasionally reflect on the many conversations you had shared back home with the Israeli *shaliach* (immigration counselor) before you set the wheels in motion? Had he prepared you well? Was his advice sound? How did you feel about leaving behind an extended family, a job you were good at, a dependable salary, a language you could readily speak? Moving to a country where at least 70% of the population lives in overdraft for part of the month and 20% for the entire month is enough to make anyone a bit jittery. Perhaps that's why the answer to a joke commonly told by new *olim*, "How do you make a small fortune in Israel?" is, "Come with a big fortune."

Whether or not there is a pot of gold at the end of the rainbow, *olim* can indeed establish themselves in their new homeland and build a comfortable financial future for their families. Regardless of their level of wealth when they arrive, they can organize and increase their net worth through earnings, investments, and diligent management of their assets. In the pages that follow, you will find explanations to help you understand how investments work, which ones might be best suited to your needs, and what strategies and ideas are most apt to help you in the quest to undo the joke and turn the small fortune back into a large one.

Chapter 1
Welcome to the World of Investing

Israel's Economic Outlook

A bird's-eye view of Israel's economic picture shows a land of growth and opportunity – a modern nation with advanced ideas, a world leader in innovation. Israel's high-tech heroics have made the country a magnet for foreign investment and earned it the nickname, "silicon wadi." Its economy, historically based on agriculture and light industry, has been updated to include the transition to a knowledge-based financial system. Recognized worldwide for its excellence in telecommunications, information technology (IT), and life sciences, Israel attracts billions of dollars of "hot money," which is a major impetus to the further building of the economy.

With thousands of high-tech start-up companies, Israel ranks among the top countries in the world as a recipient of venture capital (VC). Over 150 Israeli companies trade on international markets, with around 80 trading on various U.S. exchanges. In

1

fact, Teva Pharmaceuticals and Check Point Software* are both listed on the exclusive NASDAQ-100 list. But that's not all …

Israel is Forging Ahead

As a strong democracy with a capitalist economy, Israel often appears at the top of the list of global stock markets in terms of returns. This is due to Israeli talent working both at home and abroad. Israel's national resource of "brainpower" has enticed some of the world's most powerful companies to focus development resources in Israel: Motorola developed the cell phone in Israel; Microsoft built most of the Windows NT operating system in Israel; Intel designed its Pentium MMX and Centrino chips in its Israeli labs; the technology for instant messaging was created in Israel and eventually sold to AOL, etc.

Israeli companies have made an impact both locally and abroad: Pharmaceutical giant Teva paid $3.4 billion for U.S. generic drug maker, Sicor, in 2004, and $7.4 billion to acquire Ivax, a company in the same business, in 2005; an Israeli company now owns the prestigious half-billion dollar New York Plaza Hotel; and the internet infrastructure company BackWeb Technologies, whose clients include Hewlett-Packard, Siemens, and Kodak, finds its roots in one of Israel's first venture capital firms, the BRM Group. Sparing patients the discomfort associated with endoscopies, Given Imaging created a pill-sized video camera that can be swallowed. As it works its way through the small intestine, doctors can get a good view of what's going on inside. After 9/11, Moseroth Technologies created the Spider Rescue System, which

---

* The listing of a particular corporation in this book is *not* a recommendation to buy or sell its stock. Consult with an investment professional to determine if and when it may be appropriate for you to trade in a specific security. The author, Profile Investment Services, Ltd., and its associates and/or affiliates may take long or short positions in the companies mentioned in this book. All securities cited throughout the text are examples for educational purposes only.

uses elevator-quality steel cables to quickly lower people to safety when immediate evacuation from a tall building is required.

Israel's business success extends to many sectors, including financial services and security. Other success stories include firms such as Nice Systems, which supplies technology to record almost 90% of the brokerage transactions around the world. Not only that, but the Los Angeles and New York City police departments record their incoming calls with Nice's equipment. Nice also sells sophisticated audio interception and video surveillance systems to various government agencies to monitor terror threats. Then there's ISDS, founded by Mossad veterans, which offers security training and systems to international organizations, including Mexico's national oil company, the Olympic Games Committee, World Cup soccer, and the airport, energy, and power plant security units in Brazil, Chile, India, Italy, and elsewhere. Magal Security Systems, the firm that's building the anti-terrorist security fence in Israel, is the same company that built the security system for Buckingham Palace. The kibbutz-based company called Mofet Etzion has pioneered the concept of a lightweight ceramic material called LIBA, "Light Improved Ballistic Armor." After examining the product, the U.S. Marines bought the armor for over 1000 of their "Expeditionary Fighting Vehicles," which are used in the battle zones of Iraq and Afghanistan.

Though there's always risk associated with trying to surge ahead, consider some of these points about the Israeli economy:

- Vigorous privatization plans are lowering the administrative and financial burden on the government by letting the free market take over. (Major moves by the government included selling off its stakes in the telephone company Bezeq, the Israel Discount Bank, and the national airline, El Al.)
- Tax rates are dropping.
- Per capita gross domestic product (GDP) matches other industrialized countries.
- As a percentage of its GDP, Israel's expenditure on education

tops the United States, the United Kingdom, Spain, Japan, and many other nations. And the vast majority of adults have 12 or more years of education.

- Twenty-four percent of the Israeli workforce has a university degree.
- Key economic points include low inflation, decreasing interest rates, and a solid currency.
- Israel has an investment grade rating from Standard & Poor's of A-, which is excellent by international standards.

Israeli companies deal in a broad range of commerce. In fact, each of the industries listed below exports over $100 million to the U.S. alone (in addition to sales made to Europe and the Far East):

- medicinal, dental, and pharmaceutical preparations,
- telecommunications equipment,
- scientific, medical, and hospital equipment,
- electric apparatus and parts,
- photo and service industry machinery and trade tools,
- civilian aircraft and parts,
- industrial organic chemicals,
- synthetic cloth and fabrics, thread and cordage,
- pulp and paper machinery,
- semiconductors and related devices,
- apparel and household goods,
- gems – diamonds,
- jewelry, and more.

Despite all of these positive features, the bursting of the high-tech bubble and the tenuous political situation provide many *olim* with a sense of nervousness about their new economic reality, and they feel a degree of concern regarding the volatility of the Israeli economy. They see the great potential, but nevertheless feel more comfortable diversifying their holdings so that only part is "Blue and White," and the rest is placed elsewhere. Often they choose to keep some of their assets in the U.S. markets. Although many are well aware of some of the political and corporate disasters Americans have experienced during the last several decades, these investors also recall more positive aspects. They remember that the U.S. economy, with its strong will to succeed, continues to forge ahead even in the wake of financial setbacks.

Past Performance Does Not Indicate Future Results

Keep in mind when considering the statistics in this book (and in any other investment guide that you read) that the numbers are not necessarily indicative of how a particular investment or market segment will perform in the future. Although studying historical performance is an accepted method used to analyze and make predictions, the reviewer of such facts must always be aware that an educated estimate is not the same as an assurance or guarantee. In fact, the U.S. Securities and Exchange Commission (SEC) insists that investment companies make a clear disclaimer to warn investors that what happened in the past is not a prediction of what will occur in the future.

Opportunities for the Market to Fall

One of the most common reasons for not creating an investment portfolio is the fear of losing money. People hear woeful stories about investors who lost everything, and imagine themselves in the same scenario.

While loss of principal sometimes does happen, it is important to keep the larger financial picture in mind. The stock market has seen highs and lows, but over time has moved steadily upward. For those investors sufficiently diversified and able to accept the risks associated with owning securities, investing in the market has generally been a solid, long-term financial choice. The difference between winning and losing on financial selections often turns out to be just a matter of time, with the most successful investors being the patient ones.

Opportunities for the Market to Rise

Global and political catastrophes have made apparent the resiliency of the American markets as they coped with and subsequently recovered from adversities. Even following the terrorist destruction of the World Trade Center, the American markets soon found their balance and were able to concentrate on moving back up. A quick lineup of historical events during the last half-century demonstrates the continuing determination and drive of the American markets in the face of national and global upheaval.

During the Cuban missile crisis in October 1962, Americans were worried that nuclear war was imminent and everything they held dear might be destroyed. However, when the crisis was diffused, the markets picked up steam and by the following year, the Dow Jones Industrial Average (a major market indicator) had gained 29%, jumping from 572 to 738.

Just a short time later, on November 22, 1963, President John F. Kennedy was assassinated. Many wondered what direction the country would take after the heartbreaking loss of its charismatic young leader. While some politicians may have floundered, the markets did not fall apart, and by the next year they showed gains of 25%, climbing from 711 to 890.

On August 9, 1974, in the midst of a recession, President Richard Nixon resigned following his involvement in the Watergate scandal. The Dow, on that date, was at 777. Just one year later, it had gone up 5% to 817. Considering the state of the economy at the time, and the fact that the market had dropped significantly due to the oil embargo and the Vietnam War, this figure is actually quite impressive.

"Black Monday," October 19, 1987, shook up the market considerably. In one of the biggest losses in Wall Street's history, the market tumbled over 22% in a day, falling 508 points from 2246 to 1738. It only took one year for the market to once again regain its health. On October 19, 1988, the market was at 2137, just about

4% below its standing before the crash, and about 23% higher than it had been on the actual day of the crash. Another year later, it was up to 2683, an increase of over 19% above the pre-crash value two years earlier.

As Gulf War I began in 1990, the Dow tumbled 22% in less than three months, from a high of 3019 on July 20 to 2344 on October 11. Fear of an extended war, a spike in oil prices, and potential terrorism might have encouraged investors to sideline their money. If they had, however, they would have missed the incredible bull market of the 1990s – and they might not have participated in the millennium ending without an infection of the Y2K bug and with the Dow at 11,497.

In each of these time periods, the market survived declines that to some may have seemed insurmountable. Each downturn, however, proved to be temporary and the market recovered, lending credence to economists who say that short-term volatility doesn't necessarily hamper the long-term upward motion of the markets.

The above examples should offer encouragement to the long-term investor. International and domestic affairs may have an immediate effect on the marketplace, but their long-term impacts have often been negligible. Many shareholders, who jumped ship upon hearing bad news, ended up selling investments that, if held, would have returned huge profits. Historically, the potential for future returns outweighs the temporary risk of the catastrophe *du jour*.

Individual Companies Often Make Comebacks

In addition to the major national and international happenings that cause general market turmoil, individual corporations also experience unexpected setbacks that may prove difficult to overcome. While there are instances when hard times force companies to close their doors, sometimes problems can reverse themselves. For example, in 1989, the Exxon Valdez disaster had shareholders worried. One of Exxon's tankers had a devastating accident, polluting the waters of Alaska's Prince William Sound with oil. Damage to wildlife and to the environment was extensive, and cleanup costs loomed massively ahead. Exxon's shares dropped 7% when the news broke. However, the stock quickly rebounded, and was soon selling at multiples similar to other stocks within its industry.

In 1984, Union Carbide Corporation, America's third largest petrochemical company, was sued for over $3 billion after a deadly gas leaked from one of its plants, tragically killing over 3,300 people in Bhopal, India. The fiasco was a public-relations nightmare, and the company's stock fell 21% within a short time. However, a year later, the stock was back at its previous level, and by 1989, it had reached a new all-time high.

There are many examples of how strong firms have regrouped, restructured, and recovered after disasters have struck. Consider how many companies survived, and even prospered, after the September 11, 2001 terror attacks on the Twin Towers (e.g., Cantor Fitzgerald lost over 650 employees and today is back as a powerful financial force). Look at how the world's largest tobacco company, Philip Morris (now called "Altria"), has constantly survived the onslaught of litigation brought against it. Watch how pharmaceutical companies see their share prices rebound after sharp drops caused by problematic drug recalls.

Stories like these illustrate that while market conditions, company news, and external situations may adversely affect the price of a stock in the short term, the shares of well-managed companies can often ride out the calamities and manage to rise in the long run.

Summary

- Israel is an important player in the world marketplace and is a key leader in the technology field.
- Investors should be aware that past performance is not necessarily indicative of future results.

- Historical events show that markets, as well as individual stocks, are resilient and often recover after setbacks, sometimes even going on to new highs.

Chapter 2
More About the Markets

The informal bartering of assets is a manner of doing business that dates back to early civilization. It wasn't until the 1600s, however, that this type of trading expanded and became more regimented. Stock and bond markets in London, Antwerp, Paris, Amsterdam, and other major European cities began to take shape and draw in investors anxious to increase their wealth and take advantage of the formality of these newly-established trading venues.

The Beginnings of the American Market

During America's early days, the need for a regulated type of marketplace soon became apparent. Washington's government was deeply in debt due to Revolutionary War expenses, and cash was urgently needed by the fledgling nation. (A famous Jewish financier named Haym Salomon became one of the most effective brokers of government securities in support of the war – and, in fact, he personally gave of his own wealth to help the troops, and loaned his own money to members of the Continental Congress.) Funding was needed by new banks, public works enterprises, and various businesses being started and expanded to help build the new nation. It was important to get citizens to feel confident enough to invest their money to help their new government and to enable their country to grow. But people needed to know, before they invested, that it would be possible to liquidate their holdings in a fair manner if they chose to do so. They wanted to be able to keep track of their investments and to know that they could easily locate their representative if they needed advice or trading services. Small groups of intermediaries were organized in several of the new states to meet these needs. Perhaps the best remembered was the group of 24 brokers who decided to assemble on a daily basis beneath a large buttonwood tree just a few blocks away from Wall Street. In a short time, this group evolved into what soon became known as the "New York Stock Exchange."

The Wall Street area flourished, and additional trading exchanges opened their doors as more and more people wanted to participate in this growth. Toward the end of the nineteenth century Charles H. Dow, a leader on the financial scene and the first editor of *The Wall Street Journal*, joined up with finance reporter Edward Davis Jones. Together, they designed and calculated a mathematical average, subsequently named after them, to enable the public to see the level and trend of the stock market by following the prices of a few representative stocks. Today, the most quoted index is the Dow Jones Industrial Average (DJIA), currently composed of 30 well-known companies. (The DJIA started with only 12 stocks, all but one of which was subsequently replaced. The survivor? General Electric.)

The early twentieth century saw an economic boom, and the Dow Jones average reached a high of 386 points. (The value of the index is quoted in points instead of dollars, since it represents a mathematical average, not a specific currency value.) Financiers with large amounts of capital to invest, and occasionally the power to influence decision-making, were rapidly growing wealthier. The average person on the street, seeing how fast others were growing rich and how readily money apparently could be made, put much or all of his savings into the market. Then, with a resounding crash, on October 24, 1929 – thereafter known as "Black Thursday" – the market took a plunge. Many people who had borrowed heavily by buying on margin found themselves practically penniless. The country entered a period of depression that showed few positive signs until the new U.S. president, Franklin D. Roosevelt, began to implement his New Deal in 1933.

New Regulations to Protect the Public

Roosevelt proposed many bills to address the ongoing financial and banking crisis. New laws were passed, and new rules and governing bodies were established. Included with these laws were the Securities Acts of 1933 and 1934 that controlled the issuance of new securities, required full and fair disclosure to buyers, and regulated and monitored stock exchanges and broker-dealers. Moreover, the legislation required brokerage firms to register with the administering agency, the Securities and Exchange Commission (SEC).

A subsequent self-regulatory body, the National Association of Securities Dealers (NASD), was organized to ensure fair business practices by reviewing members' business activities and disciplining those who failed to follow regulations. Today the NASD has become the world's leading provider of financial regulatory services. It is because of the integrity of this organization that investors, regardless of the size of their accounts, can trade with confidence.

New laws were also passed to help protect bank depositors from losing all their savings in the event of bank disasters. The Federal Deposit Insurance Corporation (FDIC) was established to identify, monitor, and help member banks and savings institutions and ensure that should there be a failure, the depositors would be reimbursed up to the prescribed limit. Today, depositors and owners of FDIC-insured bank deposits would be fully compensated for principal and interest, up to $100,000 per depositor per bank, should the bank go under. The assets of FDIC-insured commercial banks exceed $8 trillion, distributed among a total of over 9000 banking institutions.

NYSE: An Auction Market

The New York Stock Exchange (NYSE), often referred to as the "Big Board," is an auction market that serves a worldwide clientele. The exchange offers an efficiently organized forum where the securities of established companies can be appraised and publicly traded. The exchange itself sets policy, lists securities, handles membership, rules on administrative matters, and monitors transactions to prevent unfair or fraudulent occurrences. The NYSE neither buys nor sells shares, nor does it determine prices. Instead, it provides an auction floor for brokers to buy and sell at the most favorable prices.

NASDAQ

Since its inception more than 30 years ago, the NASDAQ (an acronym for "National Association of Securities Dealers Automated Quotation") has been the electronic marketplace for the vast over-the-counter (OTC) trading market, surpassing the NYSE in share volume in 1994 and in dollar volume by the year 1999. Not confined to any particular location, it consists of a sophisticated telecommunications and computer network system linking OTC firms that serve as market makers for over 3000 publicly traded national and international companies. Due to less stringent listing requirements than those found on the NYSE, NASDAQ stocks sometimes tend to be more speculative and/or very low priced (factors that might lead to the delisting of a Big Board stock). However, this is not always the case, as evidenced by the inclusion in NASDAQ of some major players, such as Microsoft, Intel, Cisco, EBay, and more.

To better understand how an OTC market functions, it is important to understand the actual role of the over 500 market makers. Market makers, also known as "dealers," are independent entities who commit themselves to buying and selling shares of specific companies through a negotiation process. Usually they buy shares of a particular company and keep them in inventory at their own risk (called "taking a position") until they can sell them at an acceptable, negotiated price. They add liquidity to the market by being required to buy or sell stock for their own accounts whenever the market is open. Since various market makers may be dealing in the same security, there is ongoing competition among them to execute investors' orders. On average, each stock has around 10 market makers competing for its business, though some large companies may have over 50 market makers.

In some ways, the market maker system can be compared to the *Machane Yehuda* open-air marketplace in Jerusalem. Several market makers survey the wares of five merchants selling oranges and make the best deals that they can to purchase a supply. Then, with their own money tied up in their newly purchased produce, they turn around and offer their oranges to the brokers representing the clients, who will ultimately make the purchase based on the best price. If any one of the market makers tries to sell his wares for an above-market price, no one will buy, and he will therefore be forced to lower his price to keep in line with the general marketplace. This same procedure is followed whether the purchase is of oranges, or Intel, Dell, or Microsoft.

NASDAQ market makers are required to compete for investor orders on both the buy and sell sides, commit their own capital to purchase the securities they are dealing in, honor their quoted prices, display the quotes and orders that have been executed, and report all trades in a timely fashion.

The Tel Aviv Stock Exchange (TASE)

In 1935, well over a century after the inception of the New York Stock Exchange, Israel's top pre-state banks and brokerage firms created the Exchange Bureau for Securities. This bureau acted as an unofficial stock exchange for 18 years, until after the establishment of the State in 1948. Thereafter, the new nation's leaders introduced an official Israeli stock market in 1953, the Tel Aviv Stock Exchange. Ten years later, a group of TASE members set up the TASE Clearing House to serve as a central securities depository and to offer clearing, settlement, and custody services.

The Knesset, in 1968, anxious to correct some flaws in the system, reviewed the economic situation and enacted the Securities Law, which created a solid regulatory framework for the TASE operations. The *Reshut Neyerot Erech* (Israeli Securities Authority) was established shortly thereafter to govern Israel's markets by regulating business practices and the disclosure of information. Some years later, in 1993, the TASE opened a derivatives market to offer the public the opportunity to trade in options and futures. This allowed Israelis to use risk-managing strategies, as well as to engage in speculative trading.

The exchange, in 1997, made major computer technological changes when it introduced the Tel Aviv Continuous Trading system (TACT). Within two years, all listed securities, as well as derivative products, were trading on the new automated trading platform. During this period, too, regulators spent a great deal of time monitoring market activities and updating and expanding laws to help correct inequities. These alterations offered much greater protection to the investing public. In addition, the government created the "Regulation of Investment Advice and Investment Portfolio Management Law, 5755/1995," which called for all investment advisors in the country to be evaluated, tested, and licensed. (The website of the Israel Securities Authority, www.isa. gov.il, allows you to check the Israeli registration of any investment advisor by clicking on the "List of Licensees" link. Be aware that some advisors are only listed on the Hebrew version of the website and not on the English part. Likewise, you can check on a U.S. broker's history at www.nasd.com, and on the insurance protection of a U.S. brokerage firm at www.sipc.org.)

TASE: Four Phases of Trading

Using the TACT system, investors can trade stocks and bonds during four different phases of the market from Sunday through Thursday. The "pre-opening" phase runs from 8:30 A.M. to 9:45 A.M. during which time traders can enter an order, but no trades actually take place. Instead, the exchange simply disseminates "theoretical" prices to the public that reflect the prices that would be real if the trades were, in fact, executed. At a random time between 9:45 A.M. and 9:50 A.M., the "opening phase" marks the beginning of trading for the shares of larger companies, and then at 10:15 A.M. all the rest of the shares begin trading. The "continuous phase" begins shortly after the opening phase and lasts until 4:45 P.M. During these hours, the computer system electronically matches buy and sell trades on a bilateral and continuous basis. Finally, during the "closing (crossing) phase," last trades and "ATC – At the Close" trades are executed.

The Best of Both Worlds: Investing in Israeli and U.S. Corporations

Many *olim* have existing portfolios of American securities. Because they are familiar with the workings of the American markets and feel confident in the U.S. economy, they choose to continue investing as they have done before moving to Israel. Yet *olim*, as well as native Israelis, have faith in and want to support, and subsequently profit from the growing, well-managed, successful companies that exist throughout Israel.

Israeli corporations often represent excellent buying opportunities and may be traded on several foreign stock exchanges in addition to the TASE. The NASDAQ is particularly noteworthy for listing dozens of these companies, such as Teva Pharmaceuticals, Blue Square Israel, Compugen, Comverse Technology, and numerous others. Many *olim*, wanting to own shares in well-known Israeli companies, choose to buy them from an American listing in order to include them in their U.S. brokerage accounts.

Why would someone opt to purchase an Israeli stock on a non-Israeli exchange? The large base of buyers and sellers on the U.S. exchange scene offers traders a greater amount of liquidity. Since more people compete on each side of the trade, buyers and sellers can often get a better price. In smaller and/or less liquid markets, on the other hand, a person looking to sell his stock may not find many potential buyers and thus be obliged to lower his price, and then lower his price again, until he finally finds a customer who agrees to buy.

Banks Provide Financial Services

In addition to familiarizing yourself with the national and international financial scenes, also keep in mind that savings, borrowing, and investment opportunities may be available at your local bank. While banks are primarily thought of as providing day-to-day financial assistance in such matters as paying bills, handling credit cards, and writing checks, they can also play an important role in helping you plan for your future. Prudent investors often set up easily accessible emergency funds – enough to cover three to six months' worth of living expenses – to help carry them through any unforeseen financial difficulties (such as sickness, loss of a job, the need to relocate, etc.).

Americans residing in Israel can choose to put their dollars either in a U.S. or an Israeli bank. While there are many similarities between the two banking systems, there are also important differences.

American banks: Americans in Israel frequently find it helpful to have access to an American bank credit card or checking account. Many people who have American-based checking accounts write themselves checks periodically and deposit them in their Israeli bank accounts to cover current expenses. They feel confident in having their U.S. accounts since they know the FDIC is guarding their principal. Other times, these customers may choose to keep their cash in money market mutual funds, either at an American bank or in a U.S.-based brokerage firm. While these money market funds usually pay higher returns than savings accounts do, and are considered very safe, they generally are not covered by FDIC insurance and are not guaranteed.

Israeli banks: Israeli banks offer many of the same checking and saving services provided by American banks. However, Israeli banks do not usually offer money market accounts, so liquid assets, like money in a checking account, sit in an open account earning no interest whatsoever. Also, the Israeli government doesn't provide an insurance program comparable to that offered by the FDIC.

Israeli banks offer a variety of savings accounts in both shekels and dollars. Two of the most common are *pikdonot* (closed deposits) and *patach* (open accounts).

A *patach* account is a shekel savings account. The *patach* account is often the standard bank arrangement that people maintain to facilitate depositing checks and paying bills. This program provides check-writing privileges and access to a debit or credit card for a fee. There are no penalties for making withdrawals.

Pikdonot accounts, offered in many currencies, are generally used by people who have some money that they can afford to lock away for a while. By tying up (closing) the money for a specific period, the depositor normally receives a set interest rate (which graduates to higher levels as time commitments are increased). While withdrawals (but not checks) are permitted, there are penalties for taking out money early. New *olim* are entitled to certain Israeli tax benefits on the interest if these investments are held long term. However, the U.S. government considers these interest payments taxable income and they must therefore be reported when filing a U.S. tax return.

Tzamud l'madad, linked-to-inflation, is another type of *pikadon* (deposit). The interest paid on this shekel savings account reflects the current rate of inflation. Thus, a *tzamud l'madad* account might offer a 5% yield, of which 2% is "true" interest, and 3% represents the tie-in with inflation. Since many Israeli business transactions (e.g., buying a house or a car) are handled in U.S. dollars, banks also offer a *tzamud l'dollar* (linked to the dollar) variation to address the needs of shekel holders who require dollars at set periods of time. For example, if you purchase a home for $200,000 and plan to pay $50,000 in four quarterly installments, you need

Shmuel Ihongdim

*"Think, son! Try to remember what it said on the computer
screen before you pushed the "enter" key and transferred
all of our money to some bank in cyberspace."*

to ensure that the currency you deposit in the bank will not have
its value eroded should the shekel drop in value against the dollar.
By linking the shekel to the dollar, this account helps preserve the
purchasing power of your money. In other words, if the rate of
exchange is currently four shekels to the dollar but within the year
goes to five to the dollar, the account will pay you with more shekels, ensuring that the value of the dollars will remain constant.

Which Account Should You Choose?

Americans living in Israel often debate whether they should keep
their money in dollars or convert their dollars into shekels. How
do you determine which is most appropriate?

For a person living and working in Israel, it is important to
have a shekel account to facilitate the handling of living expenses
and to have a place in which to deposit Israeli paychecks. In fact,
one of the first things any new *oleh* or long-term tourist should
do is to set up a bank account.

When it comes to putting away money for growth and to meet

longer-term goals, squirreling your assets in a bank account may not be your best choice. Often, you can find more competitive yields and more suitable growth opportunities by putting a portion of your money into other vehicles. However, since no one can tell whether the shekel, the dollar, or any other currency, for that matter, will outpace the others, it is important to decide carefully how you will set up your account. Many people simply feel more comfortable keeping their assets in their original currency. Others look at the financial and political trends of Israel versus the outside world and feel they might be taking a greater risk with the shekel. And still others are happy to assume Israeli exposure, as they believe this may lead to higher returns over time. Diversification is the key to mitigating the risk of multiple currencies, and examining your long-term cash flow needs can help you figure out in which currencies you should invest.

Summary

- The history of the U.S. and Israeli exchanges shows ever-strengthening and ever more responsive marketplaces. Flaws in the markets' systems have been addressed and new regulations have been instituted to provide investors with greater exposure to global business and more protection against unfair practices.
- Investing in Israeli markets can be done through both American markets and the Tel Aviv Stock Exchange.
- Auction markets, such as the NYSE, allow brokers on the floor of the exchange to bid for shares at the lowest price and to offer to sell shares at the highest price on behalf of their clients. The NASDAQ enables market makers to negotiate, buy, and sell securities via an electronic trading system. The TASE uses four phases of trading throughout the day to match buyers and sellers.
- In addition to various stock markets, Israeli banks also offer important savings and investing opportunities to people living in Israel.

Chapter 3
Why Buy Stocks?

Owning a Business

Businesses take many different forms. You can be a sole proprietor and open up a shop, deal with suppliers and customers, negotiate the rent, handle the management, be personally liable for the business debts, and hopefully grow your enterprise and prosper. Alternatively, you can form a partnership with one or more associates and you can all share the long hours, responsibilities and obligations and, with good luck, also succeed. And yet there is still another way to gain from a thriving business, without having to wipe the sweat from your brow: Look around for a well-run corporation and buy a partial ownership of it in the form of a stock purchase.

Corporate Stocks

When you buy stock in a corporation, you are, in fact, buying a piece of the company. You, just as Bill Gates, can be a part-owner of the huge Microsoft company (although, most probably, yours would be a much smaller portion), and in relation to the number of shares you own, you can cast your vote on certain decisions, vote for members of the board of directors, and even voice your opinion publicly to management and to your fellow shareowners if you choose to attend a shareholders' meeting.

Some key advantages to buying equity in a company (stocks are often referred to as "equities") include:

- not having any personal liability to creditors should the company fail (the most you could lose is the amount you put in to purchase the shares),
- knowing that if top managers leave, others will be chosen to replace them, and the company will continue to function,
- not having any management responsibilities (as you would if it were your own company),
- receiving a portion of the profits in the form of dividends (this does not apply to all companies), and
- being comfortable with the fact that when you wish to sell your shares, you can generally do this rapidly.

Highest on the list of advantages, of course, is that your stock may go up in price, because it is moving in tandem with a strong market, or because the business itself is doing particularly well, or because the market perceives it will do well in the future.

A company's "real" value is often nothing more than the public's opinion of what the company should be worth. This perception factor that you, analysts, and other investors take into consideration when deciding how much a share is actually worth is often related to external events such as potential government contracts, talked-about mergers, new industrial inventions, political or military happenings, or plain rumors. Regardless of the reason behind the upward move of the share price – if your position becomes more valuable and you sell, you make a profit.

On the other hand, however, while owning a portion of a company has its benefits, you have very little say in decision-making unless you are a major shareholder. The board of directors determines policy, decides if, when, and how much you will receive in dividends, chooses the management, and decides how much shareholders will pay them from the company's coffers. And, to add to this, should the market falter, your company do poorly, or its products drop from public favor, the value of your holding will decrease.

To Buy, or Not to Buy?

The stock market has shown that over time it has been able to deliver profits that have been greater than those of most other investments. A comparison of the long-term returns of the Standard & Poor's 500 shows that savings accounts and bond programs have not matched stock performances over comparable periods.

Growth of $10,000 investment from 1955 to 2004		
Asset class	Annual compound rates of return	Value at end
Stocks	10.93%	$1,789,351
Bonds	6.63%	$248,113
Cash	5.42%	$140,323

(Source: AdvisorTek.com. Printed with permission.)

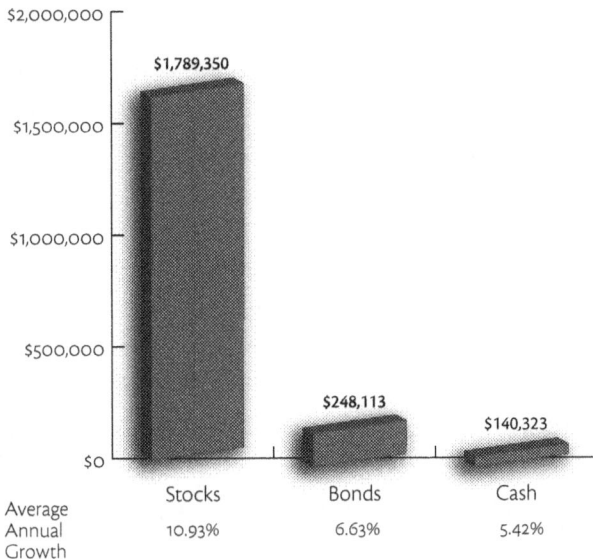

	Stocks	Bonds	Cash
Average Annual Growth	10.93%	6.63%	5.42%

Investors hope that this trend will be representative of the equities markets in the future. Stocks are often chosen for the growth portion of portfolios to enable assets to appreciate. Other times, investors choose stocks so they will have ongoing quarterly income in the form of dividends.

Choosing stocks takes time, willingness to do research, and an inclination to make decisions and accept responsibility. It also involves risk and uncertainty. Is the stock on its way up? Is the economy improving? Should you wait another week to buy? Some investors will aim for modest profits. Others will invest more boldly as they reach out to catch a rising star.

It's a Rough Ride for Short-Term Investors

Even though the long-term results of the markets have been impressive, the path to success wasn't always smooth. During the 50 years portrayed in the chart on page 25, there were plenty of ups and downs. If you had invested money and needed to use it during one of the market's drops, some, or all, of your money would not have been available to you. Wise investors remember that investing in stocks is often more suitable for people with long-term goals than for those who may need the funds for more immediate use. While trends may indicate growth, there is no guarantee that on the day you need to sell your stock, the company's price will be strong. Needless to say, the past performance of the market (both good and bad) does not mean that those returns will necessarily repeat themselves.

Let's look over an even longer period to examine how the volatility of the markets affects investors. Assume that from 1934 through 2003 you owned a portfolio that matched the return of the s&p 500 (the most common index used for this type of study). These 69 years can be broken down into 840 one-month periods. Of those 840 months, the majority showed positive returns (see chart on page 27). In fact, you would have had 521 "up" months and 319 "down" months. In other words, in 38% of the periods you would have lost money.

Holding period	# of periods	Description	# of positive returns	# of negative returns	% of "up" periods	% of "down" periods
1 Month	840	Jan 1–31 1934; Feb 1–28 1934 … Dec 1–31 2003	521	319	62%	38%
1 Year	828	Jan 1934–Jan 1935; Feb 1934–Feb 1935… Dec 2002–Dec 2003	622	206	75%	25%
3 Years	804	Jan 1934–Jan 1937; Feb 1934–Feb 1937… Dec 2000–Dec 2003	705	99	88%	12%
5 Years	780	Jan 1934–Jan 1939; Feb 1934–Feb 1939 … Dec 1998–Dec 2003	737	43	94%	6%
10 Years	720	Jan 1934–Jan 1944; Feb 1934–Feb 1944… Dec 1993–Dec 2003	720	0	100%	0%
15 Years	660	Jan 1934–Jan 1949; Feb 1934–Feb 1949 … Dec 1988–Dec 2003	660	0	100%	0%
20 Years	600	Jan 1934–Jan 1954; Feb 1934–Feb 1954 … Dec 1983–Dec 2003	600	0	100%	0%
25 Years	540	Jan 1934–Jan 1959; Feb 1934–Feb 1959… Dec 1978–Dec 2003	540	0	100%	0%
30 Years	480	Jan 1934–Jan 1964; Feb 1934–Feb 1964 … Dec 1973–Dec 2003	480	0	100%	0%

(Source: AdvisorTek.com. Printed with permission.)

Could you live with that kind of volatility? If not, try changing your viewpoint of the markets. In other words, instead of looking at monthly timeframes, consider looking at annual periods. There were 828 rolling one-year periods from 1934 through 2003 (January 1934 to January 1935, February 1934 to February 1935 ... December 2002 to December 2003). This time, 622 periods (75%) were positive versus 206 (25%) down years. As your perspective widens, the number of winning periods increases.

You Have Choices

Many buyers feel that stocks, like people, have character. Companies have certain features that different investors like or dislike. These characteristics, diverse as they may be, often appeal to the same person who wants – for diversity's sake – to have big and small, conservative and risky, foreign and domestic, and samplings of other philosophical opposites in his portfolio. Although corporations, like investors, rarely fit neatly into just one category, analysts often differentiate between companies according to market sectors. Dividing assets among these sectors is one of the fundamental ways to diversify an account.

Diversification Technique #1: *Select Different Market Sectors*

1. **Basic materials.** Companies in this group include those engaged in the acquisition and manufacturing of basic substances that go into finished products, such as chemicals, paper and packaging, wood, and steel.
2. **Capital goods.** These firms design, develop, produce, and service commercial machinery and construction-related items. Categories include aerospace and defense, construction and agriculture, mobile homes and heavy-duty vehicles.
3. **Conglomerates.** The reference here is to multi-industry corporations, a category that over the last few years has widened considerably. Examples of these are General Electric and Honeywell International.

4. **Consumer cyclicals.** Companies in this group produce durable goods, such as plant equipment, automobiles, tools, television sets, and furniture. Because of the non-disposable nature of these goods, the ups and downs in the economy greatly affect them. During a recession, for example, buyers often postpone purchasing new kitchen chairs until they feel the financial outlook looks more secure.

5. **Consumer non-cyclicals.** Goods that are consumed and need replenishing, such as food, medicines, beverages, and various household products, are referred to as "non-cyclical," "non-durable," or "defensive." Companies that produce these are less affected by poor business cycles than are more cyclical firms. They are able to defend themselves (hence the description, "defensive") against down markets since consumers need their products on an ongoing basis, even during recessions.

6. **Energy.** This group refers to companies engaged in the acquisition, harnessing, production, and distribution and service of forms of energy, including coal, oil, and gas.

7. **Financial.** Major brokerage firms, insurance companies, banks, and other financial-related institutions are included in this category.

8. **Healthcare.** This sector tracks the health and medical industry. Included are drug companies and those engaged in biotechnology, providers and insurers of healthcare, medical facilities, manufacturers and suppliers of medical equipment.

9. **Media and general services.** This very broad category includes broadcast and cable TV, publishing, movies, and various aspects of these communications companies, along with restaurants, hotels, real estate, retailing, and all of the ancillary aspects of these businesses.

10. **Technology.** High-tech companies are the core of this group, along with communications equipment, computer hardware, computer networks, electronic instruments and controls, semiconductors, software, and programming.

11. **Transportation.** This sector includes companies involved in aspects of air and sea transport, railroads, trucking, and forms of public transportation.
12. **Utilities.** These corporations acquire, furnish, and provide electricity, water service, natural gas, and telephone services to industry and to the public.

Above and beyond the most common sectors noted above, investors want to spread their exposure even more widely. Here are some additional tools to help you diversify your portfolio further:

Diversification Technique #2: *Common or Preferred Stocks*

In considering stock ownership in a company, most people think of and, in fact, buy **common stock** with its potential for growth (or decline). They appreciate having the ability to vote and perhaps influence policy, and they understand that at their discretion, the directors may declare a dividend in line with current corporate profits.

For clients who also want to own shares in the company and to receive quarterly income, but don't want to assume as much risk, and are not bothered by the fact that they will probably have no voting rights, **preferred stock** might be more appealing. Preferred stock dividends are established when the shares are first issued, and this fixed amount is paid regularly out of earnings or other corporate sources unless the company is in very serious financial difficulty. If there are additional earnings available after the full allotment of money is set aside for the preferred shareholders, the board may then declare a dividend payout for common shareholders. Another major potential benefit to preferred stockholders is that if the company fails and its assets are liquidated to pay off debts, available funds will be distributed to the holders of bonds and preferred shares until they receive the full amount to which they are entitled before common shareholders receive anything.

Diversification Technique #3: *Foreign Corporations*

The United States is just one of many countries offering investors the chance to participate in the nation's corporate growth. Markets in other regions, too, invite international traders to grow with and benefit from their national economies. Since the U.S. represents only about half the world's market capitalization, it often pays to investigate foreign investment opportunities. For those who may be concerned that foreign investing can be perilous, consider that in different countries the growth rates, politics, currency values, and general economic conditions may differ, and because of this, the upturns in certain national markets can help mitigate the downturns in others. By incorporating geographic diversity into your portfolio, you distribute the risk factor over a wider investment landscape.

American Depository Receipts (ADRS)

If you want to participate in international investing, but do not wish to deal with foreign stock exchanges, consider purchasing American Depository Receipts (ADRS). An ADR is a negotiable certificate issued by an American bank that holds the underlying shares of a foreign corporation. ADR certificates represent indirect ownership of a given number of shares in foreign companies such as Bayer (Germany), Cadbury Schweppes (United Kingdom), Fiat (Italy), Fuji Photo Film (Japan), Telefonos de Mexico (Mexico), News Corporation (Australia), and Blue Square (Israel). Since they trade on American exchanges, they have to meet certain SEC requirements. ADRS are a convenient way to provide global market exposure without the inconvenience and added expenses frequently associated with trading on foreign exchanges (e.g., foreign brokerage commissions, currency exchange fees, etc.). Because ADRS are traded in dollars, and the dividends are also paid to shareholders in dollars, be aware that the actual price per share can be affected by swings in the value of the U.S. dollar against the related foreign currency.

Diversification Technique #4: *Stock Research*

The success of the stock market reflects the constant striving by corporations to expand both in size and in ability to provide goods and services. The ways in which the companies do this, the selection of services and products they choose to offer, and the risks they are willing to assume to pursue their objectives generally determine how investors categorize them. When you are beginning to set up your stock portfolio, or are considering stocks with an eye to adding them to your holdings, keep in mind that no one can outguess the future. Today's industries that seem to hold all the answers may be out of favor tomorrow – perhaps because their key products are replaced by newer inventions, or because government contracts are few and far between. Sometimes companies decline because foreign competitors have lured away their market, or a poor economy has priced the products out of the reach of many consumers. Whatever the reason, putting all your eggs in one basket is risky business. A company, or even an industry, can falter. And should this happen, it can be disastrous if you have all your money invested there.

Stock diversification is more than just buying a random group of companies. Varying your selections requires that you study the different market sectors, choose areas that you feel provide products and services that are currently in demand and look like they will continue to be so in the foreseeable future, and then delve further to find representative stocks in those fields that meet your risk/growth criteria.

Diversification Technique #5: *Real Estate Investment Trusts*

If you want to enter the real estate market, but lack the time, money, or experience to oversee your portfolio properly, consider using Real Estate Investment Trusts (REITS). A REIT (pronounced *reet*) is a business that accumulates money through an Initial Public Offering (IPO). With the cash raised by the IPO, professional real estate managers buy and develop specific properties. The team receives management fees and rental income from their assorted holdings, and over time, they may sell the assets for a profit or loss. Some management groups have particular expertise in selecting and running niche properties, such as nursing homes, shopping malls, office buildings, warehouses, or residential complexes. Others focus on certain geographic areas that they know best or believe have the greatest potential for gain. Hundreds of REITs trade on the American stock markets and represent hundreds of billions of dollars worth of real estate. You can buy shares of a REIT in the same way that you would purchase any other stock – either as an IPO or as a purchase on an exchange. Profits from your investment will flow through to you from the income generated by renting, leasing, or selling properties, and will be in the form of capital appreciation or dividends.

With a REIT, you essentially own a physical asset with rights to the income and profits that it produces. And, regardless of whether you actually do profit, you may feel as other investors do, that the underlying assets provide a form of safety net.

One advantage of owning a REIT over holding one or two specific properties and renting them out is that owning a REIT can broadly diversify the real estate portion of your portfolio. Additionally, you don't need to start with the hundreds of millions of dollars normally required to adequately spread out the risk over a large number of properties. If you tried to mimic a professionally managed REIT, you would need to spend tremendous amounts of time and money to set up and maintain the program; and when you wanted to liquidate the portfolio or make new purchases, you would have to enter the challenging world of property agents, lawyers, banks, and competing real estate moguls. Buying or selling a REIT, on the other hand, simply entails calling your broker and placing the order.

How Do I Choose a Good REIT?
There are mutual funds and managers that specialize in REIT portfolios (see Chapter 5 for information on mutual funds, and Chapter 11 for information on money managers). If you're keen

on selecting the REITs yourself, however, consider these three points:

Management – Confirm that the management team has experience in the types of real estate they will be controlling. Do they have a track record? How are they compensated? The long-term profitability of the investment relies on this team, so make sure they have the ability to excel.

Diversification – Different sectors of the real estate market move at different times. If the economy drops, for example, shopping malls might suffer from lower rental income. On the other hand, residential properties might prosper. If you buy only one REIT, look for a more diversified portfolio. However, if you will put together a set of different REITs, you can control the overall diversification by focusing on different specializations.

Earnings – It's important to study a REIT's balance sheet carefully lest you fall into some traps. For example, when a property depreciates, that lower figure gets included in the regular income numbers; it could appear that the company is losing money because of ordinary depreciation, even though the monthly rental income remains steady. Examine the Funds From Operations (FFO) and Cash Available for Distribution (CAD) statistics that measure the amount of money available to the investors. When considering REITs, professionals usually look at the FFO in place of the EPS (Earnings Per Share) that they normally study for their other stock purchases. The FFO and CAD can generally give a better sense of cash flow from operations, which may ultimately translate into higher or more secure dividends.

Mortgage REITs

Note that there is one type of REIT called a "mortgage REIT." About 10% of the REIT marketplace consists of these companies that don't actually own any real estate; rather, they make loans secured by real estate. In essence, they are finance companies, not real estate firms. As such, evaluating their books requires a different set of glasses. If you're looking for a straight real estate play, make sure you buy a traditional REIT, also known as an "equity REIT," and not a mortgage REIT.

Why Invest in REITs?

With a relatively low correlation to other asset classes (i.e., stocks and bonds), REITs can help to soften the volatility of a portfolio by adding diversification. To summarize, benefits of REITs include:

- reasonably predictable dividend payments,
- higher dividend yields than most stocks,
- potential for dividend growth,
- liquidity (unlike owning real estate directly),
- professional management,
- diversification by holding a piece of many different properties,
- disclosure obligations (Traded REITs that are registered with the SEC must make regular disclosures that include quarterly and annual reports, and the insiders, when they trade in their company's stock, must notify the SEC promptly.).

Diversification Technique #6:
Large, Medium, and Small Stocks

The term "market capitalization," or "market cap," refers to the size and/or value of a company. This figure is determined by multiplying the number of shares outstanding times the price per share. For example, a company with five million shares outstanding at a current market value of $14 per share has a market cap of $70 million.

Large-cap stocks usually refer to companies with total market capitalization of over $10 billion. These well-established firms with names that are familiar to many are found listed on major indexes. Companies in this size category tend to be less volatile than smaller firms. They do not constantly focus on growing larger through new undertakings, but instead aim to grow more profitable by expanding and servicing markets for their existing product lines.

Mid-cap stocks are often newer, but still established companies with market capitalization in the $1 billion to $10 billion range. They have proven themselves capable of meeting their customers' needs but, in an effort to grow and achieve greater success, may choose to assume additional risk. While many of these companies will remain in this mid-cap category and continue to provide satisfactory returns for their shareholders, others will successfully enlarge their scope and join the large-cap grouping.

Small-cap is a designation that is usually associated with companies having market caps of less than $1 billion. This group generally includes new businesses in the start-up phase. These firms often aggressively seek ways to raise money, expand their production, search for new markets, and compete with others in the industry in order to hold onto their foothold and hopefully forge ahead in the field. Buying stock in these companies is considered more speculative than investing in medium- or large-cap companies.

Diversification Technique #7: *Growth or Income?*
Some corporations offer investors enhanced growth opportunities, while others provide their shareholders with streams of dividend income. Buyers can determine if they would like to focus on either of these two choices or opt for stocks that offer some of both.

When purchasing a growth stock, you are buying shares in a company that is seeking to expand its business through aggressive research, production, and marketing, and sometimes by the merging with or acquiring of other companies. A growth company can be expected to use its earnings to further these goals, and its investors forgo receiving current income in the hope that the company's policy of investing in itself will pay off with greater future profits.

If you are more interested in investing as a way of receiving current income, you may want to consider a stable, less aggressive corporation – such as a utility company – that pays its shareholders quarterly dividends. Dividends on common stock are not fixed. If the company does well and maintains a continuing flow of income, its dividends can rise over time. Since the company would presumably be flourishing, an added benefit would also be the rising of the share price. Needless to say, sometimes companies lack the financial strength to maintain the dividend, and they cut it. This generally causes the stock price to drop as well.

What if you're among the investors who want both growth and income? It's certainly possible to satisfy both goals. Many of the older, well-established corporations have steady earnings that they share with their stockholders. Slow and steady growth combined with the distribution of revenue is what the shareholders of these companies want.

Diversification Technique #8: *Look for Corporate Stability*
Blue-chip is generally a descriptive term for large, established, nationally known corporations that have solid records of earnings growth. They derive their nickname, "blue-chip," from the game of poker's blue chip. In good times, and even in bad times, these companies can usually be counted on to pay out dividends. Since changing economies cause different industries and corporations to reach economic prominence and then sometimes recede, the title of "blue-chip" can shift. Periodically, it is removed from some companies and bestowed on others. Long ago, railroads would have fallen into this blue-chip grouping, but now they are no longer regarded this way. In today's markets, corporations such as IBM, DuPont, GE, Johnson & Johnson and others, including those from the Dow Jones Industrial Average, are considered to be in the blue-chip category.

Penny stocks are at the other end of the spectrum from blue-chip stocks. They are extremely speculative, low priced, and don't trade on an exchange. High-pressure salespeople frequently downplay

*"Let's design an aggressive portfolio. I earn about 200 shekels
per month babysitting, and I'd like to retire when I'm 17."*

penny stocks' lack of revenue and limited capital, and instead present them as inexpensive golden opportunities usually selling for
under a few dollars. Since the shares are so cheap, and the story
behind them generally sounds so enticing, many people feel inclined to gamble on them in the hope that the company will beat
the odds and succeed. Unfortunately, however, the bets usually
turn out to be losers. Penny stock listings can sometimes be found
on the "Pink Sheets," a posting of lightly traded over-the-counter
securities handled by market makers.

Trading Terms
Just as most businesses have their own jargon and special abbre-
viations to enhance the sharing of ideas among those in the same
field, professional investors have their own special vocabulary, too.
Placing an order can involve more than simply asking your broker to buy or sell shares. Here are some transaction choices and
general terminology that may be useful.

   • **All or nothing (AON).** When buying shares, a trader may only be able to get a few hundred shares at a time for a client – and these may not all be at the identical price. Or, it may not be possible to completely fill the order in one day. If, under these circumstances, the investor would not want his order executed, he can specify "All or nothing." If you're interested in a large quantity of stock and stipulate AON on your trade, your order may not be filled because no one is interested in taking the other side of the transaction. Many brokerage firms have "block trading" desks that specialize in handling such large single-stock orders.

- *Bid* and *ask* price. The "bid" is the highest price an investor is willing to pay for a stock, and the "ask" (also called "offer price") is the lowest price at which a seller is willing (or offering) to sell. The difference between the two is called the "spread."
- **Day order.** An order to buy or sell that remains valid until the end of the day unless it is executed or cancelled by the client before the closing.
- **Good till cancelled (GTC).** A GTC order to buy or sell does not expire at the end of the day. Also called an "open order," it stays in effect until executed or cancelled by the client. Some brokerage firms limit the length of time open orders can remain active, so check with your broker when placing such an order. In addition, some firms will adjust the limit price you set on your GTC if the underlying stock pays a dividend. You can request that the firm not change the price by choosing "Do Not Reduce" (DNR).
- **Limit.** When placing an order, you can give instructions as to what price (or better) you are willing to buy or sell. Your trade will not be executed unless it meets, or improves upon, your request.
- **Market order.** This is an instruction to buy or sell stock at the best price currently available.
- **Settlement date.** On a sell trade, this is the date when payment is due to the seller and when the securities must be in the

brokerage firm's possession. On a buy trade, this is the day that payment is due to the broker for the purchase. On most U.S. stock and bond trades, the settlement date is three business days after the trade date. In Israel, most trades settle T+1, which means the business day immediately following the transaction.

- **Stop order.** This is an order to buy or sell a stock after it reaches or trades through a specific price that you request. After the stop price is met, an order then becomes a market order and is filled along with other market orders at the best price currently available.
- **Stop-limit order.** This order combines the stop order with the limit order. As soon as your requested price is reached, your order changes automatically to a limit order. Then, if your order can be transacted at your requested price, or better, it will be carried out. If it cannot meet this requirement, it will not be executed. For example, you could give an order to sell 500 shares of XYZ at a stop price of 40 with a limit of 39. If the stock subsequently trades at 40, your order will become active, and as long as you can get 39 or better, your order will be filled. On the other hand, if the stock is trading at 46 when you enter your order, and then there is terrible news and the stock next trades at 35, your order will be active, since the 40 stop price has been met; however, you won't be sold out because your limit of 39 can't be met. (If you had entered a regular stop order without a limit, then your trade would be executed at the market price, no matter what it is.)
- **Trade date.** This is the date on which the securities are bought or sold. (The trade normally settles three business days later.)

Summary

- One can own a business by being a sole proprietor, a joint owner, or a shareholder in a publicly traded corporation.
- A share of stock is an actual segment of ownership in a com-

pany. By owning this stock, your fortune is intertwined with corporate performance.

- Over time, the stock market has delivered returns that outperformed other investment categories.
- Having a diversified stock portfolio is a method to protect against the uncertainty of the future, but still does not guarantee that you won't lose money.
- Diversification techniques may include choosing stocks from various market sectors. One can buy investments offering worldwide growth opportunities, select holdings of large, medium, and small companies, or even make speculative purchases with an eye to complementing a blue-chip portfolio.
- Buying common stock may be a good choice for those seeking growth of capital, whereas investors more interested in equity income may select preferred shares.
- When investing in the stock market, it is important to know market terminology.

Chapter 4
Making Money in Bonds

If you are like many investors, you may have already determined that bonds are perfect portfolio companions for your stock holdings. Bonds are often safer and less volatile than stocks. They provide you with an agreement that on a set future date called the "maturity date," the value of the bond, as stated on the face of the certificate, will be returned to you. But possibly the most important aspect of owning bonds is that they furnish a steady stream of regular income. When you hear people talk about "living off interest from their investments," chances are that their portfolios are heavy with bonds.

Bonds are also known as "fixed-income" or "debt" securities (whereas stocks are called "equity securities" because they represent ownership – or "equity" in the company). Bonds are essentially corporate or government certificates given to investors to acknowledge that the investor has loaned money to the issuer, that this money will be repaid at a set maturity date, and that during this holding period, a stated amount of interest will be paid to the bondholder at specific intervals (usually every six months). Unlike stockholders, bond buyers don't have a say in the way the company conducts its business. They are not invited to attend shareholder meetings, nor are they asked their opinion in the form of a vote.

Considerations in Buying Bonds

Do bond buyers lend out their money in the hope of making a profit? In most cases the answer is "no." The majority of bond buyers, especially those who are retired or nearing that stage, are looking for a steady, reliable source of income, or a supplement to their pensions. They draw added comfort when making bond purchases from knowing that bonds are commonly traded and can be sold to raise cash, should it be necessary to do so. Not every bond buyer is a long-term investor, however. Some are traders looking to buy or sell bonds at a profit. They pay little attention to the semiannual payments, but instead focus on interest rate movements and ongoing events that affect the bond's current price. Some of these buyers and sellers, especially those who are more risk oriented, also keep a trading eye on weakened or failing companies whose stocks and bonds are dropping in price, or on various municipalities that are experiencing changes, in the hope of picking up some good buys. When Hurricane Katrina hit the American Gulf Coast states in August 2005, for example, municipal bond traders everywhere closely monitored the devastation in New Orleans and nearby regions.

For many investors, the prime reason to buy corporate bonds (often called "debentures") is for a sense of security; they know that should the company that issued the bonds fall on hard times, the loans are backed by the general credit and good faith of the underlying corporation. The bondholders' claims, as lenders, will be repaid before the claims of stockholders.

In making the decision to buy bonds, people sometimes find themselves influenced by tax considerations. Interest payments received on corporate bonds are normally taxable to U.S. citizens. Non-U.S. citizens, however, may choose to buy the bonds because the interest earned is generally not taxed in the U.S. Be aware, however, that bond income is taxable in Israel, even if it's exempt in America. Be sure to consult your tax advisor before making any investment decisions.

As you consider which bonds to include in your portfolio, note that you can find fixed-income offerings with varying features. For example, some, such as "zero coupon bonds," have an alternate style of payout structure (on these you don't collect money every year, but rather at the end of the holding period). Others are "callable" – which means the issuer has the right to return your principal and interest before the scheduled maturity date. Some are backed by specific, rather than general, corporate assets, and some have particularly long- or short-term maturities. Before making your bond purchase, therefore, review your overall financial plan and see which particular types of bonds would be most useful to you in helping you meet your investment goals.

U.S. Government Bonds: Why Lend to Uncle Sam?

Bonds issued by the U.S. government offer buyers maximum security because they are backed by the full faith and credit of the government – and its almost unlimited power to tax its citizens to fulfill its debt obligations. These bonds are bought by investors around the world, who feel that the level of safety backing these obligations is so strong that nothing, short of a global catastrophe, could endanger their funds. The bonds, also called "Treasuries," are traded actively by institutional and private investors despite the fact that their yields are lower than somewhat riskier corporate securities. Many U.S. buyers accept these lower yields readily because interest on Treasuries is not taxed at the state or local levels. It is important to note, however, that the income from such bonds is taxed by the U.S. government on the federal level as ordinary income *and*, for Israelis, by the Israeli government. Given the U.S.-Israel tax treaty, though, American-Israeli investors should normally be able to receive a credit for tax paid in one country when filing a return in the other. So in most cases, double taxation should not be a problem.

Treasury securities are sold in three different holding-period categories: short-term Treasury bills, intermediate-term Treasury notes, and long-term Treasury bonds. The U.S. Treasury Department determines on an ongoing basis the amount of each of these securities that must be sold in order to meet the needs of the federal budget. If you buy and retain a bond until it matures, your risk of losing principal is virtually nonexistent due to the government's backing. If you sell early, however, you may receive more or less than the bond's face value, depending on current interest rates.

- **Treasury bills.** These short-term securities are issued at a discount from the face value (called "par") by a competitive bidding procedure. Treasury bills are short-term (a year or less) obligations that have a par value of $10,000. When they are being priced, they are offered at auction, and large institutional investors and money-market funds submit competitive bids. They bid a discounted price, an amount somewhat less than the $10,000 face value. This establishes a price that will be offered to the public. When you purchase a Treasury bill, the income you will receive is the difference between the discounted purchase price you pay and the amount you receive at maturity. You might pay, for example, $9600 today and get back $10,000 when the bill matures. For U.S. tax purposes this $400 return is not called a capital gain. It is treated as interest and is taxed as ordinary income to U.S. citizens.
- **Treasury notes.** Treasury notes have maturities ranging from one to 10 years and are issued in minimum face values of $1000 and $5000 denominations. They are interest-bearing securities and pay semiannually.
- **Treasury bonds.** These securities, which also pay semiannual interest, have longer-term maturities, usually 10 to 30 years, with minimum face values of $1000. Some Treasury bonds have optional call dates, at which time the bonds can be called back by the government in exchange for their full face value.

U.S. Government Agency Bonds

Certain federal government agencies issue debt securities in order to help them meet their financial needs. Although federal agencies issue these bonds, they generally are not backed by the full faith and credit of the U.S. government; instead, the agencies themselves guarantee them. These securities usually provide slightly higher yields than direct government obligations because they don't have the full U.S. government backing. But, they offer somewhat lower yields than corporate bonds because, being issued by agencies of the government, they are safer and usually carry an AAA rating.

Municipal Bonds

Municipal bonds ("munis") are issued in the U.S. by states, cities, towns, villages, and various authorities, such as housing, transportation, or power supply. They are usually offered to the public as a means of borrowing money in order to support ongoing state and local expenses and to help finance specific projects, such as putting up a larger hospital, building a much-needed school, constructing a new bridge, or erecting a barrier to hold back rising waters during a hurricane.

American bond buyers who are in the higher income brackets are prime customers for municipal bond offerings because munis provide interest payments that are free from both federal and state taxes to state residents. (Although interest may not be subject to taxation, buyers still must include it when filing their income tax returns.) In some cases, municipal bond interest payments may be subject to the alternative minimum tax (AMT). If you are subject to AMT, ask your accountant if munis are appropriate for you, and if so, which ones. For *olim* owning American municipal bonds, however, the situation is different. Although the interest may enjoy tax-free status in the United States, if you live in Israel, any interest income you receive, including "tax-free" interest, would be taxable under Israeli laws.

Munis Are Not for Everyone

Frequently, when making *aliya*, the holder of municipal bonds finds that the benefits of ownership that he enjoyed while living in America are no longer relevant. Take a typical case: When David resided in the States he had been in a high tax bracket. To avoid paying taxes in his 30% tax bracket on the interest from his bond investments, he had opted to buy municipal bonds. He knew when he purchased the munis that there were corporate bonds with equally good ratings and higher yields available, but he figured out that after paying the IRS 30% of the interest income he would have fewer dollars in his pocket than if he bought a lower-yielding muni – and kept all the interest. His calculations went something like this:

A $100,000 corporate bond paying 5% provides an income of $5000 per year. Of this, 30% ($1500) would go for taxes ($5000 × 30% = $1500), leaving him with $3500 to keep. However, if he bought a $100,000 muni paying 4%, he would earn $4000 and would keep it all.

Corporate vs. Municipal bond

	Corporate bond	Municipal bond
Principal sum	$100,000	$100,000
Coupon	5%	4%
Annual interest	$5,000	$4,000
Tax obligation	30%	0%
Tax due	$1,500	$0
Net income	$3,500	$4,000

When muni investors, such as David, move to a new tax jurisdiction, their tax-free holdings need to be looked at anew. For starters, new *olim* see that foreign investment income, regardless of its municipal nature, is subject to Israeli taxation. That negates one of the muni's major benefits. Secondly, upon leaving the U.S. and their former jobs – which may have put them in a high tax bracket – they are now living and working in Israel, where they may be in a lower tax bracket (David's case) and, because of the U.S.-Israel tax treaty, they may not owe any taxes to Uncle Sam. Many *olim*, therefore, decide when reviewing these tax factors that lower-paying munis are no longer ideal choices for them and it may be time to reconsider corporate bonds.

If David, who may find himself paying 20% tax to Israel on passive income, does the calculations again, he'll see that if he buys the 5% $100,000 corporate bond and pays the Israeli government 20% of the $5000 he earns in income, he will be paying taxes of $1000 ($5000 × 20% = $1000), leaving himself $4000 to keep. This is equivalent to the $4000 he'd get from a $100,000 muni paying 4%. However, it definitely outdoes the $3200 he would actually keep after paying 20% of that to Israel. (Due to certain ambiguities in the way the recent Israeli tax reforms were written, different tax professionals have varying opinions on how to calculate the tax on foreign securities. The illustration above, and all tax examples in this book, are merely an introduction to the concepts involved. Be sure to get proper tax counsel when handling your affairs.)

Zero Coupon Bonds

Buying zero coupon bonds can be a rewarding and low-cost way to invest your money for a long period because the interest will compound continually, and a much larger amount will be available at a given date. Many investors look to the future and wonder how they will pay their toddlers' college bills, or how they will cover the distant wedding costs, or what will happen when their own retirement expenses begin. These people don't need semiannual interest payments now to supplement their salaries, nor do they even want to receive the interest payments because they may be tempted to spend the money rather than reinvest it. To them, periodically having to study current interest rates or investment opportunities just to be able to invest a small, twice-a-year payment is more effort than it's worth. These folks also know that if they just cash the checks and spend the money, in 10 years they'll be annoyed at themselves because their basic principal will not have increased. For them, zero coupon bonds may be an ideal portfolio component.

Zero coupon bonds based on government issues (also called "zero coupon Treasuries") are particularly popular with security-minded buyers. These bonds are generally long-term investments with the government's guarantee to pay back the full face value of the underlying bonds upon maturity. Moreover, these zero coupon bonds are very marketable should the owner want to sell early. Available also, for those wanting higher yields, are Treasury-related zeros issued by various brokerage firms, and zeros issued and backed by corporations. For zero coupon owners, however, there is greater interest rate risk and volatility than for standard bondholders. This is because with zeros, interest is locked in both on the principal and on the reinvested income. Thus, if interest rates should rise above a zero bondholder's rate, his principal and interest would both be locked into his lower yield. A standard bondholder, in the same interest rate environment, would only be locked into the yield on his principal. He could take his semi-annual payments and reinvest them in a higher-yielding vehicle. Of course, if interest rates move down, then the zero bondholder is in a particularly advantageous position.

How Do Zero Coupon Bonds Work?

You purchase zeros at a deep discount to the face value, called "original issue discount" or "OID," and watch them grow based on a specified yield. Throughout the lifetime of the investment, this rate is paid on your principal as well as on the interest, thus creating a compounding effect. A schedule of appreciation is calculated to determine how many years it will take for your holding to reach the face value. Thus, if you buy zero coupon Treasuries yielding 5.5% and put down $6,757, you can look forward to getting back $20,000 in 20 years.

Will you have to pay U.S. capital gains tax when you redeem

your holding? No. Instead, taxes are levied on a yearly basis on your "phantom income." Even though your profits stay in the bond until you sell it or it matures, you are responsible for the taxes when you pay your annual tax bills. *Olim*, and others living outside the United States, may have fewer tax obligations in America, so check your position with regard to your particular tax responsibilities. Similarly, it's important to discuss your holdings in zero coupon bonds with your Israeli accountant to determine your Israeli tax obligations.

How Bonds Are Issued, Traded, and Priced

When corporations, municipalities, and national governments decide to raise money through the issuing of bonds, they generally begin by looking for a suitable "underwriter." An underwriter is an investment banking firm that agrees to purchase and then distribute the new issues to the public. Banking firms, anxious to get this business (and the large fees that go along with it), bid to determine who can assure the issuer that it will get the amount of money it requires at the lowest interest rate. The investment firm that wins the tender then sells the bonds to brokerage firms, other institutions, and individual investors.

Once the underwriters have sold the bonds, and individual buyers begin purchasing them, a secondary market develops in which the bonds are traded in much the same way that stocks are bought and sold. Some bonds are traded on the NYSE through a special department called the "Bond Division," but most transactions are made in the over-the-counter markets. When investors call their broker to buy a bond, the broker searches bond inventories or goes into the market to get an offering that meets the required specifications at the best available price.

What's the Right Price?

Most bonds have a par value (also called "face value") of $1000, although many have denominations of $5000 or $10,000. The interest rate, sometimes called the "coupon rate," is also noted on the face of the bond and denotes the yearly payment the issuer will make to the holder.

The bond pricing system can be confusing. This is because Wall Street traders quote bond prices as a percentage of face value. Thus, a $1000 face-value bond quoted at 94 means the price is 94% of $1000, or $940. Similarly, a bond quoted at 120 would cost $1200.

Why would an investor pay $1200 for a bond when he knows he will only get back $1000 at maturity? Suppose that the seller bought this bond many years ago and got 10% interest. Each year he received $100 in payments ($1000 × 10%). Now he needs money and wants to sell it. He looks around and sees that interest rates are down, and bonds such as his are only paying 4%, which provides only $40 in annual payments to owners. He, of course, would want to get much more than par value for his higher-yielding bond and you, if you were the buyer, seeing how large the annual payments would be, might be willing to pay much more than the $1000 face value.

Take the opposite scenario: You bought a 5% bond for $1000 that paid $50 interest annually. Two years later, when the market rate on similar bonds had increased to 6%, you found it necessary to sell. If you tried to get back your $1000, nobody would offer to buy it from you. Why should they, when they could buy other bonds paying 6%? Without some type of adjustment on your part, your bond would lack resale value. The only incentive someone would have to buy your lower-yielding bond would be if you agreed to sell it at a discount. Thus, you would need to lower your asking price from $1000 in order to compete with the market.

Trading with Interest

What happens if you want to sell your bond before your next semiannual payment is due? Perhaps you've owned it for three months since your last payment. Are you entitled to three months' worth of the interest? Yes. The new buyer must compensate you, the seller, for the portion of the interest accrued while you owned the bond. Thus, at the time of purchase, the buyer will pay you the cost of the bond plus the appropriate amount of "accrued interest" owed. When the upcoming interest payment comes in, however, the entire six-month amount will get credited to the new owner (normally by having the cash directly deposited into his brokerage account).

Understanding Bond Yields

- **Coupon rate.** When a bond is issued at par, the interest that the bond will pay – the "coupon rate" – is clearly stated. For example, a $1000 bond with a coupon rate of 6% will pay the owner $60 annually.
- **Current yield.** As long as the price of the bond remains at $1000, the current yield will be the same as the coupon rate – which, as noted above, is 6%. However, if you buy a 6% coupon bond and pay $1200, your current yield will be only 5% (which is the $60 coupon divided by the bond price of $1200).
- **Yield to maturity (YTM).** If you buy bonds on the secondary market, understanding what you are actually earning on the investment means knowing what the yield to maturity is. YTM is a calculation that gives you a realistic impression of the total return that you can expect from your bond. The YTM takes into account the amount paid for the bond (whether more or less than the face value), the coupon rate, and the number of years remaining until maturity, when you will get back the face value (par). Thus, if you paid $100 over par or $50 below par, this sum is included in the equation used to determine your YTM. Because yield-to-maturity calculations can be very complex, a financial calculator is usually used to get an accurate reading. Before making a bond purchase, you might want to use such a calculator or check with your financial advisor.
- **Yield to call.** Many bonds are issued with call provisions. This call option, stated on the original bond, gives the issuer the right to redeem the bond prior to its maturity date. Why

would an issuer want to do that? Let's say a corporation needed $10 million. To get the necessary cash, the company brought to the market 8% bonds with a five-year call feature. If, after five years, current interest rates were in the neighborhood of 8% or higher, the corporation would do nothing except continue to pay semiannual interest. But what if interest rates on similar bonds were being offered at 5%? At this point the corporation would probably call the bonds, pay the owners par (or sometimes more than par if that was in the original call stipulation), and no longer be obliged to pay 8% per year. Then, if the corporation still needs $10 million for ongoing expenses, it might issue another bond at the current 5% rates. Including a call feature on a bond is, therefore, advantageous to an issuer even though it generally must offer a slightly higher yield in order to entice investors to buy. It is somewhat less advantageous to the buyer, who understands that if interest rates drop, his principal will probably be returned to him. Then, since current rates at that time will be lower, if he wishes to reinvest, he will have to accept a bond offering a lower yield.

Callable features vary, but most callable bonds cannot be called by the issuer until a certain amount of time, such as a year or more, has elapsed. This period is known as "call protection." Whenever buying a bond, it's a good idea to check on the call features. Consider the very real possibility that the attractive coupon rate may be short-lived and, if that happens, your overall return may be much less. Ask what the yield to call on your purchase will be. (Note that the yield to call is calculated in the same manner as the yield to maturity.) Then decide if you will be satisfied with this yield should your bond actually get called.

Premium Bonds: A Great Opportunity

A premium bond is one that you buy on the secondary market for more than par value ($1000). For example, if you purchase a bond that has a 9% coupon (when most other bonds are only paying

7%) you might pay $1150 for it. You are willing to pay more than $1000 for the bond because it generates more income every year ($90/year) than 7% offerings ($70/year). When it matures, you will receive $1000, which is less than you originally paid. The difference, $150, is called the "premium." The reason you would accept that $150 loss is because you would have made it up by getting higher annual interest payments than if you had simply bought a lower-yielding bond at par ($1000). If you are an investor who looks forward to receiving a predictable cash flow, consider the advantages of buying premium bonds:

- Because many people are price-conscious and never like to pay more for a product than the listed value, the market price for premium bonds will often be a little lower than you might expect (based on your calculations of returns), and their yield to maturity a bit higher than low-coupon bonds selling at a discount or new bonds selling at par. Since yield to maturity is a good measure of a bond's return, you may actually be getting a bargain by buying a premium bond because, at maturity, your net return could be higher than if you had purchased a bond at a discount.
- Premium bonds pay a higher coupon rate than discount or par bonds. Thus, each year you will receive more cash in your hand. With that money you can go shopping, pay your bills, or, hopefully, reinvest it and earn interest on your earnings. The effect of this compounding interest is, as Albert Einstein is credited with remarking, "the most powerful force in the universe."
- During a period of increasing interest rates, premium bonds can make sense. Since premium bond coupons are closer in value to current yields in the marketplace, they are more favorably looked upon by buyers than are discounted bonds with notably lower coupons. If you hold a 7% bond while your neighbor keeps his 4% issue, as rates move up to 7% and beyond, your coupon will seem more in line with general

expectations compared with his lower return of 4%. Therefore, your bond is poised to hold its value better.

Convertible Bonds: Another Way to Buy Stocks

Convertible bonds, like other debentures, have a par value, a coupon rate, and a maturity date. But they are very different in one respect: They can be converted into a specific number of common shares of the issuing company when the shares reach a specified price. This convertibility feature can be positive or negative, depending on your point of view.

On the plus side, the bondholders enjoy semiannual interest payments and know that their investments can appreciate more dramatically than non-convertibles if the underlying corporate shares do well and climb in price. They also know that if the share values appreciate they can convert, at the predetermined price, and benefit from the upswing.

On the downside, however, convertibles usually are more risky than regular corporate bonds. Often a corporation, fearing that it will not get a positive response to a new stock issue (because of inferior earnings, poor market conditions, or other reasons), and not wishing to dilute the value of the existing shares by immediately putting an additional number of shares on the market, chooses to issue convertible bonds instead. Such a company often cannot or does not wish to pay the current yields being offered on non-convertible debentures, and so they offer potential buyers lower yields with convertibility as a sweetener.

How can you calculate the potential profit in a convertible? Along with the duration, coupon, and rating, you need to know the conversion ratio. Let's say you choose to buy XYZ 4% convertible debenture with a 20:1 conversion ratio. That means that for every bond (with a $1000 par value), you can make an exchange to get 20 shares of the underlying stock. One thousand dollars divided by 20 is $50, so if the price of the stock rises to $55, you might exchange your bond and get 20 shares of stock worth a total of $1100 (20 × $55). Until you make an exchange, you will continue to get $40 per year in interest payments until the bond matures.

If the company should go bankrupt while you own the bond, you and all of the other bondholders have a priority claim on the assets. But if you've already converted to shares, you'll have to wait in line along with all the other stockholders to receive payment (if there is anything left after everyone else has been paid off). Because assessing the true value of convertible bonds can be complex, investors often invest in convertibles through a mutual fund or money manager.

Secure or Not? Check the Rating

Some bonds offer great security; others do not. There is always the possibility that bond issuers will fail to meet the periodic interest payments, or worse, will default on their debts and be unable to repay all, or even part of the bond's principal upon maturity. You should know the issuer's reputation, financial integrity, and future prospects for success before you purchase a bond. A high-yielding bond may cause you to sit up and take notice, but it could turn into a poor investment if the issuer runs out of money before it returns your principal to you.

The question then arises: How can you know if a company is having fiscal problems? One of the easiest ways to get an evaluation of an issuer's financial situation is to consult the ratings published by some of the major independent rating services such as Standard & Poor's and Moody's. These services measure the probability that an issuer will pay back the principal at maturity and make timely interest payouts. They base their ratings on the issuer's existing debt, stability of cash flow, asset protection, management ability, and perceived capability to meet obligations. S&P cautions investors against using their ratings as a recommendation to buy, hold, or sell any specific security. Nonetheless, when the rating agencies change their opinion by upgrading or downgrading a bond issuer, the prices of the securities usually change.

Bonds with higher ratings normally offer lower interest rates, and issuers can generally borrow money relatively cheaply. Lower-rated bonds, sometimes called "junk bonds," pay richer yields, commensurate with their higher risk. Issuers of these bonds often require cash more desperately than their higher-rated peers, and they know that the only reason buyers will take on the added risk associated with their bonds is if the yields are higher than the better-quality issuers offer.

The table on the next page outlines the grading system for bonds. In order to further clarify the ratings, Standard & Poor's sometimes adds a plus or minus sign to indicate that a bond falls at the top or bottom of its category. Likewise, Moody's sometimes adds a "1" after the grade to show that the bond is at the top of its category.

Junk Bonds (a.k.a. High-Yield Bonds)

As you can see on the table, non-investment grade bonds get progressively more risky and more liable to default the farther down the scale they go. For this reason, the issuers of these obligations know that the only way to create interest among potential buyers is to offer unusually high returns. Similarly, the current owners of bonds issued by corporations that have fallen on hard times may find their ratings have dropped to B, C, or D. When this happens, these bondholders can keep their bonds and hope the issuers do not default or skip interest payments. Or, they can try to sell their bonds on the secondary market at a price well below par. At such a price, the daring new buyers will be getting very high yields as compensation for taking on these risks.

In the 1980s, high-yield, lower-rated bonds, commonly called "junk bonds," were issued when companies needed large sums of money quickly in order to take over other companies and do leveraged buyouts. They found they could rapidly raise cash by offering higher-than-average yields on new bonds. Speculative buyers, anxious to profit from the corporate expansion, were eager to buy these junk bonds and profit from the high coupons. In the end,

BOND RATINGS

Standard & Poor's	Moody's	Meaning
Bank Grade (Investment Grade) Bonds		
AAA	Aaa	Highest rating. High capacity to repay principal and interest.
AA	Aa	Very strong. Slightly less certain than highest ranking.
A	A	Slightly more susceptible to adverse economic conditions.
BBB	Baa	Good capacity to repay principal and interest. Slightly speculative.
Speculative (Non-Investment Grade) Bonds		
BB	Ba	Speculative. Significant chance the issuer could miss an interest payment.
B	B	Issuer has missed one or more interest payments.
C	Caa	No interest is currently being paid on the bond.
D	D	Issuer is in default. Payment of interest or principal is being held back.

changes in the economy, an overabundance of high-yield instruments, corporate buyouts not turning out to be as profitable as hoped for, and high general interest rates all forced the high-yield bond market to teeter. Sellers, aware that they were holding risky investments, then decided to convert their holdings back into cash. Within a very short time, those wishing to liquidate rapidly outnumbered those willing to buy. Although the vast majority of junk bonds didn't actually go into default, a number of issuers were unable to meet their interest payments, and many investors felt themselves lucky to come out with partial repayment on their bonds at maturity.

Today, the junk bond market, valued at over $600 billion, represents an important segment of the fixed-income market. Interested individual investors generally access the junk bond arena by using a mutual fund, since the risks of owning an undiversified portfolio of just a few bonds may outweigh the return possibilities. Moreover, "round lots" of these bonds normally exchange hands between professional traders in values of $25,000 to $1 million. That means that if you want to place $5000 in each of 10 different junk bond positions, you would probably buy them at prices far higher than if an institutional investor were to buy them. Despite the title of "junk bonds," it is important to note that the majority of such bonds do not default and are indeed able to repay their promises.

What is Junk Worth?

Four main variables dictate the motion of the junk bond market niche: default rates, economic strength, the direction of interest rates, and bank lending conditions.

Bond players on the institutional level keep an eye both on the average default rate and on the average recovery rate. They know that unlike stocks, where you lose all your money if the company goes under, junk bonds can still repay after a default. In fact, on average, junk bonds have paid back approximately 44 cents on the dollar *after* they've recovered from defaults. Top-tier traders use this type of analysis for making clever buy and sell decisions.

Economic strength, the direction of interest rates, and bank lending conditions affect all bonds, but their impact is magnified in the junk bond market. As the economy improves, buyers may race out to buy more junk bonds than other bonds because they believe the lower-rated companies can recover more strongly. Similarly, the up-and-down moves in interest rates and the ever-changing availability of credit from banks can sway the sensitive and volatile junk bond market.

Since it's generally unwise for a retail-size account to hold a large position in individual junk bonds, there are mutual funds and money managers that specialize in this area. In selecting the specific fund, find one that is large enough to diversify broadly and has managers with enough experience to understand and navigate through this turbulent market.

"Put Junk in the Garbage. I Want the Safety of CDs!"

If high-risk bonds don't sit well with you because you are a safety-oriented person, perhaps you should consider buying bank certificates of deposit (CDs). CDs are similar to corporate and government bonds in that they pay a stipulated interest and they mature at a specified time. If banks insured by the Federal Deposit Insurance Corporation (FDIC) issue CDs, you can feel comfortable knowing that your money is insured up to $100,000 per institution. You can check with the bank, or go to the FDIC's web site to see if the bank is listed with them.* If you are a frequent CD buyer, pay attention to your total CD value at any given establishment. Don't accumulate more than $100,000 per investor in any one banking institution, since the FDIC only covers this amount should a problem arise.

Both American and non-American investors have a choice of buying CDs at U.S. banks or brokerage firms. In either case, buyers' main concerns usually center on the length of maturity and the interest rate being offered. When brokerage firms handle CDs, they generally buy a large quantity and negotiate a favorable rate with the issuing bank. Then, they offer these CDs, usually in $1000 units, to clients. Should you, as a client, want to sell part, or all, of your holding prior to maturity, there will be no penalty. Instead the broker will sell the CD and, depending on the going interest rate, you might get more (if current rates are lower than

---

* http://www2.fdic.gov/structur/search/findoneinst.asp

your CD is paying), or less (if rates have risen since the CD was issued) than you originally paid.

A particular advantage in buying the CD in lots of $1000 is that if you make a $25,000 investment, for example, and soon thereafter you need $3000 for a personal expense, you can sell off $3000 worth of CDs, and still keep the remaining $22,000 until maturity. This is particularly advantageous if the CD rate is higher than the current interest rate, as you can continue to enjoy the high rate on your remaining holdings. If you buy your CD directly at a bank, there is generally an early withdrawal penalty, often amounting to the equivalent of three to six months of interest, if the CD is cashed in before maturity. Also, when you ask for details, you may be told that CDs are automatically renewed at maturity for a matching period at the new current rate, unless you contact the bank and request that this is not done. For example, if you buy a 12-month 4.5% CD and a year later the rates drop to 3% for a one-year CD, you will get 3% on the rollover if you do nothing – even if the bank is featuring a 5% 18-month CD at that time. It is important, therefore, to check with a bank salesperson before you buy, as the rules at different banks vary. Additionally, if you are like most customers buying a $25,000 CD at the bank, you may find it inconvenient to purchase 25 $1000 certificates and instead buy just one for the full amount. Unfortunately, if you need only some of the money before the term is up, you will have to break the whole CD, and you will be hit with penalties.

In recent years, CDs have taken on more sophisticated aspects as various features have been added. Now you can buy variable rate CDs, inflation-linked CDs, CDs that are callable, and even CDs that have a "death put" that allows an heir to cash it in at full value before maturity should the owner die. (For up-to-date information on different CD choices, go to www.profile-financial.com.)

Two Bond-Buying Strategies

Many investors living on fixed income are partial to bonds because they find comfort in knowing interest payments will arrive on a regular basis. Although most fixed-income obligations pay semiannually, an easy buying program called the "check-a-month" strategy can supplement other cash inflows. Also, for bond buyers concerned that the interest they are now enjoying on their high-yielding CD or bond may disappear when the investment matures, a plan is available for them, too. They can use an approach called "bond laddering."

Check-a-month: This plan is constructed using a selection of six fixed-income securities that pay out interest semiannually. The first holding will pay out in January and July, the next in February and August, and so forth. If you have varying needs at different times of the year, you can buy bonds of differing denominations and then flexibly set up this plan so that you get the largest interest payments in the months when you need them most. For example, if you normally pay your car insurance premiums in the summer, you could tailor your portfolio to supply an extra or larger interest payment in June.

Bond ladders: Let's say you are planning to invest $100,000 in a five-year bond paying 6%. You want to enjoy a steady stream of $6000 yearly income, and in five years roll the bond over again for another five years. However, if interest rates have become lower in five years, for example, 4%, you would find your yearly income dropping from $6000 to $4000.

Laddering your bond portfolio can help you limit the risk of dropping interest rates and can provide you with two potential investment advantages. Let's look at a laddering alternative to the example of $100,000 described above. With your initial investment, instead of buying one large bond, select five $20,000 bonds with successive maturities of one, two, three, four, and five years. When the one-year $20,000 bond comes due, you can reinvest the principal in a five-year bond at the prevailing interest rate. Since at that point in time all of the bonds have advanced one year up the maturity ladder, the five-year position has been vacated and is ready to accept this new investment. Similarly, the following year you do the same with the original two-year bond, and so on. Generally, longer-term bonds pay higher yields than do shorter-term ones, and by following this rotating pattern, your replacement bonds will soon each be purchased on an attractive five-year yield basis. That's the first potential investment advantage.

The second advantage of this fixed-income strategy is that the ladder can often serve as a type of hedge against adverse moves in interest rates. For example, if the entire principal were to be invested in a five-year bond and if interest rates were to drop around the time of maturity there might be few available income choices to your liking, leaving you little alternative but to invest your entire sum at the lower rate. (This is called "reinvestment risk.") But, if it were necessary to invest only one-fifth of your principal at the new low rate and, if over time, you have accumulated some higher-yielding five-year bonds on your ladder, your average rate of return will be higher.

Follow the series of charts below to see how a hypothetical bond ladder might perform if interest rates remain steady over a five-year period. In the first box, examine how you might diversify into a one, two, three, four, and five-year bond. Assuming long-term rates beat short-term ones as shown, your one-year bond will pay 2% and your five-year will pay 6%. The average of the whole portfolio at the beginning will be 4%.

One year	2%
Two year	3%
Three year	4%
Four year	5%
Five year	6%
Average	4.00%

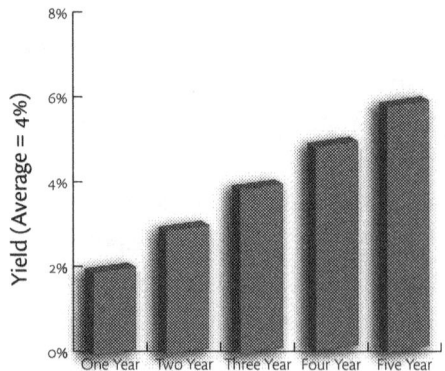

After the first year, your 2% bond matures. Take the proceeds and buy a new five-year bond. Presuming rates hold steady, that piece of your portfolio will start earning 6%, instead of 2%, thus upping your average return to 4.80%. Take a look:

One year	2%
Two year	3%
Three year	4%
Four year	5%
Five year	6%
Five year	6%
Average	4.80%

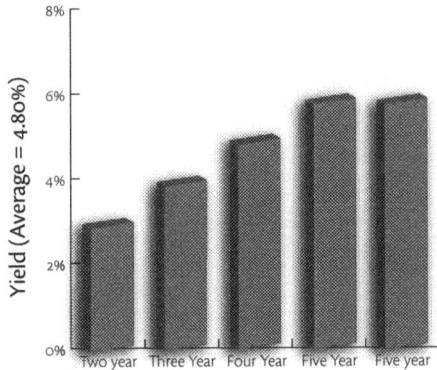

Note that even though more of your money has been used to buy longer-term positions, you nonetheless always have a fifth of your portfolio maturing in a year or less. When the next bond matures, you'll roll that 3% payer to a five-year, perhaps once again receiving 6%. Now your average return on the whole program rises from 4.8% to 5.40%:

One year	2%
Two year	3%
Three year	4%
Four year	5%
Five year	6%
Five year	6%
Five year	6%
Average	5.40%

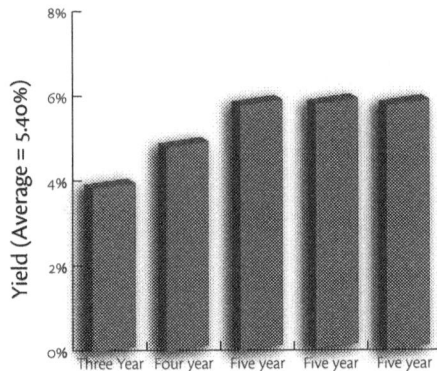

Each time your shortest-term bond matures, you get to replace it with a longer-term position. Though it's unrealistic to assume rates never change, this example shows the concept. Even if rates drop, you still have the flexibility each year to re-evaluate and reinvest your maturing sums. And if rates rise, you come out ahead, since you'll lock in some higher yields. Here's what happens to your average when you replace the maturing 4% with a 6% position:

One year	2%
Two year	3%
Three year	4%
Four year	5%
Five year	6%
Five year	6%
Five year	6%
Five year	6%
Average	5.80%

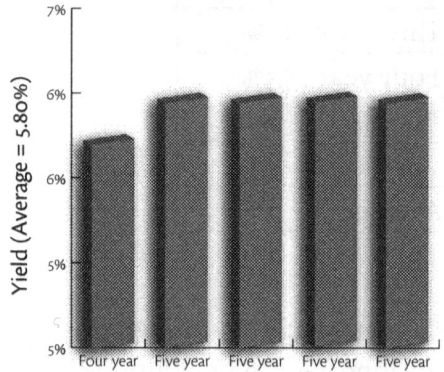

Finally, when your last bond from the original series matures, you can replace it, too, with a longer-term one. When all the bonds yield 6%, your average return equals 6%. You will have produced a bond ladder that has both an excellent return and lots of liquidity since a bond matures every year.

One year	2%
Two year	3%
Three year	4%
Four year	5%
Five year	6%
Five year	6%
Five year	6%
Five year	6%
Five year	6%
Average	6.00%

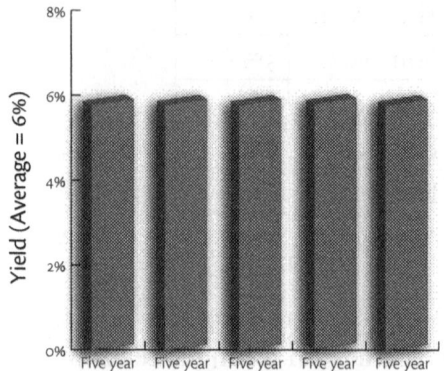

Depending on your needs, ladders can span from several months to many years. Overall, by staggering maturities, your money won't be locked into one position for either too short or too long a period. This strategy is another useful way in which to spread out your risk – time diversification. Also, having bonds maturing regularly allows you to adjust the cash flows they produce in accordance with your situation. If you lose your job, or have some other large, unexpected expense, you'll have money maturing to help you cope.

The Parts of a Ladder

In customizing your own ladder, consider the three important sections:

1. **Rungs**. Calculate the total amount of money you want to place in bonds and divide it over the number of years you wish to invest. That number tells you the total number of issues, or rungs, on your ladder.

2. **Height of the ladder**. Depending on your needs, you could have a short ladder, using fixed-income investments that mature every few months, to a very high ladder, which reaches the longer-term bonds, hopefully giving you a strong cash flow and higher yields.

3. **Materials**. Some ladders are made of wood, some are aluminum. Your bond ladder can consist of corporate bonds, Treasuries, CDs, municipal bonds, and other fixed-income securities, all of which have different strengths and weaknesses. Note that if your bonds are callable, which means the issuer may redeem them before the fixed maturity date, that could disrupt your ladder while you're climbing.

Buying Israeli Bonds

State of Israel bonds, guaranteed by the Israeli government, are popularly sold in America at fund-raising events, where people buy them to show confidence in and offer financial support to the State of Israel. Similarly, Israelis frequently support the Israeli government by buying shekel-denominated bonds at Israeli banks. In general, the bonds sold in Israel work like bonds sold in any other country. However, in order to address investor concerns about inflation and about the volatility of the shekel against the dollar, the Israeli Finance Ministry has issued special types of obligations, including CPI-Indexed bonds and U.S. Dollar-linked bonds.

The Index that Tracks Inflation

The Consumer Price Index (CPI) is a statistical measurement employed by many countries to describe how the prices of household goods and services fluctuate with time. Following these movements enables economists to keep track of the rate of inflation. These indexes are designed to monitor a "market basket" of items in eight basic categories: food, housing, clothing, transportation, recreation, education, medicine, and personal care. Each month, representatives are sent on shopping trips to observe and record changes in the prices of a specific set of items. (The same items are used from month to month.) The compiled results are based on a scale to allow easy comparison with previous sets of price data.

Inflation Reduces Your Purchasing Power

Potential bond investors may be concerned about inflation because it causes erosion in the purchasing power of the shekel and this, in turn, lowers most or even all of the real return on the investment. For instance, bonds that yield 5% annually may seem attractive when one is making the purchase, but if the inflation rate is 3% for the upcoming year then the real return would be only 2%. In other words, an investor who puts 1000 shekels into a 5% one-year bond will get back 1050 shekels at maturity. However, if during the year the inflation rate was 3%, then the jacket he could have bought last year for 1000 shekels would now cost him 1030 shekels and, if he makes the purchase, he will be left with only 20 shekels in hand.

cpi Bonds

To help alleviate bond buyers' problems of effectively losing real return on their investments due to inflation, the Israeli government, in 1985, began issuing cpi-indexed bonds that would produce a true income which would not be diminished by these economic conditions. Buyers of cpi-indexed bonds agree to accept a lower yield than they might get on other debt obligations because they are promised that the inflation rate will be added to their principal for the duration of the bond. This assures them that the effective buying power of their return will not decrease due to inflation. Regardless of whether the inflation rate is 0%, 1%, or even 10%, their real yield is unaffected since the payout is adjusted to compensate for inflation.

U.S. Dollar-Linked Bonds

Although a particular Israeli bond may be of high quality and possess the features that the buyer wants, if the value of the shekel declines against that of the U.S. dollar, the buyer may be at a disadvantage. For those investors who frequently convert shekels to dollars, the erosion in the value of the shekel is akin to the inflation problem discussed previously. If the shekel were to decrease by 3% in its value against the dollar, then once again, an investor in the 5% bond would receive only a 2% real return after converting to the dollar.

Therefore, since 1988, the Israeli government has issued dollar-linked bonds. These securities are linked to the official exchange rate with the U.S. dollar and thereby guarantee that the investors' shekel return on the bond will not be affected by any shekel/dollar price fluctuations.

Summary

- Bonds are generally less volatile than stocks, have a set maturity date, and provide a steady stream of income.

- Corporate bonds have varying features, yields, call dates, and lengths of maturities.
- U.S. government bonds offer excellent security as they are backed by the full faith and credit of the government. These bonds, along with U.S. government agency bonds, corporates, and municipals, meet different portfolio needs.
- Zero coupon bonds help the buyer prepare long in advance for upcoming large bills.
- Bonds selling on the secondary market may be priced above or below par, depending on current interest rates and other market conditions.
- To determine a bond's return, you need to know the following: coupon rate, current yield, yield to maturity, yield to call.
- Investors buy convertible bonds because they believe the underlying stock will go up in price.
- It is important to check a bond's rating before making a purchase. Some buyers prefer high-yielding, lower-rated "junk" bonds while others opt for obligations with higher ratings. Still others will only buy top-rated issues, government Treasuries, or CDs.
- Two bond-buying strategies often used by investors are the check-a-month program and bond laddering.
- Take into account the rate of inflation when determining the real return you are receiving on your bond investments.
- The State of Israel offers various types of bonds, including indexed bonds to help buyers combat the inflation factor, and dollar-linked bonds to overcome problems of currency depreciation.

Chapter 5
Are Mutual Funds for Everyone?

It may be true what the ultra-wealthy industrialist Andrew Carnegie said: "The way to become rich is to put all your eggs in one basket and then watch that basket." However, what if you choose the wrong basket, or forget to watch it one day, or if your eggs just never hatch? In fact, when dealing with your own hard-earned savings, spreading out the risk may make the most sense. One of the most commonly used tactics to spread the risk is to use a basket called a "mutual fund."

A mutual fund is an investment company through which investors pool their money in order to gain ownership of a wide selection of stocks, bonds, or other securities. The fund itself operates as a single large account, owned by the many shareholders. If you invest in such a fund, you own a proportional amount of every security in the portfolio. (In Hebrew, a mutual fund is called a *keren ne'emanut*.)

Why would you want to invest in a mutual fund and give up your right to choose the holdings you like? Moreover, why would you willingly agree to take on the various management fees and expenses? What added value do you get from holding securities through the fund rather than on your own? The answer is that it takes a great deal of time, experience, and general know-how to analyze and track a company properly and to be aware of its potential to move up and down in a changing economy. Mutual funds are investment vehicles that hire professional management teams who address many of these concerns, minimize some of the risks, and provide increased diversification.

People from all walks of life and all degrees of investing sophistication buy mutual funds. Trillions of dollars are invested worldwide in an array of these national and global investment companies. Whether mutual funds are part of retirement programs or are bought in general investing accounts, they meet investors' needs in a variety of ways. Perhaps the key benefit of mutual funds is their ability to help the shareholder own a highly diversified, professionally managed portfolio with one simple purchase.

Four Reasons to Buy Mutual Funds

1. **Save time and lower your stress level.** If you don't want to worry about which individual stocks to buy, when to buy them, and what criteria to use in deciding when to sell, then perhaps mutual funds are for you.

2. **Diversification.** Although diversification is an important investment strategy for minimizing risk, it isn't practical to own hundreds – or even dozens – of individual issues. Notwithstanding the large outlay of cash necessary to get started, there would be a tremendous amount of research and paperwork involved in establishing and maintaining such a diverse portfolio. A mutual fund, on the other hand, offers "turn-key" diversification.

3. **Professional management.** An experienced team, led by a senior manager, researches potential companies that fit the criteria and meet the goals of the mutual fund. They analyze stocks' financial statements, consider the value of the products or services in line with current needs in the economy, and then purchase those securities that they feel will do well. The man-

agers continue to monitor the holdings until they determine that the goals have been met, the financials are no longer so positive, or that other available choices are more suitable – at which point they sell.

4. **Focus on your interests.** Mutual funds come in many varieties and have a wide array of themes, risk factors, and general goals. For example, you can choose a conservative bond fund designed to provide moderate ongoing income and limited price risk, or a bond fund that will pay handsomely on a monthly basis but with a much higher share price risk. You can delve into the world of computers by buying a potentially volatile high-tech fund that you hope will bring you big bucks, or buy into a package of more conservative blue-chip corporations that will distribute some income along with more modest appreciation. There are funds specializing in international markets, small companies, large companies, precious metals, health care, transportation, conservative securities, risky stocks – you name it. There are thousands of mutual funds available, and should you have a special interest, there is probably a fund out there for you.

Your Tolerance for Risk

Mutual funds are considered good vehicles to help mitigate the risks inherent in owning individual stocks and bonds. Individual corporations can – and sometimes do – falter due to external circumstances beyond their control. Politics, the economy, wars, fashion fads, advances in technology (who still buys typewriters?), and even the weather (insurance executives watch the progress of every hurricane and hope the winds subside before reaching their policyholders' homes) can all lead to corporate loss or failure. Of course, so can faulty decision-making and business practices. Remember Enron and WorldCom, two major companies that collapsed virtually overnight due to negligence and mismanagement?

The question then is: Can mutual funds avoid or lessen these market risks? In some cases they can. By owning portions of many corporations, mutual funds are not overly exposed to the troubles of any one company. If you, as an investor, buy a mutual fund with 30 holdings, and one of these holdings drops considerably in value, chances are that you and the other shareholders will not suffer much of a loss in share price. But if you and your fellow investors owned shares directly in the afflicted company, or had bought bonds issued by that company, the value of these holdings would probably have diminished markedly.

What Is Your Real Rate of Return?

In considering your personal tolerance for risk, however, don't only think about market fluctuation. Be aware that changes in the rate of inflation can also affect your returns. Many people don't think about the very real risk of inflation when they buy mutual fund shares. They do not consider their "real return." As discussed earlier in the section on bonds, view your mutual funds in terms of their return on top of inflation. Remember: "Real return" is your yearly return minus the rate of inflation. Let's say you invest $10,000 in a mutual fund. If the fund is worth 5% more at the end of the year, but inflation for the year was 3%, then you are only ahead by 2% with regard to actual buying power. And worse still, if inflation was 6% for the year, your ability to purchase goods with your $10,500 ($10,000 plus the 5% growth) would be less than if you had made the purchases a year earlier with your original $10,000.

How Mutual Funds Really Work

Every fund is a separate company with its own elected board of directors, whose job it is to employ and oversee third-party providers of services. This includes hiring investment advisors to select and manage holdings, transfer agents to keep the records, accountants to monitor the finances, and custodians (usually banks) to hold the investments and cash. The mandate of the board is to protect the interests of the shareholders by overseeing performance, approving contract and fee arrangements, and supervising compliance issues.

Which Fund Suits You Best?

Although you can purchase thousands of different mutual funds, it is neither necessary – nor practical – to consider them all. So how can you narrow down the choices? A good place to start is to review the general categories into which most funds fall and then begin honing in on specific selections.

- *Growth funds.* Buyers of these funds look for long-term appreciation and expect to find names of familiar, established stocks in the portfolio. They believe that as these large, well-known corporations expand and flourish, their earnings will surpass those of smaller, less prominent companies. As this happens, general stock market investors will be willing to pay more for their shares and this will increase the total value of the fund.
- *Aggressive growth funds.* As the name implies, these funds seek to maximize their returns by investing in smaller, usually riskier companies with new products and new ideas. When, and if, these small-cap companies succeed, their share prices generally shoot up dramatically, thus elevating the share prices of the mutual funds that own them. In addition to researching and selecting hopeful winners, managers of aggressive growth funds may also try to enhance the bottom line by using leverage and more aggressive financial strategies.
- *Growth and income funds.* The managers of these funds tend to take a more conservative slant by including dividend-paying stocks that distribute some of their earnings to shareholders rather than using all of it for expansion, acquisition, and other forms of growth. Additionally, many funds in this class also include bonds and preferred stock that produce income and have moderate appreciation potential. Fund investors willing to forego some growth opportunities in return for income

and a greater feeling of safety may choose a fund from this category.

- *Equity income funds.* The managers of these funds, less interested in growth than in income, concentrate on companies paying high dividends. This dividend income often comprises a larger proportion of the total return than does the profit from growth. Why would income-oriented buyers choose these funds over higher-yielding bond funds? Generally, it's because they are willing to make do with the lesser income stream in exchange for the potential growth of the equities.

- *Balanced funds.* These funds usually contain a fixed proportion of stocks and bonds, with an emphasis on conserving principal, while providing the buyer with reliable income and some growth potential. The large quantity of bonds and cash equivalents in a balanced fund create a steady flow of income, while the equity component protects against inflation. Be wary if you have developed your own personal asset allocation model (e.g., what percentage of your money should be in stocks, how much in bonds, and what amount in cash). A "balanced" fund could make it difficult to adhere to your personal asset allocation model since the fund management may adjust their allocation from time to time, and this could knock your own model off kilter.

- *Global and international funds.* Similar, but not identical, these two classes provide an opportunity to invest on a worldwide scale and take advantage of the fact that more than half the world's business takes place outside the United States. By including overseas investments in your portfolio, you can participate in the growth potential of foreign economies, which often do not rise and fall in conjunction with each other. Following the American markets and, for people living in Israel, keeping track of Israeli companies may not be too difficult as news coverage and share prices are often carried in local media. However, buying individual foreign stocks and bonds, and monitoring overseas markets and monetary rates, is a different matter. For those people interested in investing in many different countries, mutual funds of foreign holdings are generally a wise choice. "Global" funds, which include investments in U.S. and non-U.S. companies, and "international" funds, which do not contain American companies, offer share buyers a chance to participate in growth in foreign developed economies as well as in those of third world nations. Managers of these funds research and track prospective corporations, convert and manage foreign currencies, and follow the various political and economic regional scenes.

- *Sector funds.* These funds generally focus on a specific aspect of the economy or on a particular geographic region. There are health care funds, energy funds, transportation, communications, biotechnology, banking, and gold funds. There are Israeli funds, Australian funds, and emerging nation funds. And the list goes on. One concern that some investors have with sector funds is that although they may include a large number of stocks, this diversity is confined to one specific investing area. In non-sector funds, "diversity protection" means that if one company falters, or even if one representative industry is suffering, the entire fund will not necessarily be decimated. But in sector funds, if the representative focus is under pressure, all of the holdings can get hit hard. During the late 1990s, when technology stocks were the rage, tech funds were doing very well. When the market crashed in 2000, though, all the tech funds took a beating.
- *Bond funds.* The term "bond funds" includes various subgroups of funds focusing on: maturity (long, intermediate, short, and ultra-short term), taxable government issues, tax-free municipals, corporate borrowing, high yield, convertible, international, and more.
  a) *Risk level*: Bond funds, unlike equity funds, serve as a source of continual income for buyers with low risk tolerance. "Low risk," however, does not mean *no* risk. The underlying companies (and sometimes municipalities) can

fall on hard times and default, or partially default, on their periodic interest payments or final repayments of principal. This can lower the share price of the fund that owns some of these bonds. Of course, just as in stock funds, if one holding goes sour, the entire fund may lose some value, but will probably still retain much of its strength. When bond fund managers select holdings, they look at the creditworthiness of the underlying companies. They know that firms that are having problems often offer higher yields to bond buyers because these buyers are taking the credit risk that the payments may not be forthcoming or that the investment may not be repaid. More secure lenders (such as the government, government agencies, and highly rated corporations) offer lower interest since buyers are not assuming as much risk. When you are buying shares of a bond fund, therefore, it's a good idea to review its portfolio and see if its bond selections match your personal tolerance for risk.

b) *Economies of scale:* One of the key benefits to bond funds lies in the economies of scale. Bonds normally trade in large pieces, anywhere from $25,000 to $1 million or more. Traders who buy larger quantities can demand better pricing. If you decide to purchase an individual issue for $5000, you will pay a going-rate price. If a fund were to buy the same issue at the same time, but purchase $500,000 worth, they would get a much better deal. That's why, even though you pay added fees by buying a mutual fund, you may still be getting a better price on bonds than if you had bought them yourself.

c) *Interest rate risk:* In addition to the many risks that can cause your investments to decline in value, there is also the risk that interest rates could move against you. If interest rates begin to rise, bonds with lower rates – which looked perfectly acceptable when they were originally purchased – will go down in price and this will drive down the value of your bond fund. Conversely, in a falling interest rate scenario, bond prices will rise and so will the value of your fund. Compare this with owning bonds directly: If interest rates cause the value of your bond to vacillate, you can choose to hold it to maturity to receive the full face value. Bond funds have no maturity date; if rates move against you, you can't just "wait it out" until the end.

Are Index Funds for You?

With the abundance of theme funds available, and the ever-expanding number of growth funds, value funds, balanced funds, bond funds, tax-free funds, socially conscious funds, and more, it may be overwhelming to try to focus on a limited number of funds that will provide you with a broad range of inclusions. This is where index funds come in.

Index mutual funds are designed to replicate, not outperform, the underlying market index. The point of such a fund is to mirror the results of the investments listed on a particular index – such as the S&P 500. The S&P 500 measures the performance of 500 widely held large-cap stocks (General Electric, Coca Cola, Merck, etc.). There are indexes monitoring the NASDAQ 100, the Russell 2000, the Wilshire 5000 and various other small-cap, precious metals, international, and emerging markets listings as well. Whether the underlying index represents blue-chip corporations or more speculative third-world companies, a mutual fund based on a particular related index enables shareholders to own a portion of every included stock.

Is it a bad idea to buy into an index fund knowing that you will only reap an average return? Not at all. In many cases, index funds have outperformed diversified, general equities, and sector funds. Since the composition of most indexes rarely changes, the turnover (amount of trading each year) inside the corresponding fund is limited. Limited trading means commissions and taxable capital gains often seen in other funds can be kept to a minimum.

And as far as costs go – because computers do much of the work in keeping each fund matched to its index, the expenses stay low. It's important to keep in mind, however, that since many indexes are "capitalization weighted," often a few stocks (like General Electric and Microsoft) represent a disproportional amount of the fund. In other words, an index such as the s&p 500 will give more weight to larger companies, and thus its value will reflect the price movements of a fairly small number of stocks. So even though the "500" does mean that there are 500 stocks in the portfolio, more than half the return of the index is attributable to around a dozen stocks – which is not much diversification.

Open-End Mutual Funds

Most fund companies come under the heading of "open-end mutual funds." This means that they issue new shares to meet buyer demand (at a cost calculated daily, based on the net assets of the company divided by the number of outstanding shares) and buy back the shares when investors wish to sell (based on the same calculations). There is a constantly changing capitalization as well as a fluctuating number of shares on any given day. Often there are built-in charges associated with these purchases and sales (explained in the "Cost and Fees" section on page 89).

Closed-End Mutual Funds

Most of the time, when people talk of mutual funds, they're referring to open-end funds. But closed-end funds (cefs) have been on the scene for a long time and share many similarities with their more popular counterparts. Both types of funds are managed by professionals (sometimes closed- and open-end funds are run by the same management), and both provide a diverse selection of holdings (often with a particular theme). The big difference between the two, however, is the way in which the shares are traded. With open-end funds, the company issues and redeems shares. If you want to buy shares, the fund receives your money (either directly or through your brokerage firm) and then creates new shares for you. When you sell, the fund liquidates shares and sends the proceeds to you or to your brokerage account.

In the case of closed-end funds, however, the managers hire an investment bank to help them raise capital by bringing out a new issue and presenting it to the public in an initial offering. The number of shares is finite. Investors thereafter wishing to purchase shares or get rid of their current holdings have to go to the stock exchange and buy or sell at prices set by supply and demand.

For example, if ABC Investment Strategists, Inc. wishes to create a closed-end stock fund, they may hire XYZ Brokerage Firm to help them raise $100 million. Once the money has been collected, ABC will begin trading with that cash. The people who put money in originally will each own a piece of the ABC portfolio. If you missed the original offering and want to own some of those shares, you would then have to buy them from a current owner at the market price. You would not have any direct interaction with ABC itself, because they no longer create new shares; they simply manage the closed portfolio.

Discount or Premium

In many cases, the price per share of a closed-end fund will closely correspond with the actual value of the securities within the portfolio. The total value of all the holdings is called the "net asset value," or NAV. Sometimes, however, the price per share and the NAV fall out of line. If the price at which the shares are trading is less than the NAV of a fund, you can say that the fund is "trading at a discount to NAV." In the opposite case, where the price per share is greater than the NAV, it's trading at a "premium."

Factors That Create a Discount or Premium

If the NAV of a fund is $10 per share, why would an investor be willing to pay $11 per share – thus buying at a premium? Likewise, why would someone holding a share with a $10 NAV be willing to sell it at a discount? Many different factors influence the trading price of a closed-end share versus its actual, underlying net asset value. For example:

- **Out of sight.** Unlike open-end funds that advertise in order to increase their asset base, closed-end funds operate in relative obscurity. These funds have no reason to advertise, since they don't collect more money if more people own shares. In fact, if they spend money on advertising, they'll diminish their asset base and negatively affect their performance. Moreover, less money in the fund will lessen the management fees they collect since these are based on a percentage of the total assets under management. Because these funds lack the exposure of their more conspicuous cousins, there will generally be less demand for them in the market, and they may trade at a discount to NAV.
- **Lagging performance.** If a fund's results trail a comparable index, large numbers of investors may leave, and new ones may be hard to find. This lack of demand for shares will erode the price. In addition, as shareholders lose faith in the managers of the fund, the share price will drop even if the underlying assets that define the NAV retain their value. There have been cases where the shareholders of funds trading at deep discounts have voted to disband the fund, sell off all the assets, and then actually profit by walking away with their share of the true value of the underlying companies and not the prevailing price per share. Even though many CEFs may trade at a discount, this type of scenario is very rare.
- **Priceless portfolios.** "Priceless" here doesn't mean expensive. Rather, for some investments – like unusual bond issues, private placements, bankrupt companies, and more – it's difficult to establish a price. CEFs that specialize in these securities, which are often relatively illiquid, tend to trade at a discount because investors, even professional traders, have a hard time getting a firm price for the underlying assets.

Taxes

Like open-end fund buyers, CEF investors must also bear the brunt of the capital gains that the funds return. Often, a long-established

CEF may hold large positions in highly appreciated stocks. If the fund sells those shares and pays out a capital gains distribution, its current shareholders must pay the tax on the gains. Immediately following these distributions, the share prices usually drop. Knowing the potential tax liability could cause investors to shy away from a CEF, causing it to trade at a discount to NAV.

Investing in Foreign Companies

Some stocks or more unusual assets may be difficult for an individual to obtain. When a country limits foreign investment or imposes certain restrictions, sometimes the only way for individuals to get in on the action is through a fund. That exclusivity may cause a greater demand for the CEF, thereby creating a market premium.

The Pros and Cons of Open- and Closed-End Mutual Funds

In addition to structural differences between open- and closed-end funds, there is also a variance in investing methods. Managers of open-end funds have to deal with fluctuating amounts of available money as ups and downs in the markets often convince investors to buy in large amounts – thus overwhelming the fund managers with an influx of cash – or sell on bad news, making it necessary for management to dig into cash reserves, or even sell positions in order to be able to redeem investors' shares. Closed-end fund managers, on the other hand, can invest following a pre-determined plan since they know in advance how much capital they have available. Along these same lines, closed-end fund managers can more easily invest in speculative or less liquid investments that they feel have great promise because they know they will not be forced to sell at an inopportune time in order to redeem shares. Note that open-end funds trade only once per day, whereas CEFs, because they trade on a stock exchange, can be bought and sold whenever the market is open.

Unit Investment Trusts: Another Way to Buy Diversification

A Unit Investment Trust (UIT) is a registered investment company that buys and holds a relatively fixed portfolio of stocks, bonds, or other securities. Investors in the UIT who buy units of the trust receive their proportion of the interest payments and, when the trust ends and its holdings are liquidated, share in the principal as well. Unit Investment Trusts differ from open- and closed-end mutual funds in that UIT holdings are retained for a fixed period and are not continually traded. In fact, they are generally not traded at all. They are monitored, however, by managers. If the managers feel a dramatic change is occurring that will adversely affect one of the holdings, they may choose to sell it to protect investor interests. In such a case, the proceeds will be divided among the unit holders. Because management is usually less active in UITs than in most mutual funds, the overhead fees on these investments may be lower than on other types of more actively traded programs.

UITs are a useful tool for portfolio diversification as they are geared toward specific industries and/or market sectors in much the same way as mutual funds are. There are UITs focusing on telecommunications, pharmaceuticals, various market indexes, foreign markets, etc., as well as on different categories of fixed-income holdings. Some UITs focus on extremely specialized sectors. For example, you can direct your investment to biotechnology, aerospace and defense, or Dow Jones trading strategies (a well-known one is called the "Dogs of the Dow," also known as the "Select 10"). More specifically, there are programs that concentrate primarily on companies tackling diseases such as Alzheimer's, breast and ovarian cancer, or diabetes. Buyers of UITs can follow their units on an ongoing basis and can, if they choose, sell their investment prior to maturity at the then-current net asset value.

For many investors, the distinct advantage of buying unit trusts rather than mutual funds is transparency. The holdings within the UIT are clearly stated and, generally speaking, do not change during the lifetime of the program. Thus, a buyer knows exactly what he is getting and can determine if these securities are ones that he wants to own. This is useful in order to avoid the scenario of owning different funds that hold the same stocks. It is also easier to avoid style drift and stay true to your asset allocation model with a UIT than with a mutual fund. Additionally, since holdings aren't as actively traded as they are in mutual funds, taxes may be minimized. Dividends and interest are taxed on a yearly basis but taxes on capital gains, if applicable, are due only after the trust has been liquidated.

Note that the term "unit investment trust" can sometimes be misleading to international clients. British investors use the term "unit trusts" to describe what Americans refer to as "mutual funds." Before making a purchase, therefore, be sure you know what you are buying.

Seven Reasons for Selling Mutual Funds

If you sell your funds, or any investment for that matter, without making a large profit, you may feel as though you are admitting a mistake. People often have a lot of emotional baggage tied to their sell decisions, and they frequently maintain positions long after they should be liquidated. However, keep this in mind: Good portfolio management means that when there is just cause, you should sell. In fact, you should see selling as the logical conclusion to buying. Moreover, disposing of a fund at the right time will improve your overall position. But how will you know when it's the right time? Here are some guidelines:

1. **Changes in management.** Because a mutual fund's success is, in large part, based on the knowledge and experience of the manager of the investment team selected by the board, you should carefully review the manager's past performance and style. If, after you buy into the fund, you note that the advisory group has had a great 10-year track record but the manager is being changed, be aware that the new leader may begin to institute a different philosophy. Will it work? Will it coincide with your philosophy? Monitor your fund closely, and sell if the new manager's approach no longer meshes with your goals.

2. **Style drift.** A noticeable change in the management's choice

of investments may indicate a potential style-drift problem. If your large-cap fund wanders heavily into the small-cap field, even if it continues to perform well, this move might adversely affect the diversification within your portfolio as a whole. It may also indicate that the manager's philosophy is veering off track. Although the management team has leeway in choosing appropriate investments, marked deviations from the stated goals are not encouraged. For instance, a fund designed to represent conservative long-term holdings may, according to the prospectus, be permitted to purchase up to 45% in small cap stocks. If you bought into this fund because, in the past, it focused on blue-chip holdings and now it has suddenly changed its character to include the maximum allowed percentage of more risky small caps, you might determine that this fund no longer meets your needs. Interestingly, in a recent industry report, approximately 40% of mutual funds were seen to be classified inaccurately when their stated goals and their actual investments were compared.

3. **Drop in performance.** When returns diminish, or when share prices drop, many investors rush to sell. However, counterintuitive as it may seem, poor results do not always lead to further poor performance. In fact, one study examined mutual funds over a 10-year period. It found that the top performers in the first five years had about a 50–50 chance of maintaining their glory in the second half of the period. Similarly, the poorest performers at the beginning also had about a 50–50 chance to be a top performer toward the end. So believe the phrase, "past performance is no guarantee of future returns." When investigating a fund's drop in performance, look to see if the fund itself is experiencing intrinsic problems, if there has been a change in management, or in management style, if this particular market sector is suffering economic woes, or if the entire market is losing ground. Try to determine why your fund is dropping. Benchmark your holding against a relevant index or against other funds with similar aims. If your fund is

below par within its own class, then this investment may no longer be worth holding.

4. **Changes in your personal goals.** Life's events, such as job changes, moves, and family happenings all affect financial decision-making and influence mutual fund buyers to favor one type of investment over another. For example, when investors are young, they can often afford to be aggressive in their investing choices as they have many years ahead to recoup if losses should occur. As they grow older, however, their financial needs and obligations may change. A more conservative attitude should prevail as the number of years until retirement grows fewer.

5. **Tax issues.** For some people, the tax efficiency of a fund may represent an important factor in considering whether to sell or continue holding. Those in high tax brackets should look for funds that trade in a most efficient manner. (For these investors, "managed money" accounts may be more appropriate than mutual funds. See Chapter 11 on managed money, or go to the "education" tab at www.profile-financial.com.) In addition, if you know you are selling a fund with a large capital gain, you might want to select one of your "loser" funds to sell at the same time. Balancing your losses against your gains can serve to lower your overall tax bite.

6. **Too big.** Sometimes a fund does well and attracts a lot of attention. Whereas the managers may have handled $50 million efficiently, they may not have the infrastructure to quickly accommodate large additional inflows of cash. They may end up holding a lot of money in reserve, making rash decisions, being unable to increase existing positions due to the possibility of exceeding legal limitations, or lacking enough staff to research new ideas. Furthermore, if the fund focuses on a specific market sector, there may not be enough liquidity in that field to absorb additional significant sums of money. Imagine this: If you were the manager of the Fidelity Magellan fund, one of the world's largest such companies with assets

in excess of $50 billion (as of 2006), and if you wanted to put 1.5% of your fund's money into a new holding, you might be hard-pressed to find a corporation that you liked that was large enough to buy into. There are over 5000 traded companies that have capitalization of under $1 billion. So if you put a mere 1.5% of your cash into one of them, you might own the whole company. Your goal (as fund manager) is not to buy and run companies, but to invest in them. As a mutual fund shareholder, if your fund grows too quickly, examine it closely.

7. **Too many.** Some people collect mutual funds like kids collect baseball cards. If you have too many funds to track and analyze, maintaining your investments becomes a full-time job. Moreover, there could be so much overlap in the specific issues that the different funds hold, that you could have a large concentration in one stock because several of your mutual funds may own it in their portfolios. Frequently, people who hold 20 or 30 different funds could achieve all their goals with five to 10 well-chosen positions. Some additional advantages of consolidating mutual fund accounts are that fees normally drop when breakpoints are reached and administration becomes easier.

Research Your Funds

There are many guides and sources you can review to learn about the financial history and current statistics of mutual funds. One of the best-known and most comprehensive research companies is Morningstar. Details on annual and quarterly return rates going back many years are provided, along with income, dividends, capital gains distributions, sales loads, expense ratios, management fees, portfolio turnover, and performance data. Information is given on equity fund style and the size of the companies contained in the portfolios. Details are provided for bond funds describing quality, lengths of maturities, and yields. In addition, Morningstar uses a rating system going from one star (lowest) to five stars (highest) that buyers, as well as financial professionals, often deem very useful. While Morningstar clearly states that such ratings are indicators of past results, and not predictors of future outcomes, many people still count on these stars to screen and choose investments.

Whether you use Morningstar as your reference source or *The Wall Street Journal, Financial World, Barron's, Forbes,* Lipper, s&p, or any other financial journal or service, be aware that a sizable number of mutual funds that are given top ratings one year often drop way down on the scale the following year, and a glowing report in no way guarantees your principal.

The Best Place to Look for Fund Information

The ideal place to get detailed information about the funds you are seriously considering is to go to the source. Contact each fund company (or your financial advisor) and ask for a copy of the prospectus. A prospectus is a detailed legal document conforming strictly to sec requirements that provides in-depth information to a fund buyer or potential buyer. Each prospectus includes sections on investment policy and objectives, administrative procedures (how to buy, sell, and exchange shares), a review of risks, historical background about the fund, financial highlights listing net assets, net investment income, realized and unrealized gains and losses, total returns going back 10 years (or less for newer funds), turnover ratio (how often holdings are bought and sold), expenses and fees (including sales loads, contingent deferred sales charges, 12b-1 fees, and management fees), and other financial data.

In conjunction with studying the prospectus, many investors also request an annual report to get additional and more in-depth understanding of the company's financials. Since mutual fund performance does not always follow a steady path, once a purchase is made, shareholders are well advised to continue to keep up with annual reports in order to keep current on their fund's performance.

Costs and Fees

Detailed in a fund's prospectus are applicable sales charges, fees, and general expenses incurred in running the fund. Mutual funds are for-profit businesses, so even if they call themselves "no load" funds, they are not working for free. Normally, a "no load" fund doesn't charge an entrance or exit fee, but simply takes its management fees from the fund's asset base. All funds have to cover their own expenses for operational and administrative costs, and they do this through an expense ratio that gets assessed daily. Many mutual funds offer multiple classes of shares, with the only difference between them being how they assess charges (not the stock selection within). Therefore, in addition to their regular expense ratio and trading costs that are paid out of the total assets, funds may charge as follows:

- **Front-end load (A-shares).** Front-end loads are charges imposed by some funds when shares are purchased. Usually these are in the neighborhood of 3% to 6% of the total investment. Sometimes this load is charged when shareholders choose to have their capital gains and dividends reinvested in additional shares. It is possible to receive discounts on the commissions of A-shares by using a few different techniques:
  a) *Breakpoints* give you a volume discount on sales charges when making purchases of $25,000, $50,000, $100,000 or more.
  b) *Letters of intent* allow you to tell the fund that you plan to invest enough additional money in the next year to reach a breakpoint. You therefore request that the lower breakpoint level be assessed on the current smaller purchase. The fund will grant you the discount, but if you fail to fulfill your "LOI," they will retroactively charge you the higher fee.
  c) *Rights of accumulation* allow you and your family to effectively view all of your investments in one mutual fund family (not just *one* of their funds, but *any* of their funds) as one big investment with regard to breakpoint benefits. Thus, if you put $60,000 into a stock fund and your

wife invests $40,000 in a bond fund, you can claim the $100,000 breakpoint in order to get a lower commission. Also, if you invested $20,000 in a fund last year (with a $50,000 breakpoint) and now add $30,000, you should get the discounted charge on the newly invested money, as you have now reached the required breakpoint.

d) *Transfers* allow you to move money between different funds in the same family of funds without having to pay a charge for the trade. Sometimes there is a small transfer fee imposed.

- **Contingent deferred sales load (B-shares).** Sometimes referred to as a back-end load or a redemption fee, this charge is imposed on a gradually decreasing scale, and there is no up-front charge. For example, if shares are sold in the first year after the purchase, the fee may be 5%, in the second year the fee may be 4%, and so on until there is no fee. As with the A-shares, you can move between different funds within the family without incurring a sales charge, and without forfeiting accumulated time on the holding pattern. In general, if you liquidate shares and withdraw money, the fund assumes you are selling the oldest shares first, so you end up paying the lowest possible fee.
- **Level-load (C-shares).** This class of shares doesn't have a front-end load, but usually charges around 1% upon surrender if you sell within the first 12 months. After that, there is no surrender charge. While you hold the fund, management normally takes a "level-load" of around 1% per year.
- **Investment advisory fees.** Covering the fund's overhead, this expense can often range from half a percent to well over 1%.
- **Administrative costs.** This pertains to general operating outlays and fees for related fund services.
- **12b-1 fees.** These fees are named after an SEC rule that allows the mutual funds to use shareholder assets for certain marketing expenses.

With more mutual funds than stocks on the New York Stock

Exchange, you will find a great variety in fee assessment methods. Along with the standard share classes listed above, you may also find "institutional" class shares that have even lower fees, but normally require investments in the millions of dollars. It's important to read the prospectus that comes with the fund to understand how much you're paying and why you're paying it.

Paying Taxes

When purchasing individual corporate stock, a buyer knows that the corporation pays taxes on earnings and then, when some of these earnings are passed along to him in the form of dividends, he must also pay taxes on this money. In the case of a mutual fund, however, the situation is somewhat different. For tax purposes, the fund is not treated as a corporation but rather as a conduit for the money. Thus, the fund does not pay taxes on the interest, dividends, and capital gains earned on the securities in the portfolio, but passes most of these obligations directly on to its shareholders. (Mutual funds do pay taxes on other forms of fund income, such as fees and sales charges.)

Certain funds with a high turnover ratio (the rate at which securities are bought and sold during the year) may generate a great number of tax obligations for their shareholders. It is not unusual for the ratio to be 80% to 100% or more, which means that the holdings of the fund may completely change throughout the course of a year. Other funds with a more buy-and-hold philosophy may do fewer trades. Information about a fund's turnover ratio can be found in its prospectus.

Don't Pay Tax on Someone Else's Gains

Sometimes timing can save you money. Most funds make their capital gains and dividend distributions around the end of the calendar year. If you are planning to buy into a fund, consider doing so after these distributions have been made or else you will be on record as a shareholder and will be responsible for paying taxes on this money (which may have come into the fund months before you bought your shares). For example, let's say you buy shares in January at $8 each and during the year earnings of $2 come in. At the end of the year, when the stock is selling for $10, you will receive a distribution of $2 and a statement indicating you owe taxes on the $2. After this distribution, the price of the share will be worth $2 less and so the share price will fall to $8 (to take into account the amount deducted from the fund and distributed to shareholders). Now let's consider what would happen if your neighbor bought the shares in December, just two days before the distribution date. He would pay $10 per share. Two days later, he too would receive a distribution of $2 per share and a statement saying he owes taxes on this $2. In January, his shares would also be worth $8, just as yours are. Now, although he got back $2 on his $10 purchase (in effect he only paid $8) he had to pay taxes on the $2. Had he bought the shares a week later, in January, he would be out-of-pocket the same $8, but would not be liable for taxes on the $2 distribution.

More on Taxes

In addition to paying taxes on distributions – which must be paid regardless of whether the value of the shares have gone up or down since you purchased them, you are also responsible for long- or short-term capital gains taxes when you sell shares at a profit. If the market didn't move in your favor, you can record them as a loss to offset other profits.

In order to calculate gains and losses, it is important to keep statements and records showing your "cost basis." The cost basis is the price you paid for the shares you bought. If you acquired more shares through a reinvestment program, it is the price on the day that you took ownership of the shares. If you inherit shares from a U.S. citizen, for U.S. tax purposes the cost basis is stepped up to the value of the shares on the date of death of the person who bequeathed the stock.

Not every shareholder is concerned with the cost basis of his shares. U.S. citizens with mutual funds in their tax-deferred

*"After deducting income tax, national insurance, and health
insurance, I can only grant you 40% of your wish. And
then don't forget, you still have to pay VAT."*

investing accounts (e.g., IRAS) do not pay U.S. taxes on distributions or capital gains on an annual basis. Instead, when money is withdrawn from their accounts for their retirement needs, as per the regulations of their programs, it is treated as ordinary income.

Keep in mind when reviewing your mutual fund returns that, in general, Israel does not distinguish between short- and long-term capital gains, so that issue may not come into play as it does with the U.S. tax code. Since Israel and the United States have a tax treaty in place, if you pay tax in one country, you may be able to use that sum as a credit in the second country, thus avoiding double taxation. However, because the calculation may be complex, and the laws frequently change, you should certainly contact a qualified tax professional to fully understand your situation.

Summary
- A mutual fund is an investment company in which investors pool their money to buy a wide selection of securities.
- Securities in a mutual fund are researched, analyzed, selected, traded, and monitored by investment professionals.
- Mutual funds can be used to diversify a portfolio by providing financial exposure to different categories of investments.
- Mutual funds vary in their investment outlook. They may focus on growth, growth and income, tax-free or taxable fixed income, international holdings, and various sectors of the economy.
- Index funds aim to mirror the results of specific market indexes as closely as possible.
- Closed-end funds differ from open-end funds in that there are a fixed number of outstanding shares, and these shares trade on the open markets.
- A Unit Investment Trust (UIT) is a diversified portfolio that has a fixed set of securities that generally don't change during the life of the fund.
- Mutual fund shareholders may choose to liquidate their holdings due to changes in management, style shift, a drop in performance, or changes in personal goals.
- The fund prospectus, annual report, and other research sources should be reviewed before making a purchase.
- Timing a mutual fund purchase or sale may save money on taxes.

Chapter 6
Invest Like a Pro

After learning about stocks, bonds, and mutual funds, it's time to explore some of the strategies that professionals use when they invest and see if you can apply their methods to your financial situation. Keep in mind, of course, that it is not necessary to delve into complicated investing ventures in order to reap financial rewards. Buying, monitoring, and taking periodic profits on basic stock and bond holdings has turned many an investor into a wealthy individual. However, if you wish to learn more about how the pros invest, read on to familiarize yourself with some of their techniques.

Know What's Going On

Before you begin a formal investing program, and certainly during the entire period that you are involved in the world of finance, it is useful to be aware of the general economic climate. Learn the language the pros use so you can better understand why they take certain actions and how these moves relate to the total economic picture. The glossary at the end of this book lists some of the most frequently used economic phrases. Read the newspaper, listen to business news on TV and radio, attend seminars, take a course in basic economics, or browse the web. (Feel free to take advantage of all the resources at the Profile website, www.profile-financial.com.)

Follow the Analysts

Before honing in on a particular company, financial managers often spend time reviewing the general economic environment. They note at what point of the business cycle they believe the economy is currently in, listen to industry analysts, compare opinions, and then thoroughly review corporate reports and forecasts. Listening, reading, questioning, following up – and always seeking to learn more – that's what the pros do. And so can you.

The Pros Listen to the Analysts

Security analysts understand that in order to determine a fair or intrinsic value for securities it is necessary to concentrate on corporate numbers detailing current, past, and future earnings and expenses. They also know it is essential to include in their calculations data related to economic happenings, as well as to specific industry and market trends. Certain analysts rely more heavily on one or the other of these calculation philosophies and become known as "fundamental" analysts or "technical" analysts. While some individual investors subscribe to the ideology of one particular school, others learn from both and then make case-by-case decisions.

Fundamental Analysis

Followers of this philosophy concentrate on basic economic conditions such as inflation rates, yields, international trading, unemployment figures, and the fiscal budget. From these broad trends, they try to draw conclusions about long-term market movements.

In their research, fundamental analysts study the political situation and the economy at large to get an overall picture of what's to come. Then they turn their attention to industry surveys, trade publications, and specialty business and financial journals to gain insight into various industry sectors. From there they go on to review individual companies and carefully go through their annual reports to track balance sheets, income statements, and related fund projections. Ultimately, their goal is to reasonably predict the future earnings potential of various corporations and then determine if, at the current market values, the shares are a good buy.

Once fundamental analysts feel they have a grasp of the big picture, they then focus on particular industries to find those they believe will outperform the market in the next few years. Questions they might address are: Will there be an ample supply of oil so that consumers will be encouraged to buy new cars? Or, will the music industry suffer as people buy less music now that they can download songs from the internet?

After a particular industry or sector has been selected for consideration, fundamental analysts turn to individual corporations and study certain statistics to determine which companies have the greatest potential to succeed. In their research, they use ratios to compare various companies, much as sports fans use ratios to compare baseball players' batting averages. Baseball fans don't only want to know how many hits the players make, but they want to know the ratio of hits to the number of times their heroes came up to bat. Similarly, analysts use ratios to compare companies. They look at the current earnings of various companies and figure out the price/earnings ratios. In each case, they try to determine if an individual stock is worth its price.

The price/earnings (P/E) ratio is calculated by taking the current share price and dividing it by the annual earnings per share (EPS). Earnings per share denotes a company's total earnings divided by the number of shares outstanding. For example, if XYZ stock is selling at $40 per share and the EPS is $4, the P/E ratio is 10. Speculative stocks often sell at P/Es that are very high, perhaps even in the double or triple digits. Their share price may be overvalued with limited corporate earnings, as happened a short time

"I didn't really fail, Dad. It's called a 'correction.'
The fundamentals still look strong."

ago with many of the start-up tech stocks. Or, the P/E ratio could be very low. This might be due to worry about a company's ability to sustain its earnings. Sometimes low P/E ratios occur when high inflation causes prices to shoot up, only to fall sharply when the government institutes anti-inflation measures. Then again, the P/E might decline if public interest in the company or industry fades, or if major changes occur on the political or economic scene.

Keeping Track: Using Indexes

Before moving on to the next group of specialists, known as "technical analysts," who base much of their thinking on studying charts instead of companies, let's quickly review why indexes are considered so important, and what aficionados of these guideposts look for.

The S&P 500

A stock index is a representative compilation of holdings. Analysts, as well as the public, monitor various indexes to get a feel for the general market – or for a particular market sector. One of the most popular indexes is Standard & Poor's. S&P's Ratings Service has been a leading provider of stock market information since 1916. The S&P 500 index traces 500 of the market's most important companies. The stocks are chosen based on each corporation's representation in the U.S. economy, its financial profile, and its liquidity. Often investors use the S&P 500 as an investment benchmark, relying on the index to gauge their overall progress. For example, a person who lost 6% on his investments might claim success when comparing his loss to the S&P's drop of 9.2% during the same period.

The Dow Jones Industrial Average

With over a 100-year history, the Dow Jones Industrial Average (DJIA) follows 30 stocks (see table on next page) that the editors of *The Wall Street Journal* feel most represent American business. Why are these editors the ones to choose? Because the Dow Jones company owns the *Journal*.

Indexes for Other Markets

The third most frequently watched listing is the NASDAQ 100, a heavily high-tech index that tracks the 100 largest companies on the NASDAQ. There's also the S&P Mid-Cap 400, the Russell 2000 (small caps), the Morgan Stanley World Index (global markets), and a variety of other indexes dealing with categories such as health care, energy, transportation, specific countries, and more.

As the financial scene changes, new indexes are sometimes created to represent certain significant categories. A company

COMPONENTS OF THE DOW JONES
INDUSTRIAL AVERAGE

3M Co.	Home Depot Inc.
AIG	Honeywell International
Alcoa Inc.	IBM
Altria Group Inc.	Intel Corp.
American Express Co.	Johnson & Johnson
AT&T	JPMorgan Chase & Co.
Boeing Co.	McDonald's Corp.
Caterpillar Inc.	Merck & Co. Inc.
Citigroup Inc.	Microsoft Corp.
Coca-Cola Co.	Pfizer Inc.
DuPont	Procter & Gamble Co.
Exxon Mobil Corp.	United Technologies
General Electric Co.	Verizon Communications
General Motors Corp.	Wal-Mart Stores Inc.
Hewlett-Packard Co.	Walt Disney Co.

choosing to create a new index can design, copyright, and publicize it. In fact, anyone can set up an index and try to market it. Perhaps one day you might see the "Profile Investments 50 Financial Index." If enough people cared about that list, the newspapers might start to quote its daily fluctuations and soon it would be well known.

Indexes in Israel

In Israel, the Tel Aviv Stock Exchange is also tracked by a number of indexes. TASE investors watch the TA 25, also known as the Maof Index, and the TA 100 (which includes some of the same stocks as the Maof, such as Teva Pharmaceuticals, Bank Hapoalim, Bezeq, Koor, and Bank Mizrahi). Additionally, investors interested in the nation's prominent high-tech stocks focus their attention on the Tel-Tech 75.

Technical Analysis

Technical analysts take a different slant from fundamental analysts on viewing potential buying opportunities. They believe that trading history affects stock prices more than general economic factors and current balance sheet results. Technical analysts will also sometimes apply their strategies to other types of securities trading, such as futures, currencies, and options, and to more esoteric trading instruments such as "interest rate swaps" and "inverse floaters." A word of caution: If you're considering trying sophisticated trading patterns using investments like these, be very careful; most amateur investors lose money quickly. Even if you've read a few books on the topic, don't get too confident. Remember the words of the humorist and essayist Clarence Day: "Information's pretty thin stuff, unless mixed with experience."

"Technicians," as technical analysts are sometimes called, follow market and individual stock price trends and focus on charting price movements, tracking indexes, and monitoring trading volume. They do this in an effort to anticipate how buyers and sellers will react to the latest news, and to estimate what will motivate them to continue or to change their patterns in the future. They focus on investor behavior and market psychology. Short-term investors, as opposed to those more inclined to buy and hold, frequently use technical analysis.

In comparing different historical periods, short-term industry trends frequently differ from one another. But, trends covering longer periods often depict the major averages and indexes moving together. Clues like these are what technicians look for in planning their moves. The main tools used by technical analysts are charts and graphs reflecting averages such as the Dow Jones Industrial Average, the Standard & Poor's 500, and the Russell 1000, 2000, and 3000 (which track a broader spread of companies). They also look at measures of volume, meaning the number of shares that are traded over a certain time frame. Changes may indicate an upcoming move in a stock's price. If a stock begins trading more actively than usual, the technical pros may predict a "breakout." This term indicates that a stock has begun to move out of its normal price range and may represent a good trading opportunity.

Another statistical line that technical analysts track is one that records "moving averages." The analysts note the prices of a stock over a set period of time – say a month, and then calculate the average daily price. Thereafter, if the stock price rises above this number, it is considered a bullish (optimistic) sign and conversely, if a lower price appears, a bearish (pessimistic) mindset is formed.

Here are a few terms that technical analysts may use when considering a position:

- *Open* – This is the first trade of the day. The price is considered important because it reflects the feeling of the market after everyone has had a chance to think about the price of the security and "sleep on it."
- *Close* – This is the last price before the market closes. Technicians will examine the difference between the open and close prices to look for trends.
- *Bear trap* – When a price level descends and stays low, the bears may start to sell rapidly. If the price then bounces back up, it's known as a "bear trap."
- *Support and resistance* – Imagine that buyers and sellers are constantly battling to come to an agreed-upon price for a stock. Optimists push the stock up and pessimists push the price down. When the price peaks, more people will start to sell, pushing the price down. This peak is called a "resistance level." On the other side, when the price drops low enough so that more people start to buy, that point on the chart is known as a "support level" (see chart on next page).

For technical analysts, interpreting charts accurately enough to be able to gauge when is the best time to get in or out of the market is a form of art as well as science. A great deal of thought must go into the decisions, and constant oversight of a position must be

SUPPORT & RESISTANCE

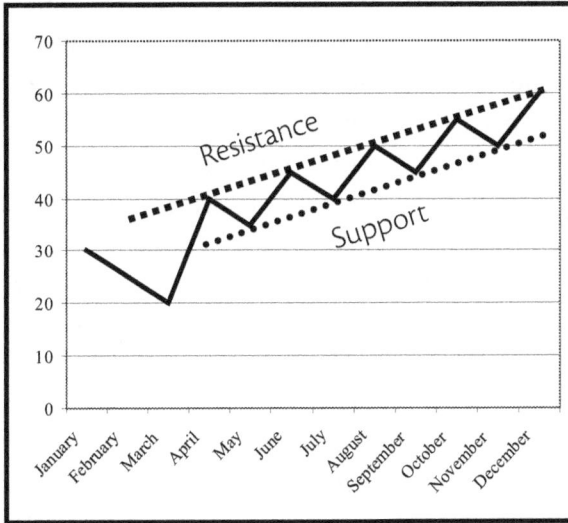

maintained. Technical analysts heed the words of General George Patton, who said, "Take calculated risks. That is quite different from being rash."

For the average person, timing the market will probably be successful some of the time – but not always. That's why for an investor, as opposed to a professional trader, *time in* the market is often more rewarding than *timing* the market.

Pros Look to Monte Carlo

Although the casinos of Monte Carlo attract those trying to strike it rich, the possibilities that these people might lose great sums are always present. In the investment world, however, the reference to Monte Carlo brings thoughts other than gambling casinos to mind. Pros in the financial field know that investments do not return the same gains year after year, nor do interest yields or rates of inflation remain constant. If they did, determining future value would simply be a matter of accurately estimating how much money to allocate to various investments in order to be assured of an adequate cash flow throughout future years.

Many people plan for the years ahead by averaging investment returns of the past and then, using these figures, make assumptions about the future. Thus, if they earned 8% last year and 4% the year before, they average their total return and decide it is reasonable to count on a 6% average return for the years ahead. This type of simplification can sometimes be grossly misleading. For example, let's say a client has a $100,000 portfolio and he assumes that he'll average a return of 6% on it, or $6000 per year (not counting taxes and expenses). He then plans to withdraw $6000 per year for an annual family vacation, believing that, over time, his basic portfolio will maintain its value. This may not always be the case. Indeed, here's where a reality check must be made.

Take a look at the chart on the opposite page. In Example A, we see a series of 10 years' worth of returns on a $100,000 initial investment portfolio. The average annual return is 6%, and the investor withdraws $6000 per year for vacations. Look carefully. Strangely enough, his initial capital is only worth about half after 10 years. Why? Although the portfolio did average 6% over the total 10-year period, the actual portfolio value did not grow by that amount on a yearly basis. During the first few years, the market value of the portfolio went down. Then, since the investor was also withdrawing his preplanned annual $6000, his total net worth actually diminished even more during each of the early successive years. By the time the market turned around and started its strong recovery, there was a much smaller principal sum.

Example B has exactly the same annual returns, but run in reverse order. In other words, the first year's return in Example A now becomes the tenth year's return in Example B – and so forth. Since the percentages total up the same, the 6% average annual return is also the same in both examples. In this example, the $6000 annual vacation sums are also being withdrawn. The surprising bottom-line results show that even though the average annual return is exactly the same (6%), the resulting portfolio values are vastly different.

COMPARISON OF TWO PORTFOLIOS
WITH SAME AVERAGE ANNUAL RETURN
BUT DIFFERENT OUTCOMES

Initial portfolio value = $100,000
Average annual return = 6%
Annual withdrawal of $6,000

EXAMPLE A

Year #	Return	Value of account
1	-15.00%	$79,000
2	-9.00%	$65,890
3	-5.00%	$56,595
4	-4.00%	$48,331
5	-3.00%	$40,881
6	8.00%	$38,152
7	12.00%	$36,730
8	22.00%	$38,811
9	24.00%	$42,125
10	30.00%	
Average Annual Return	6.00%	$48,763

EXAMPLE B

Year #	Return	Value of account
1	30.00%	$124,000
2	24.00%	$147,760
3	22.00%	$174,267
4	12.00%	$189,179
5	8.00%	$198,313
6	-3.00%	$186,364
7	-4.00%	$172,909
8	-5.00%	$158,264
9	-9.00%	$138,020
10	-15.00%	
Average Annual Return	6.00%	$111,317

Because pros need to account for future variables while planning for the future, they cannot necessarily settle for estimated averages. Therefore, they rely on a statistical modeling technique known as a "Monte Carlo Simulation." This sophisticated format provides in-depth gauges to help an investor determine the probability of meeting specific future goals.

Monte Carlo Simulation (MCS) is an analysis tool that deals with uncertainty. The goal behind its use is to find a way to put order into a large body of data (such as capital market results) so that practical decisions can be made (e.g., how much money can

I spend annually?). By using computer-driven MCS programs to analyze answers based on mathematical probabilities, pros in the field of investing greatly improve their chances of following the right roads to financial success. In the previous charts, there was a wide range of possible returns, based on two numerical configurations, for an investor who wanted a yearly $6000 income stream. However, two such examples are insufficient to use as a basis for making a reasonable estimate of future returns.

How can a Monte Carlo Simulation help? As a very simplified response, imagine taking a fish bowl and filling it with 10 slips of paper on which various stock market annual returns are written. Then draw a slip, note the result on a chart, and throw the paper back into the bowl (as this same answer could be a possible return for a future year too). After repeating this nine more times, there will be one possible estimation as to what might happen if you invested over a 10-year period. If this exercise is repeated numerous times, a pattern might develop. Investment pros know, however, that a pattern based on relatively few examples (10, 50, or even 100) may not provide very reliable potential outcome estimation. Therefore, they turn to MCS programs to determine – based on very large numbers – the probability of achieving successful outcomes as a result of choosing particular investing paths.

How do these specialized computer programs arrive at conclusions? They use random number generation while taking into account capital markets information, standard deviation patterns, distribution curves, etc. They produce thousands of possible market results and, in so doing, create vast numbers of in-depth probability outcomes. Monte Carlo reports can lead to conclusions such as, "If you continue spending the way you plan, and if your asset allocation is kept in the current position, you have a 55% chance of success." You can then decide if that probability level of success is satisfactory for you. Generally, people feel reasonably secure with a 70% to 80% chance of success in their financial plans. Of course, as they get older, they tend to look for an even greater probability of success.

What Other Investing Strategies do the Pros Use?

Professional managers, experienced traders, and other savvy investors rely on a variety of investment strategies to make their money grow and, hopefully, to outperform the market. Some may be conservative, some risky, and some in between. Below are other investment strategies commonly used by the pros. See which ones match your own investing outlook and might work for you.

Strategy #1: *Buy and Hold*

Simply put, this practice encourages a person to buy quality stocks and hold on to them. It is not designed for people who want to profit from a few points and then sell, nor is it suggested for those who can't bear to see their holdings lose a couple of points. Basically, it works best for purchasers who carefully research and determine that the companies they are buying should do well because they are well run, well funded, and well placed in the business sectors in which they operate.

A benefit of this investing strategy is that by accumulating and holding on to a steady portfolio, the buy-and-hold investor minimizes transaction costs and may reduce capital gains taxes caused by frequent trading. Should the positive factors for owning specific stocks change – as determined by frequent monitoring of the holdings – the investor should consider selling.

Certainly, pros such as Warren Buffet, Peter Lynch, and Charles Brandes have demonstrated that the buy-and-hold approach has great merit. They have created billions of dollars of wealth for themselves and for their shareholders by holding their investments for the long term.

Strategy #2: *Dollar-Cost Averaging*

Followers of this strategy invest a fixed dollar amount at regular intervals to buy additional shares of the positions they hold. They want to acquire as many shares as possible with the sum of money they are putting in, regardless of the price per share on the day of the transaction. As a result, when prices are low, more shares are purchased with the fixed amount than when the prices are higher. Since market prices fluctuate over time, investors using this plan end up owning more shares purchased at lows than at highs.

For example, let's look at a one-year chart (see below) for a person who has decided to invest $100 per month in the ABC mutual fund. (Dollar-cost averaging normally works best with mutual funds.) Over the 12-month period, he invests $1200 and, based on the monthly purchase price, he accumulates 84.58 shares. (You cannot normally buy fractional shares of stocks, but you can with mutual funds.) By taking the total cost ($1200) and dividing it by the number of shares (84.58) we find his average cost per share is $14.19. Take a look at the chart to see that in June and July, when the shares were at their lowest price, he purchased 20 shares, whereas in the two months that the shares were highest, January and December, he only bought a total of 10 shares.

Month	Amount invested	Share price	# Shares bought
January	$100	$20	5.00
February	$100	$18	5.56
March	$100	$16	6.25
April	$100	$14	7.15
May	$100	$12	8.33
June	$100	$10	10.00
July	$100	$10	10.00
August	$100	$12	8.33
September	$100	$14	7.15
October	$100	$16	6.25
November	$100	$18	5.56
December	$100	$20	5.00
Total	$1200		84.58
Avg. cost per share:		$1200 ÷ 84.58 = $14.19	

By dollar-cost averaging, his average cost per share ($14.19) was less than it would have been if he had simply invested the full $1200 at the beginning. Then he would have bought 60 shares at $20 apiece. On the other hand, had the market gone steadily up over the one-year period, he would have been better off buying all the shares at once at the beginning. Since there is no way of knowing how the market will move, it may be wise to minimize risk by spreading out purchases over time.

One complaint that people have with dollar-cost averaging comes when they sell their position and have to calculate their capital gains. Each purchase has its own separate cost basis. So in this example, you would have to figure out the gains you made on each $100 that you invested. Good software and/or clear brokerage statements can help with this task. Also, many mutual fund companies provide cost basis information on periodic statements or upon request. One way to avoid the hassle of having to make these calculations is to use this strategy in tax-deferred accounts (such as IRAs), where taxes aren't paid each time a security is sold at a profit.

Strategy #3: *Market Timing*
Market timing is a strategy that is essentially the opposite of dollar-cost averaging. Pros who believe they can put their money into the market at "optimal" times carefully adhere to trends and other financial criteria. They believe that markets follow predictable patterns and that market timers, as astute observers, can select stocks when they are just ripe for picking. One major problem with this approach is that even when a person has wisely chosen a sector or correctly analyzed a cyclical pattern, the specific stock he chooses may not consistently conform to his expectations. Equally upsetting to the market timer is that he can never know with certainty that when he sees a bargain, the prices might not drop even further after he buys. Many academic studies have demonstrated that market timers underperform the market as a whole. If they

were simply to buy an index fund, they could spend all day on other activities rather than watching the market, and still come out ahead. As onlookers of this strategy observe, jumping in and out may not make you money; it may only make you tired.

Perhaps one group of people most attuned to market timing, but often without the emphasis on research and analysis, are the investors referred to as "day traders." These players, by and large, are not investment pros, and often buy and sell based on their hunches, hot tips they get on the internet, and their willingness to take a chance. They win some, and lose some, but in the end there are far more losers than winners.

Strategy #4: *Buying IPOS*

Toward the end of the 1990s, buying IPOs (initial public offerings) became the investing sport of choice. Although IPOs are still issued when businesses need additional capital for development, the buying frenzy from past years has slowed down. Buyers who want to participate in the growth of a new company giving up its private ownership and going public now buy shares based on their belief that over time, the corporation will grow and its earnings will expand. In the days of the hot IPOs, many high-profile new companies made headlines by doubling, tripling, or more in price during the hours or days after going public. Investors wanted a piece of the action and begged their brokers to get them involved. Due to the tremendous demand for new shares, prices skyrocketed, and those who got in at the offering prices made a fortune (if they sold in time). IPO mania was strong with technology stock offerings, and many would-be pros began basing their investment strategies on buying IPOs and selling them rapidly. Often they did not pick up a prospectus, study a company financial report, or even look at the management history. It was all a gamble, and many players lost. Hopefully, people have learned the lesson that they should study new companies just as carefully as they do the more established ones. If and when they buy an IPO, they should do so based on in-depth research and analysis – just as the real pros do.

Strategy #5: *Short-Selling*

Selling a stock "short" means that an investor sells a stock he does not own. How can you sell something you don't own? Let's say an investor feels XYZ stock is markedly *overpriced*. He calculates that, based on earnings and other factors, the price per share should be about $20. Yet he sees the stock is currently selling for $40. He believes that new competing products are coming out in the sector that will cause the company to lose its market share. He anticipates that investors will begin dumping their XYZ shares, which will cause the price to plummet. He therefore decides to sell shares today at the $40 price and wait until the stock goes down. At that point, he will then re-buy the same number of shares at a lower price – thus making a nice profit. Profits from selling short relate to the same principal as trading "long" (the normal way of trading): buy low, sell high. The difference, however, is in the order. Short-sellers hope to sell high first, and then later buy back at a low price.

Short-selling transactions are done through a brokerage firm that handles the paperwork involved that allows a person to borrow the shares from another account to effect the sale. The individual selling short has to have sufficient funds in his account to cover this loan lest the stock go up, rather than down in price, and he has to pay back more money than the sale proceeds.

The pros who sell short are well aware of the risks involved. They know that if the underlying company has some good luck, or if the prevailing bear market suddenly becomes bullish, their potential gain may turn into a terrible loss. They also know that if they buy a position long, (for example, if they pay $10 a share for a stock, and the company fails) the most they can lose is their $10 per share. But if they sell a stock short at $10 per share (intending to cover their short when the stock drops to $5) and the stock price begins going up, there is no limit to how high the price can go nor to how much money they could lose until they buy back the shares. Theoretically, they could lose an unlimited amount of money.

Sophisticated professionals often include various protection techniques, such as placing stop orders or buying call options to hedge their short positions, but even with these, they are still dealing in risky business.

While short-sellers may hope that prices will go down, there are stock market rules that try to prevent individuals from influencing the market to benefit their own interests. When a stock is already losing value, the last thing the company (and the market as a whole) wants to see is a group of short-sellers pushing the price down further. Therefore, regulations were established to implement the "uptick rule" in an effort to control a downward spin. This rule states that the last trade must be higher than the previous trade in order for an investor to be allowed to sell short. Thus, this ruling both prevents short-sellers from forcing down the value of a stock, and simultaneously limits the potential profits of a short sale. (Note that this rule applies to company shares, but not necessarily to those of exchange-traded index funds.)

Short-sellers also need to be aware of the possibility of an early call. When a stock is shorted, shares are borrowed; the lender doesn't know that his stocks have been lent to someone else. What happens if the original owner wants to sell those shares? Ordinarily, the brokerage firm simply borrows the shares from a third investor. Complications may arise, however, if the brokerage firm cannot get the requisite shares of the stock in question to cover the transaction. This scenario is more likely to occur with stocks that have low volume. In this situation, the short sale will get "called" early, and the short-seller will be forced to close his position immediately, regardless of the stock's current value. If the stock's value is up, the short-seller will lose money on the investment. The possibility of this scenario occurring makes short-selling less liquid companies a particularly risky endeavor.

There may be additional costs associated with shorting stocks. If you sit on a short sell when a dividend is paid, you will have to cover this amount so it can be credited to the lender's account. If the company announces a 50-cent dividend per share, you must pay that amount out of your own pocket to the person who actually owns the stock.

Margin fees can be another expense of selling short. When you short a stock, the brokerage firm will demand that you have sufficient cash available to cover any potential loss. To ensure that you have enough funds, you may have to use your other holdings as collateral and borrow money from the brokerage firm using margin. Borrowing money on margin is not free (see the section below on using margin). Regardless of how profitable your short-sell is, margin interest payments can effectively minimize your total return. Thus, these extra expenses – not to mention the basic commissions you'll pay for executing the stock trades – need to be factored into any calculation of the profit you hope to make.

Strategy #6: *Buying on Margin*

Professional investors often believe that their intended purchases are so worthwhile that they would like to buy a larger number of shares than they can currently afford. How do they do it? They borrow money from the brokerage firm to buy the additional shares "on margin." The brokerage firm extends credit to the investor, that is, it lends him the money to purchase the extra shares in accordance with both the federal rules (called "Regulation T") and with the brokerage firm's own requirements. Margin accounts offer investors the ability to buy many extra shares of stock for a specific amount of money; it gives them "leverage" (a term the British call "gearing").

How does buying on margin actually work? Let's say you feel that the ABC Company will soon move up from its $20 price. You have $2000 available, which would allow you to buy 100 shares. But you are enthusiastic and would like to buy 200 shares. You sign the required paperwork, open a margin account, and then place an order for 200 shares. The brokerage firm will lend you the additional $2000 (and charge you margin interest for the amount you borrow) to buy the extra shares. The stock you buy must remain in your brokerage account as collateral for the loan.

If ABC goes up to $30 and you sell your 200 shares, you will receive $6000. From this, you can repay your $2000 debt (plus commissions and interest), deduct the $2000 you originally put down, and still have a profit of about $2000. If, however, you had only bought 100 shares because that is all you were able to afford at that time, then when you sold at $30, your profit would only have been $1000. In the first case your $2000 outlay enabled you to make a $2000 profit (a 100% return on investment); in the second case your $2000 only put you ahead $1000 (a 50% return).

What would have happened if you guessed wrong and ABC went down in price? Under Regulation T, your brokerage firm can only lend you 50% of the total value of the purchase. So, if the stock went down from $20 (remember your original 200-share purchase cost $4000 – you put up $2000 and the firm put up $2000) to $15 per share (now the total value of the holding is only $3000), a problem would be created. Since the firm's $2000 loan to you is now more than half the total value, you will be asked to pay the firm an additional $500 so that they will only be putting up half the $3000 value. Alternatively, you could deposit other "marginable" securities in the account to protect the firm's loan, or sell off some of the holding to equalize the debt.

Buying on margin can be risky, especially if the stock market turns bearish. As a margined security starts dropping in price, the broker will keep calling the investor for the additional funds necessary to maintain the required collateral. If the investor cannot come up with the additional funds, or if the investor has purchased many stocks on margin and is getting many margin calls, he may finally have to sell his investment at a big loss. Had he paid in full for his purchase and not borrowed, he might have decided to hold onto the security and wait for the market to recover.

The most an investor can lose when buying stocks without margin is the amount of money he invests. A margined investor, though, stands to lose his initial investment *plus* the amount of money he borrowed on margin. Beware! Margin trading is blamed for some of the greatest drops in stock market history. If you use margin, make sure that the added dangers are appropriate for your personal risk profile.

Strategy #7: *Buying and Selling Options*
Options trading, with its many intricacies, can be complicated. The pros often use basic options know-how along with unique investing twists in executing their strategies, but these techniques are not generally recommended for the average investor. Nonetheless, there are times when options make sense for personal portfolios.

Let's consider how an option is used. For a certain sum of money, an investor can buy the right to purchase or sell a set number of shares of stock at a stated **price** (called the "strike price") within a specified period of **time** (the final day of which is called the "expiration date"). When an investor buys an option, he is, in effect, controlling a certain number of shares. His option usually covers a 100-share lot, called a "contract." Thus, when he buys one contract of ABC stock at $2, he pays $200 for the purchase. With that in mind, let's consider the two main option categories: *Calls* and *Puts*.

Calls
When you buy a call option (a contract) from a seller (sometimes called the option "writer"), it gives you the right to buy a specific number of shares of a stock from him at a set price (strike price) for a limited period of time (until the expiration date). For example, if BCD stock is now selling at $34 per share but you feel that within the next six months it is likely to go way up, you might buy an option to purchase 100 shares of BCD at $35 at any time during the next half a year. For the right to buy the shares at $35 (regardless of the market price at that time) you must pay the current owner (the seller) a premium, for example, $1 per share ($100 for the 100 share contract). If you predicted correctly, and the stock starts moving up, as the price bypasses $35 and reaches, say, $38, you can exercise your option and buy the 100 shares at

the strike price ($35 per share for a total cost of $3500). Then you can turn around and sell the holding for $38 (total amount $3800) and come out $300 ahead. Excluding taxes and commissions (as do all examples in this book, unless otherwise noted), you will profit $200 – and your total risk was your $100 outlay. Your $100 investment profited you $200 (Sale value: $3800, minus purchase cost of the shares: $3500, minus option cost: $100, totals a profit of $200, or 200%).

Proceeds from sale of stock	$3,800
Cost to purchase stock when exercising option	-$3,500
Cost of option	-$100
Total profit	**$200**

Is it Better to Buy the Stock or the Option?

What if you had decided not to buy an option but simply bought 100 shares of the stock at $34, for a total outlay of $3400? In this case, instead of putting only $100 at risk, you're putting $3400 on the table. Should the stock move up to $38, as shown in the above example, you could sell the stock for $3800. The $400 profit represents a 12% gain from your original investment. The 12% gain is lower than the 200% gain in percentage terms using the options strategy, but the $400 profit is double the sum earned with the option.

So why buy the option? Let's say the stock drops to $30 per share after your purchase of $3400. You would be down $400, or 12%, since your position would be worth only $3000. If, however, you purchased the option and the stock dropped to $30, you would not exercise your right to buy at $35 – after all, why would you buy the stock at $35 when it's available on the stock market at $30? In this case, you would have lost your $100 premium, which is a 100% loss; however, the actual loss of $100 is much less than the loss of $400 you might have incurred with the stock purchase.

Puts

A "put" is an option that gives the buyer the right to sell a certain number of shares of a stock at a specified strike price on or before an expiration date. In effect, it is the opposite of a "call." An investor who believes a stock currently selling at $36 per share is about to drop in price might buy an "April 35 put" contract from a seller who is not so pessimistic and who, in fact, would be happy to purchase the shares from the put-buyer, should he choose to sell them. The put-buyer pays a premium, for example, $1 per share ($100 for the contract) and then waits for the stock price to start falling. (He knows that if the price does not fall by the April expiration date, he is not obliged to execute the option; he will let it expire and simply forfeit the premium.) He watches the stock drop from $36 to $35 (which is the strike price) but does nothing. When the price falls – perhaps to about $32 – he buys 100 shares on the open market (at $32) and turns around and exercises his option by selling 100 shares at $35. With this quick exchange, he captures the three-point difference and earns a $300 profit (minus the $100 premium). During this period, the put-seller also waits. He knows that either the stock price will go down and he will wind up buying more shares at $35 per share, or the price will go up, in which case he'll get to keep the $100 premium.

In these examples of calls and puts, we presume that the options trader would actually exercise his right to buy or sell shares of stock at the strike price. In general, however, pros normally buy or sell options, wait for the price of the option to move, and then sell or buy the option. They don't usually exercise their options, so they don't have to actually trade the underlying stocks – they just move the options back and forth.

Strategy #8: *Using Futures Markets*

The Derivatives Markets

"Derivatives" refer to a general category of investments that include options and their riskier counterpart, futures. A derivative is an investment based on an underlying financial asset (e.g., oil futures are related to the underlying asset – oil). Derivatives have expiration dates at which point they become worthless. Because derivatives are affected by the performance of the underlying asset and a specific time frame, they are considered particularly risky; that is, since either one of the factors could create a drop in value, there is sizable exposure to loss. Even if you are correct in guessing the direction that the asset will move, you must also correctly predict when the upsurge or downturn will occur. Derivative trading is often employed by agricultural entities and large corporations to help protect their future earnings from unforeseeable changes in currency values, weather (which affects crops), oil prices, and other phenomena. Hedge fund managers and other professional traders also use derivatives to help them manage risk.

One type of derivative, futures, are exchange-traded contracts that specify a price and future delivery date of various types of commodities. Most often included in the grouping are wheat, soybeans, cattle, precious metals, foreign currencies, and oil. Traders anxiously study everything from the weather, to overseas economic happenings, to disease epidemics among cows, in order to try to outguess the future direction of these highly volatile markets. Even with all of this research, individual investors tend to lose more than 75% of the time when they speculate in these markets. The attraction of futures trading is the enormous *potential* winnings, but because of the huge leverage frequently involved in this arena, individuals' accounts can get flattened in a matter of hours should their guesses be wrong. (As an example of leverage, consider that for a margin deposit of a few thousand dollars, you might be able to buy or sell a futures contract on 37,000 pounds of coffee.)

If you've been considering engaging in futures trading, or have seen a fund or broker who claims to have had stellar results, remember that when something sounds too good to be true, it probably isn't true. Don't let someone pressure you to "act now!"

or to borrow money to fund an investment. Professional investment advisors or traders who engage in futures transactions must
have special licenses, and are overseen by the National Futures
Association in the United States. Before you invest in commodity pools or funds, you should receive a disclosure document that
spells out all the terms of the investment. It should address such
important details as:

- To what extent is your principal at risk?
- Can you lose more than your initial investment?
- Is there a maximum amount you can lose?
- What are the fees and expenses? Are there other management,
  brokerage, or advisory fees?
- What percentage return must the fund achieve for you to
  break even (after taking into account all fees and commis-
  sions)?
- Does the management have any actual or potential conflicts
  of interest?
- Are there restrictions on how and when you can withdraw
  your money?
- Are there periodic distributions, and what are the tax consequences?

In most cases, trading in futures is best left to the institutional
investors. Trading techniques are beyond the scope of this book.
If you're considering this subject nonetheless, you can learn more
from the National Futures Association at www.nfa.futures.org.

Strategy #9: *Buying Hedge Funds*

Unlike regular mutual funds, which are generally open to all investors, hedge funds are sophisticated, private investment groups
that cater to wealthy individuals who can afford to put up large
sums (often $1 million or more). The reason hedge funds are only
appropriate for the ultra-wealthy is that unlike traditional mutual funds, hedge funds are largely unregulated, frequently specialize in complex trading techniques, and generally expect their

FINANCIAL PLANNING

"I'm all tied up in futures. I have to pay for my kid's wedding next year, make next month's car payment, and buy tomorrow's dinner."

investors to be willing and able to take risks and be knowledgeable enough to know what's going on with their money.

During the last few years, the hedge fund concept has become more accessible and attractive to a greater number of investors as minimum entry requirements have been lowered in some cases and regulatory bodies have become more involved. Certain large investment houses, as well as independent companies, have even begun to set up groupings of hedge funds under one roof to form funds of funds. This allows smaller investors an opportunity to become involved with minimum investments in the thousands, instead of in the millions of dollars.

Strategy #10: *Investing in Real Estate*

If you own your home, you are technically a real estate investor. But for the majority of homeowners, the term "real estate pro" would not be appropriate. Although homeowners might turn a profit upon selling their abode, or sometimes sustain a loss, the purpose in purchasing an apartment or house generally is not to make a business investment; it's to have a nice place to call home.

Buying and renting out property as an investment strategy may not be an easy way to earn money. Unless you enjoy a very good return on your investment, the time spent repairing broken pipes, trying to collect the rent, or looking for tenants, may not be worth the profits you receive. At frequent intervals, you will be obliged to come up with cash to cover insurance costs, *arnona* (Israeli property tax), legal fees, mortgage payments, management fees, agents costs, etc. In addition, you have to keep in mind the possibility that the value of your property may decrease. People who invest heavily in real estate, and have relatively small liquid investment portfolios, moreover, run the risk of interrupted cash flow (in between tenants) and limited diversification (if they have tied up most of their money in the rental property). Should you also decide to own a rental property, it could mean that you may find yourself unable to accurately determine your net worth, as values can and do change – and these variations are not listed on an ongoing basis as are the prices of stocks and bonds. And, very important to consider, is that in a best-case scenario, when your property value appreciates, you will only benefit if you find a buyer to purchase your asset at the elevated price. This is normally a long, drawn-out process. With the securities portion of your portfolio, on the other hand, if the prices rise, you can call your broker and sell on the very day that you need the cash.

What If You Believe in Real Estate?
Mark Twain believed in the value of investing in real estate. "Buy land," he said. "They're not making it anymore." Buying and managing properties takes skill, devotion, financial backing, time, research, and hard work. But people do it.

Knowing the ins and outs in the field and finally arriving at the point where you are making a lot of money takes both dedication and luck. Consider real estate moguls such as Donald Trump – who owns, among other things, over 18 million square feet of prime Manhattan office and hotel property, Samuel Zell, who made his billions buying up and then rehabilitating cheap office space and apartments (he owns over 200,000 of them) throughout America, or Mort Zuckerman, who built up over 45 million square feet of commercial real estate and now rents it out. If you want to participate in the great potential of land but don't think you can be the next Donald, Sam or Mort, consider using Real Estate Investment Trusts. These investments trade like stocks but give you direct access to the real estate market (see the discussion on REITs in Chapter 3).

Do-it-Yourself vs. Using a Pro

Many people feel that stocks and bonds are a familiar subject and, as such, they believe that they can handle decisions relating to them on their own. That may or may not be a good idea for you. As you consider whether you should trade your own account, ask yourself, "Would someone else be wise in hiring me to handle his portfolio?" If you answer "No," that people really shouldn't appoint you to invest their money, consider whether you should hire yourself to oversee your own assets or if you should look for a professional money manager.

If you decide to put yourself in charge of your portfolio, then consider how you would like to transact the actual buy and sell orders. This is an important matter since it can potentially either save you or cost you a lot of money. Does the benefit of working with professionals outweigh the costs involved?

Over the past decade, online discount brokerages have crowded the investment market, offering a wide range of financial services. Their easy-to-use forums and their affordability have attracted many millions of dollars to Wall Street. Knowing this, certain questions come to mind: Is computer online usage better for the investor than personal investment service? Are online discount investors as pleased with their results as are people using professional guidance? And finally, since several studies have shown that those with on-line accounts frequently trade more actively and often more speculatively than those working with personal advisors, are online traders making as much money and keeping their assets as safe as are their brokerage-client counterparts? Consider some of the differences between full service and online brokerages:

- **Price.** Online brokerage sites charge lower commission rates than full-service brokerage firms. How can online firms be profitable if they charge less? One way is by eliminating skilled advisors, who build relationships with their clients, know clients' needs, and have both the access to information and the ability to interpret financial data relating to potential trades. Instead of personalized service, online firms provide websites or toll-free 800 numbers where different order takers respond each time a client calls. This may be compared with contacting a personal family physician who may be better able to diagnose illness based on knowing the family history, as opposed to going to a clinic and seeing whichever medical advisor is on call.
- **Personal professional guidance.** Once you turn on your computer there is a plethora of financial information, opinions, and chat rooms with "hot tips" and guidance from assorted analysts as well as from the man down the street. This information overload can leave you feeling lost in deciding which stock to buy.

Should you decide to do your own trading online, carefully consider the following three points:

1. **Time.** Keeping track of your investments is a time-consuming endeavor. Skimming the financial news, even daily, won't necessarily give you enough information to make the best decisions. Do you have sufficient time – and inclination – to spend hours per day (as do professional money managers)

monitoring holdings and researching new investment possibilities?

2. **Expertise.** Are you well educated in the world of finance? Do you know how to read financial statements and balance sheets and how to decipher the important information? Money managers may not always pick the winners or bail out before they slide, but with their extensive background and experience, they are generally far more qualified to identify and screen investments than untrained individuals are.

3. **Temperament.** Savvy investors know that financial decision-making is not an exact science. Do you make snap decisions based on gut feelings, investing trends, or hot tips? Should you sell a stock after it gains two points, buy more, or hold on and ride it out for further profits? You need to have the stomach to weather tough times, and have the stamina not to sacrifice your edge when the market is going well. Novice investors often lose out in this game of wits because they have so much at stake.

Investing Advice from the Pros

Pros often employ different theories and may use original or time-proven strategies in their efforts to manage their financial holdings successfully. However, on certain basic tenets, there is wide agreement. Below are some of their generalized words of wisdom:

- **Buy what you know.** When possible, buy companies in industries with which you are familiar. This will add personal insight into your observations and facilitate your research.
- **Buy what you like.** Invest in companies whose products and policies are in line with your beliefs. Since you will be interested in the companies, it will be easier for you to follow their progress and monitor their statements and reports.
- **Ease into the market you are entering.** If events are such that you feel it's a good time to enter into a specific industry, move in slowly. Just because you may believe that some stocks are

priced low, don't feel pressured to invest as much as you can immediately. Take time to research and watch ongoing performance. You can always add to your positions at a later point if you are satisfied. In most instances, you will find that the market as a whole, or the particular sector of your choice is not a "one-day sale."

- **Experience is the best teacher.** Whether you are a beginner or an investor of long standing, you will probably misjudge some of your investments some of the time. Use your mistakes, as well as your successes, to guide your future actions. Start with only the amount of money you can afford to lose, and don't be surprised if you actually do lose some. If you happen to be lucky on the first try, don't assume you're a stock-picking genius and start managing money for friends and family.

- **Be wary of hot tips.** Fellow investors love to tell everyone about their favorite stocks. Use caution before accepting advice. Beginners tend to rely on more experienced investors' opinions. However, an opinion is only as good as the research and understanding that went into it. Do the same amount of vigorous research on stocks recommended to you as you would do on your own picks.

- **Diversify.** Spread your assets among a number of stocks and other types of investments to minimize the risk. Holding only one or two positions exposes you to major losses should those holdings fizzle. Consider that during the bear market that spanned from September 2000 to September 2002, the s&p Total Return Index dropped 44.7%. Someone with $100,000 invested in those stocks would have ended the period with $55,300. On the other hand, had he split his money equally between stocks, bonds, and cash, his total portfolio would have only decreased by 2.6%. Diversification would have saved him over $42,000.

Summary
- Successful investors know what's going on in the world of

finance. They make it a point to follow the news, learn related vocabulary, and monitor what the professionals are saying.

- Two prominent investment philosophies are technical analysis and fundamental analysis. While some investors lean toward one or the other, it is also common to pay attention to both theories.

- Monte Carlo Simulations are used to estimate the likelihood of future economic outcomes.

- Professional investors use strategies to help them maximize profits while limiting risk. Serious amateur investors can study the pros' techniques and follow those that best match their own needs. Some strategies include buy and hold, dollar-cost averaging, market timing, short-selling, and buying on margin.

- Professional and sophisticated individual investors may use derivative markets dealing in options and futures to speculate and/or to hedge their investments.

- Real estate may be bought for personal use or for investment purposes.

- Investing without professional guidance can provide rewards, but often the risks involved outweigh the potential advantages. Having enough time to follow the markets, sufficient expertise to analyze available information, and the temperament to act swiftly and make difficult judgment calls are all factors that should influence your decision to seek professional guidance or invest on your own.

- Research carefully before purchasing, and continue to monitor holdings after buying them. Diversify your portfolio, be cautious about buying and selling, and beware of hot tips and advice from other investors.

Chapter 7
Work-Related Benefit Plans

Whether you had IRAs, 401(k)s, social security, national insurance, or any other forms of pension plans in your port of origin, as an *oleh*, it's time to learn a new system. All countries have complex retirement savings arrangements with volumes full of rules and regulations, and Israel is no different. Take some time to learn about the programs that you may one day rely on for some of your income.

Common Israeli Pension and Benefit Plans

Bituach Leumi
Bituach leumi, Israel's national insurance service, provides some sense of economic security and well-being to the country's citizens, both before and after retirement. Services such as child allowance, maternity leave, unemployment and work-injury compensation, aid to the disabled, rehabilitation care, and more are available for younger and older people alike.

While the government of Israel offers a stipend to qualified elderly citizens, the pension's amount, generally speaking, is too small to be the sole source of income during retirement years. According to the *bituach leumi* website (www.btl.gov.il), as of

2005, the basic government check for a worker is NIS 1079 per month. This amount may increase somewhat if you have worked more than 12 years, and even more if you continue working past the standard retirement age (which is gradually increasing to 67 for men and 64 for women). However, these additions may only increase your pension by a few hundred shekels per month. (To find out more about the specific *bituach leumi* benefits you might expect to receive, go to www.profile-financial.com and click on the "Financial Planning" tab to download the *bituach leumi* worksheet.) Realistically, to enjoy a comfortable and relaxed retirement it is imperative to have a source of additional funding to supplement this governmental pension program.

Keren Hishtalmut

One important benefit package Israeli workers (including non-Israelis with work permits) often receive is *keren hishtalmut* (continuing education fund). This is a savings plan/mutual fund that uses money set aside by both the employer and the employee. While all full-time workers are eligible to participate in this program, employers aren't legally bound to offer it to employees; rather, it is established in an agreement between employer and employee. Generally, the participating employer contributes up to 7.5% of the worker's gross salary and the employee puts in 2.5%. If the monthly base salary is under a set sum (about NIS 15,400), the funds deposited are untaxed. Money contributed on wages in excess of this amount is taxable. These funds are left to grow for six years and then can be withdrawn and used as the recipient sees fit. One can take out money from the account at any time during the six years, but there will be a tax penalty. Originally, *keren hishtalmut* funds were meant to be used for further education, but there is no statutory limitation on their usage. Frequently, individuals use the windfall to pay for current expenses (family celebrations, renovations, overdrafts, etc.). However, depending on one's personal situation, the wisest course is often to reinvest the funds for retirement savings.

Bituach Minahalim

Bituach minahalim (manager's insurance) is a three-tiered retirement plan consisting of savings, insurance, and severance pay. Usually, a boss arranges this plan in conjunction with an insurance company when he wants to give certain benefits to the employees. Both the employer and employee put in a percentage of the salary – generally about 5% of the gross paycheck. Within the savings component of the pension fund, the money can grow in value. Since taxes are not paid on this growth, the value of the holding can increase at a faster rate than it would in a general investing account. Then, after the employee retires, he can redeem these savings either in a lump sum or by taking monthly paychecks, depending on the terms of the plan.

With regard to the insurance component of the *bituach minahalim* plan, the employer and employee split the expenses for purchasing and maintaining life and disability insurance. The employee has the right to elect how he wishes to have his insurance premiums apportioned.

The third component of the plan is *pitzuim*, the severance pay fund. Normally, the employer pays 8.33% of the worker's gross salary into a *pitzuim* fund. An employee receives this money if he is fired or forced to leave work for other reasons, such as mandatory army service or retirement. If an employee leaves work voluntarily, he is not entitled to collect accumulated *pitzuim*, though the employer, at his own discretion, may choose to grant him some or the entire amount. It should be noted that if a worker is fired or leaves involuntarily, both the *keren hishtalmut* and the pension component of *bituach minahalim* are released to him. While the *pitzuim* segment is generally considered part of the *bituach minahalim* plan, it does not have to be. It could be set up as a separate fund via a bank or insurance company, or could simply remain as an unfunded obligation of the employer. In other words, if the employer doesn't set aside any money to pay *pitzuim* and if he fires an employee, he simply pays the required severance amount from company assets. If *pitzuim* funds are not set aside, employees face

"I've been with you for four years now, Abba. I think it's time we spoke about a bituach minahalim plan."

the special risk that if the company goes bankrupt, they may not receive any severance pay.

Customize Your Pension Plan to Your Needs

Good financial planning is the key to determining the best structure for your *bituach minahalim* policy. Like any investment portfolio, your *bituach minahalim* accounts should adhere to a logical allocation model. If you own sufficient life insurance directly with an insurance company, you may prefer to focus your *bituach minahalim* on savings (especially with the tax-deferred advantage) and minimize the insurance dimension. Check with your insurance agent to determine what your insurance coverage is, and see if the insurance selection offered by your *bituach minahalim* account provides additional or better insurance benefits. (Many times the insurance selections provided by *bituach minahalim* plans tend to offer fewer options than do policies sold by independent insurance agents.)

You can often direct what percentage of your monthly deposits should be put into the savings or insurance component of your plan. Be careful to choose sensible proportions. From time to time, you may hear stories about someone who arranged for his plan to lean heavily on the life insurance side because he had young children. Then, decades later when he retired, he realized that he had almost no pension savings. All his accumulated shekels had paid for life insurance premiums instead of going toward building his nest egg. Had he reviewed his plan periodically throughout the years, he may have made corrections in accordance with his changing needs.

When you reach retirement age and decide to withdraw your pension savings, you can arrange (depending on the plan details) to receive a lump sum or take an annuity. "Annuitizing" means that the insurance company promises to pay you a certain amount on a monthly basis for the rest of your life. Though this can prove to be advantageous in terms of the total number of shekels you receive in your lifetime, make sure that you understand the pros and cons of such an annuity. Specifically, if the insurance company promises to pay you NIS 2,000 per month for the rest of your life, what would happen to the principal that you've worked so hard to accumulate if you die *early*? If you had just put the lump sum pension payment in the bank and lived off the interest, your heirs would inherit the whole sum instead of the insurance company keeping some or all of it. Also, taking a lump sum versus choosing an annuity may have different tax consequences. Discuss your choices with your tax advisors before electing one option or the other.

Naming the Right Beneficiaries

Often retirement plan mistakes revolve around the naming of beneficiaries. In the event of death, the assets in a plan get distributed according to the beneficiary form you completed when signing up, not according to your will. There have been times when a husband named his wife as beneficiary and then years later got divorced and then remarried. When he eventually died, his first wife collected all the benefits from his retirement plan because he neglected to update the forms. Along the same lines, people have named children as their beneficiaries, but then forgot to add subsequently born kids to their policies, thus disenfranchising the younger ones.

Are Changes Necessary?

How will you know if, and when, changes in your benefit plan are necessary? Go over your statements and forms to clarify all the details and see if everything is accurate. It is particularly important to review your pension plan records when you switch jobs, or when you have a change in your personal status (e.g., marriage, divorce, death in the family, more children). From time to time, the insurance companies make mistakes. The only way that you'll ever catch them is if you analyze the paperwork closely; in fact, simply comparing one year-end statement with the next can sometimes help you to uncover errors, missing policies, or problematic investments. Another important way to keep track of your plan is to meet with your insurance agent or your company's human resources manager on a yearly basis. You might find it useful to print out the "Retirement Benefits Worksheet" that can be downloaded at the "Financial Planning" tab at www. profile-financial.com and bring it to the meeting. As seen on the next page, the form clearly lists the specific points that should be raised during this conversation. Also, when meeting with your insurance agent, you may find it useful to review all your different insurance policies – life, disability, long-term nursing, supplemental medical, etc. Use the insurance tracker (also located at the Profile website) to help manage this crucial part of your financial picture.

RETIREMENT BENEFITS WORKSHEET

Available at the "Financial Planning" tab of www.profile-financial.com

Client's name:	
Plan name and/or name of administrator of plan:	
Current value of client's retirement plan	
Total amount contributed to the retirement plan each year	
What percent of the monthly/yearly deposits that go into this plan go into the *savings* component of the plan?*	%
Estimated amount client will receive yearly at retirement	
OR Estimated amount client will receive as lump sum at retirement	
Is this amount in "today's" shekels	YES NO
Will the annuity or lump sum be taxed?	YES NO
If "yes," at what rate?	%
Will spouse continue to receive retirement benefits upon death of client?	YES NO
If "yes," what percent will spouse receive?	%
Estimated annual growth (above inflation) of the principal	%
Retirement age	
Earliest age that client can begin to receive funds	
In the event of death, what will heirs receive?	
In the event of disability, what will client receive?	
Other information	

*   Note that the monthly sums that go into retirement accounts are often
     split between savings and insurance; find out what percent of the monthly
     deposits go towards savings. Normally, it's between 60% and 95%.

Employee Stock Options

In addition to *bituach minahalim* pension plans, another form of compensation that many employees enjoy (especially those in the high-tech world) is the acquisition of employee stock options. Companies sometimes offer these options in lieu of giving raises, or they make offers of corporate stock options to job candidates as a means of enticing them to accept employment. Frequently, when the company is privately owned, the options are of low value at the time of the offer. However, if the stock goes public and the share value increases, the options could prove to be quite lucrative.

Stock options usually come with restrictions as to when and how they can be redeemed. Certificates given to employees in these cases often have the notification "Restricted – See legend on reverse side for details" stamped across the front. These certificates are not in "good deliverable form" and cannot be sold until they are given to a broker who submits them to the transfer agent who, after ascertaining that the proper requirements have been met, clears them for trading and they are put back into the employee's brokerage account.

Since employees receiving stock options often get a large number of shares (because the price per share is very low), which eventually appreciate in value, it is important that the sale of the shares be done with careful oversight. Frequently, Israeli high-tech companies have a relatively small trading volume. This means that if you were to attempt to sell 50,000 shares of a stock at the beginning of the day, and the stock normally only trades 250,000 shares per day, your trade might flood the market. Inadvertently, you could single-handedly drive down the price significantly. In a scenario such as this, it's helpful to have professional traders who specialize in "block" trading conduct the trade for you. They are trained to get a good price for shares without causing too much disruption to the stock's underlying price.

Sometimes Israeli companies make arrangements with the Israeli tax authorities to withhold money for taxes from those exercising their options to ensure that the newly rich won't spend all their gains before the tax bill comes due. Also, when discussing corporate stock options, be aware that U.S. citizens may still owe additional taxes above and beyond what they paid to Israel, and they should consult an accountant on the proper handling of their tax paperwork.

Stop and Think

Sometimes, when a person comes into a large sum of money all at once, he feels that it is "burning a hole in his pocket" and he must spend it immediately. Don't rush! Before your big day comes and you exercise your options, or you gain access to your *keren hishtalmut* or *bituach minahalim* accounts, stop and plan. You have many choices and they should all be given careful consideration. You can spend the money immediately – whether from the exercised options or from withdrawals from the pension plans – to pay off an overdraft or other debt, buy a car, take a vacation, or upgrade your residence. If you do these, of course, you will no longer have the funds. You can leave money in the pension accounts and continue to receive the prevailing rate of return. While it may be tempting to leave the funds under the insurance company's management (as no special action is required on your part), be aware that insurance companies frequently offer relatively weak returns. Better rates, terms, and diversification may often be found elsewhere. It may be wise to sit down with your spouse and a professional financial advisor. Together, you can work on developing an investment portfolio that will enable your nest egg to grow and, when the time comes, provide you with a stream of income.

Review of American Plans

Even though you have made *aliya* and left behind your American jobs, you might still be able to benefit from your old pension plans. Below is a discussion about some of the more widely used programs currently in effect.

Many American companies offer their employees some kind of employer-funded (or combined employer/employee-funded) retirement plan. In addition, many firms and organizations also choose to allow their employees to make tax-deferred contributions to a 401(k) (for corporations) or 403(b) (for government workers, teachers, hospital personnel, etc.) and often provide matching funds up to a certain amount. Keogh and SEP (Simplified Employee Pension) plans (generally designed for small businesses and the self-employed) and the very popular tax-deductible and tax-deferred IRAs (Individual Retirement Accounts) and the newer, not tax-deductible Roth IRAs are other types of U.S. Government-approved savings programs established to help American workers prepare for retirement.

More About IRAs

People who worked in the United States, even as teenagers earning low wages, may have opened and funded some type of IRA. They understood that the money they deposited could grow in a tax-free environment until they would begin to draw it out (at which time it might or might not be subject to taxation, depending on how their IRA was established). These IRA holders look forward to a much higher long-term bottom line than they could have achieved by investing in similar offerings within regular accounts subject to yearly taxation of capital gains and income.

Often workers with employment-related pension accounts decide, when leaving or retiring from a job, to roll over their work-related plan assets, (401(k)s or 403(b)s) into their IRAs. This maintains the tax-deferred status of the money, and allows them to have more control over the specific investments.

If you already have an IRA or an IRA Rollover account from your previous employment retirement plan, it is important to monitor the investments on a continuing basis and to integrate the selections with those in your financial portfolio as a whole when making investment decisions.

Often Rollover accounts contain a large amount of corporate stock issued by the company for which you worked. Be sure that you do not inadvertently let your overall portfolio become too top-heavy with one stock. Also, if you are receiving a salary from the same company that you are heavily invested in, be aware of potential diversification problems. If the company goes bankrupt, both your salary and stock position would both disappear. Is that a risk you're willing to take? Analyze your total financial picture and decide what percentage of the holding you wish to keep and what part you might want to exchange for other assets.

In making new asset purchases, take note that it may be wise to keep investments with the highest yearly tax bites – such as dividend-paying stocks, high-yielding bonds, and certain mutual funds (especially those with high turnover ratios) – in IRAs, and maintain holdings that are less subject to yearly taxation in regular accounts.

Roth IRAs

A few years ago, the U.S. government created another type of IRA called a "Roth IRA." Rather than letting a person put in pre-tax dollars, the U.S. Government allows an individual to deposit money that has already been taxed. The tax benefit accrues to the investor *after* the money goes into the Roth IRA because all earnings are tax free; when he eventually withdraws the money at retirement, he doesn't pay tax (unlike a regular IRA, where one gets hit with income taxes when he withdraws his funds). In fact, with a Roth IRA (unlike with a regular IRA), you have the right to withdraw the principal that you deposited *before* age 59½ without a penalty, though certain restrictions apply. Moreover, Roth IRAs don't have requirements for mandatory distributions when you reach age 70½, whereas folks with regular IRAs must take distributions at that age or get charged severe penalties. Add to that the benefit that if you die holding a regular IRA, your heirs must pay income tax on the money inherited. Not so with Roth IRAs. Just as you could have withdrawn your money income tax-free, so can your beneficiaries. (Nonetheless, estate taxes may apply with either type of IRA.) In certain cases, you can convert a regular IRA to a Roth IRA. Many *olim* find that there are significant long-term tax benefits in doing so. Ask your U.S. accountant if you are eligible to fund an IRA, and if you should consider a Roth IRA for your retirement savings.

Contributing to Your IRA from Abroad

Unfortunately, once you work outside the United States, the terms of contributing to an IRA change. Although income earned outside of the United States generally cannot be added to the account, if your earned income is over $80,000 and is taxed in the U.S., you may be eligible to make a contribution. A general guideline to the rule is that if you benefit from the $80,000 tax exclusion, you cannot also put money into an IRA and claim that as a tax deduction. The only money that can go into an IRA is money that would be taxable in the United States.

U.S. Social Security

Many American retirees living in Israel receive U.S. social security payments. Even if you didn't retire before making *aliya*, but you completed 40 quarters of work in the U.S., you are eligible to collect social security when you reach retirement age. Furthermore, if you worked for almost 40 quarters before making *aliya*, it may be possible to earn the points necessary for those extra quarters while in Israel, thus making you eligible to get benefits one day. In this case, to help you with your planning, you may want to contact the Social Security Administration. A form to use for this inquiry can be found on the Profile website (www.profile-financial.com under the "Education" tab). For people living in Israel, social security income is tax-free both in Israel and in the United States (because of the U.S.-Israel Tax Treaty). Furthermore, the size of the monthly stipend increases periodically based on American cost of living calculations. For speed, safety, and convenience in receiving payment, you can ask the Administration to deposit your checks directly to your brokerage account or to your U.S. or Israeli bank account.

Working for an American Company in Israel

Some *olim* from the United States feel that an ideal situation would be to move to Israel but still work for an American company. They believe that having ongoing access to American paychecks and pension plans will benefit them as they build their new lives abroad.

For those finding employment with an American company in Israel, however, there may be disappointment, too. American firms often open branches overseas not only to gain access to the local talent, but also to utilize cheaper labor. As an employee, you may not necessarily get the same salary or benefits as your counterpart in the United States receives.

Another important point to consider is that Israelis (or even people whose residence and/or center of life is in Israel but who have not declared *aliya*) must pay income tax to Israel. As long as you work in Israel, you will have to pay taxes, even if you haven't officially changed your status to "Israeli citizen."

Moreover, paying Israeli taxes does not exempt you from filing a return in your country of origin. American citizens earning $80,000 or more annually while living in Israel, whether they work for an American company or for an Israeli one, are subject to U.S. income tax on the portion above $80,000. Even though earnings below this threshold amount are exempt from most American taxes, U.S. returns must usually still be filed. This doesn't mean you'll owe money to America. In fact, if you've paid income tax to Israel, you may be able to get a credit for the amount paid to Israel when you file your U.S. return. If your Israeli tax bill exceeds your U.S. obligation, you might not have to give anything to Uncle Sam, even if your income topped the $80,000 foreign earned income exclusion. In order to use this exclusion, you must complete IRS Form 2555 in addition to your regular 1040 form.

To qualify for the foreign income exclusion, you must pass two IRS tests: (1) You must have a tax home in a foreign country, and (2) you must pass the physical presence test (which means you actually have to be in that other country, not just visit it every so often). Because of the many complexities involved, it is very important to check out your tax situation with a knowledgeable accountant or tax lawyer. The information in this chapter, and the more complete discussion on American and Israeli taxes and tax treaties presented in Chapter 12, should be considered only a starting point, and not a definitive tax guide.

Working for Yourself

American self-employed *olim* working in Israel must pay social security taxes to the United States. Thus, the earnings of *atzma'im* (independent contractors) are treated differently from wages earned by employees of established companies. Since social security tax can be 15% of net self-employment income, and since American social security tax may not be a deductible business expense on an Israeli tax return, accountants sometimes recommend that independent contractors become incorporated. If your company is classified as a corporation, and you are an employee of the corporation, you may not be required to pay social security taxes. On the other hand, if you don't pay into the system, you're not entitled to receive the social security pension one day. Again, an accountant's expertise in analyzing your choices can be helpful to you in navigating this taxing situation.

Summary
- Salary perks add value to one's income. Employers offer a variety of benefits as incentives to keep and reward current staff and to recruit new employees.
- Israel's national insurance service, *bituach leumi*, provides a range of services to the country's citizens.
- *Keren hishtalmut* and *bituach minahalim* are common benefits programs offered to Israeli workers. These investment accounts, contributed to by both employers and employees, are geared toward long-term and retirement savings and may also provide insurance.

- Stock options are a way of sharing in the profits of a company. Cashing them in may involve working with a stockbroker, transfer agent, and specialized trader who deals with large "block trades."
- Many *olim* benefit from IRAS, social security checks, and income from American corporate retirement plans.
- Tax implications should be considered by *olim* working for American companies, for Israeli companies, or for themselves as independent contractors.

Chapter 8
Creating a Budget

When Benjamin Franklin said, "Time is money," what did he really mean? Most people will agree that he equated the two because he considered time to be a valuable commodity that shouldn't be wasted. Certainly, time and money both share certain of the same attributes. They are used on a daily basis. The supply of each is not limitless. And perhaps most importantly, they must both be apportioned and spent wisely lest they disappear while you still need them.

Creating budgets to manage your expenditures of time and money may be the keystone to allowing you to enjoy a more relaxed, yet productive life. Start considering how much of the day, week, or year you want or need to devote to your job, family, house upkeep, volunteer work, hobbies, or any other of your many activities and obligations. Once you begin to think about these and start writing them down, you'll find that a properly developed time-management schedule will help you immensely.

Now, what about budgeting your money? There are many aspects to consider. How much money is coming in? How much is being spent, and on what? How much must be saved for the future? How can this best be accomplished? A properly constructed financial budget highlights your present and future needs in a clear manner. Once you know your needs, then you can plan for economic security in the years ahead. So when you sit down with pen in hand to begin recording your allocations, be aware that "budget" doesn't automatically mean deprivation. It's just a way of helping you balance your finances so that you can meet your short- and long-term goals.

Are You Making Ends Meet?

Making ends meet means having a positive current cash flow, plus having enough extra to put away for future needs. In other words, you need enough cash to pay your bills, meet non-periodic financial obligations, and add to your savings programs without slipping into overdraft at the bank. Many people think they are living within their means because they are able to pay off their bills at the end of the month. However, if all you can do is minimally satisfy your obligations – and don't have anything left over for savings – then you are living dangerously. Think of your retirement savings plan as one of your most important bills, like your mortgage, utility, and grocery payments.

It is easy to gradually begin living beyond your means, even if your spending habits do not significantly change. This happens because inflation, which is the general increase in the cost of living, turns moderate spending patterns into lavish lifestyles. In addition, unexpected circumstances (such as family sickness, loss of a job, etc.) or even planned events (like weddings, buying a new car, or taking a long-awaited trip) can upset the most carefully worked out strategy. And, as if these challenges were not enough, some families have one or more members who indulge in spending sprees that make it impossible for the family to stay in the black.

By understanding exactly how much you can afford to spend each month, you can keep a collar on overspending. When you prepare a budget, your income sources and expenses are set forth in front of you and you can check whether you can afford to purchase a given item. In addition, by studying your figures, you can make well-educated estimates as to how much capital you will need in the future, which expenses you can minimize or eliminate, or when sufficient funds will have accumulated so that you can make future purchases.

Often, business owners focus their attention on their company expenditures and don't pay much attention to personal or family budgets. But, keep in mind – a budget is an essential tool, both in the workplace and in the home, and it is necessary in both situations to help you achieve your business and family objectives.

Building a Budget

The first step in creating a budget is to classify and list all of your set expenses. It is best to work with the numbers on a monthly basis since many expenses, such as rent or mortgage payments, remain the same throughout the year. Other expenses, such as electricity, may vary from month to month, but you can use an average in your planning. Payments that are due quarterly or annually (such as insurance premiums or tuition bills), or money needed for once-a-year spending (for gift-giving, the family vacation, or for car registration) should also be averaged and converted to monthly amounts. Even if you don't pay every bill monthly, there is nothing wrong with having a few extra shekels in your bank account waiting for the anticipated "pay" date.

Money Coming In

If you have irregular paychecks (because you run your own business or are a freelancer), try to estimate your potential earnings and then review these estimates periodically during the year. Check with your accountant to get an accurate figure showing how much net income you brought home last year. Use that amount as a guide. Don't forget, you need to know your net income (*netto* in Hebrew), which means what your actual paycheck is after taxes, expenses, and savings plans have been deducted.

"Look, dear, I can balance the checkbook, too."

The gross income (*bruto*) tells you how much it costs your boss to keep you on staff, but does not give you an accurate cash flow entry in terms of how much money you deposit into your bank account each month.

Begin your accounting by listing your (and/or your spouse's) salary, pensions, *bituach leumi*, social security benefits, investment dividends and interest, alimony, royalties, commissions, rents, and any other income sources you may have. Don't include non-usual payments, such as proceeds from a lottery, an inheritance, or an unexpected gift (although this money can be used to eliminate a debt, enhance a savings program, or buy an item that was not on the budget). However, you may, if you wish, choose to include in your income stream an annual monetary gift that your Aunt Sara has been giving you every year on your birthday since you were a child. Refer to the sample chart at the end of the chapter – or download a printable copy of this budget worksheet along with other useful budget material by clicking the "Financial Planning" tab at www.profile-financial.com.

Money Going Out

To create a list of expenses that you will probably incur in the coming year, look through your checkbook and charge account records for last year. Many of the entries shown will match expenditures you will encounter in the year ahead. An often forgotten line item in a budget is the cost of borrowing money. For example, if you borrow $5000 on your credit card and your finance charges are 15% a year, that means you will owe $750 above the principal loan each year.

Helpful Hints for a Successful Budget

- **Save your receipts.** In the beginning, it can be daunting to watch every expenditure. However, with practice it will become a habit for you to request a receipt, even when "just" buying an ice cream at the neighborhood kiosk. If a storeowner refuses to give you a receipt (even though the law obligates him to do so), record the expenditure yourself, and put the slip in with your other receipts. Then, by reviewing the numbers either weekly or monthly, you can better understand where your money is going.
- **Track your expenses.** When you first begin a budget, keep close track of your spending for at least three to six months so that you can develop a sense of where your money is going. Thereafter, if you are satisfied with your balance sheet, you can determine if you want to relax your vigilance a bit. To make the task of recording expenses easier, use a computer program that can help you track your numbers. Alternatively, you can opt for the "envelope" method – simply put all receipts into categorized envelopes.
- **Use cash.** If you have difficulty living within your means, try to use cash instead of credit cards or checks. When your wallet gets light, you'll have to stop spending. You probably only

notice your overdraft or credit card bills once or twice a month. A diminishing cash supply in your pocketbook, however, will constantly remind you to shop with care.

- **Add details to your written budget.** Make separate listings to subdivide some of your expense categories. For example, as seen in the budget chart at the end of this chapter, the entertainment category offers subdivisions covering gym membership, CDs and tapes, cable TV, etc. You may want to add (or delete) a few lines to customize the budget for your family. The more exact you make your budget, the better tool it will become. Keep in mind that it is often difficult to cut spending in an entire category (e.g., entertainment), but if your budget is detailed you can focus on specific areas that need trimming (e.g., sporting event admissions).

- **Set priorities.** Make lists that separate what you want from what you need. Your "wish list" must always take second place if funds are limited.

- **Be a smart shopper.** It never hurts to polish your negotiating skills. While you may not want to haggle, there is nothing wrong with inquiring if there is a discount available. Or, if you use a large quantity of the same item, you may want to ask if buying in bulk would save you money. Often, smart shoppers do comparison shopping. If a bargain can be found readily, this can result in a money-saving opportunity. But keep in mind that running yourself ragged to save a few shekels on a purchase may not be worthwhile.

- **Resist impulse buying.** Be aware of selling techniques used by high-pressure salespeople. When in doubt, pull out your copies of your "wish vs. need" lists and refer to them *prior* to making a purchase. Below are some top "come-ons" used to induce you to buy:
  - Show the client a cool product or feature: The newest pen, car, computer, eyeglasses, skirt, jacket, CD, video game, shoes, etc.
  - Make it easy: Offer easy payment schedules, no-interest

loans, round number prices (NIS 100 even – no change so it's a quick transaction), easy delivery, "quick click" purchase orders on the internet, or some other approach so you don't have a good excuse not to buy now.

- Entice the buyer with a discount: "Buy one now and get one free" or "free shipping" are common mantras. "One day only" works well, too. Remember, never buy just *because* there's a sale.

• **Money-saving techniques.** Now that you're beginning to tune into the ways to avoid impulse buying, here are a few other techniques to use to hang on to your shekels:

- Give yourself a time limit in the store. Put a half hour on your parking meter and you won't have time to browse leisurely.
- Don't go to malls.
- When you spy a great deal, wait 48 hours. If you think about it for two whole days, and still want/need it, and if you can't find something at home that you're just as happy with, then check your budget. If you can afford it, go ahead and buy it.
- Make a "miscellaneous" items line on your budget that allows you a certain amount to spend each month on non-essential or impulse purchases.
- Keep a "money diary" to record the money that comes in, when it comes in, and the money you spend and *why* you spent it. This exercise may keep you from making a purchase that you can't readily justify.

Will Your Budget Work?

Don't be intimidated by your budget. Think of it as a tool to help you spend wisely rather than imagining it as a lock on your wallet. Creating a budget means understanding and making the best use of your cash flow so that you can live within your means. A budget tells you where your money is coming from and where it's going. The best budgets are flexible, changing with your circumstances.

"Your allowance? I'm sorry. I don't recall seeing that on this month's budget."

But what if your budget does not run smoothly? If you find your money runs out before the end of the month, what should you do? If unexpected expenses cause you to go over-budget, re-work your plan to include more emergency funding. Or, perhaps, adjust your budget to reflect reality more closely. If, however, you find yourself going over your budget and falling into debt because you are indulging in non-essential purchasing, then maybe you have to give yourself an ultimatum: Earn more or spend less.

Can Your Budget Keep up with Inflation?

Inflation can definitely have an adverse affect on your budget, especially if your earnings are not keeping pace with the changing economy. If your grocery order costs you NIS 100 today, with an inflation rate of 5%, the same items will cost you NIS 105 next year. Similarly, national and global events can alter prices, and even seasonal changes can cause costs to vary. When prices increase, your money loses "real" value, and has less purchasing power.

Will your budget be able to keep up with inflation? In an effort to address this problem, many salaries in Israel are linked to the Consumer Price Index (CPI). This helps to maintain the real value of your shekel salary. In this way, wages increase in conjunction with the rise in the overall price level. The *tosefet yoker* is a system used to measure the link between price level changes and salaries. It was developed by Israel's most influential union, the *Histadrut*, in an effort to protect workers from rampant inflation. When inflation rises rapidly over a six-month period, wages are supposed to increase to keep pace. (No adjustment of wages takes place for minor inflationary moves.) These calculations were originally created to adjust wages for *Histadrut* workers, but now many other employers use them in determining salaries for their own employees.

If you are self-employed or are not covered by this inflation-related wage increase program, you will need to calculate an inflation factor when you periodically review your budget. If costs have increased on the items you usually buy, then in order to maintain your current lifestyle you will have to lay out more money. Once again, your choice will be to earn more or spend less.

The Need to Save

Even though it may be tempting to spend your entire paycheck every month, don't feel obliged to single-handedly support the economy. Instead, earmark a part of your salary for savings. Putting away even a small amount on a regular monthly basis will help you toward achieving your long-term goals.

A portion of your savings should be set aside in an interest-bearing account as an emergency cushion. What would happen if you lost your job or became ill? What if your car unexpectedly stopped working and needed pricey repairs? Another part of the savings can be put into your investment portfolio. Even if you can only afford to save NIS 250 or NIS 500 per month, that's a fine beginning. By adding a set amount of cash on a periodic basis, you will soon have a respectable amount of savings.

"Uh oh! I'm just about to turn one and I haven't put anything into retirement savings."

Overdraft

What about people who are unable to save? Or those who would like to save but find they just run out of money before the end of the month? Many Israelis are guilty of spending more than they earn and wind up going into overdraft at their banks. In fact, well over half of all Israeli bank accounts are in overdraft. Banks extend credit to these customers when their accounts drop below a zero balance, and in return for these loans, the customers owe the banks hefty interest payments. Even though the depositors then have a negative balance in their accounts and owe interest, the banks allow them to continue writing checks and spending money. The government enacted regulations requiring banks' overdraft parameters to be reviewed and kept within a limit in order to avoid having people tumble further and further into overdraft. Regardless of the *Knesset's* intention, though, it is often difficult to escape this snowballing debt.

Banks sometimes offer to exchange your high-interest overdraft for a lower-interest fixed loan. For example, if your current account shows minus NIS 20,000 with a 14% interest charge, they'll convert it to a three-year loan at 8%. While this sounds tempting and should be considered, don't mortgage the future to pay for today. Do you really want to be paying for this year's Passover vacation for the next few years? Restructuring debt gives people a false sense of security and often leads them further into debt.

Where Does Your Money Go?

By keeping tabs on your money – as it comes in and as it goes out – you will have a well-organized budget that you can rely on to help you track your financial situation. Creating a budget can help catch a small spending problem before it becomes a big problem. This, in turn, may keep your bank balance intact and keep you out of overdraft.

Budgeting does not mean skimping; it is not a diet for your pocketbook. By constructing a budget for your household, you can see how and where your money goes, and you can then reconcile this knowledge with your fiscal and personal priorities.

Summary

- Devising and following a budget enables you to balance your finances so that you can meet your long- and short-term goals.
- In building a budget, work with the numbers on a monthly basis. If certain expenses arise quarterly or yearly, average them out as a monthly cost.
- Helpful hints for a successful budget include: Save and organize receipts, track expenses for at least three months, use cash instead of credit to better recognize spending habits, subdivide

budget categories, set priorities, resist impulse buying, and be a smart shopper.

- If your budget doesn't provide you with logical answers in organizing your finances, think of ways to increase income and/or reduce expenses. Budgets are flexible tools that should work for you.
- Determine if your budget keeps up with inflation. If not, you may have to adjust your spending or your earnings.
- Budgeting your resources carefully should allow you to contribute to a savings plan, either for short-term needs or to meet long-term goals.
- While overdraft is often considered as Israeli as *falafel*, taking advantage of the overdraft option offered by your bank can quickly increase your debt. A good spending plan and a well-designed budget may help avoid this situation.

PROFILE BUDGET WORKSHEET

Available at the "Financial Planning" tab of www.profile-financial.com

INCOME

	Monthly	Quarterly	Annually
Income from employment			
Salary (1)			
Salary (2)			
Commissions			
Kollel stipend			
Tips			
Other			
Income from pensions and benefit plans			
Bituach leumi			
Pension			
Social security			
Additional retirement plans			
Income from other sources			
Alimony			
Annuities			
Bonus payments			
Child allowance from *bituach leumi*			
Child support payments			
Family gifts			
Income tax refunds			
Investment income			
Rental income			
Royalties			
Other 1			
Other 2			
Other 3			
TOTAL			

EXPENSES

		Monthly	Quarterly	Annually
Auto	Car loan payments			
	Gas			
	Maintenance/upkeep			
	Parking			
	Registration			
Bank	Credit card fees			
	Fees (*rishum peulot, rebeet,* checkbooks, etc.)			
	Other			
Charity	(List your charities)			
	Synagogue dues, building fund			
Clothing	Adults			
	Children			
Child-care	Daycare			
	Babysitting			
Com-puter	Internet access			
	Purchase			
	Repair/service			
Educa-tion	Adult tuition			
	Camp			
	Children's tuitions			
	Enrichment programs			
	School supplies			
	Tutoring			
Enter-tainment & recre-ation	Books, magazines, newspapers			
	Cable TV			

		Monthly	Quarterly	Annually
	Entry fees to sporting events			
	Gym membership			
	Lottery tickets			
	Music – CDs, tapes			
	Movies			
	Shows, theater, concerts			
	Video/DVD rental			
	Other			
Food	Groceries			
Gifts				
Hobbies	Photography, collecting, painting, etc.			
Home	Alarm/security service			
	Cleaning help			
	Garden			
	Improvement projects			
	Maintenance			
	Rent/mortgage			
	Repair			
	Va'ad ha'bayit (tenant's association)			
Insur-ance	Auto – compulsory and supplemental			
	Bituach leumi payments for children over 18			
	Disability (1)			
	Disability (2)			
	Home			
	Life (1)			
	Life (2)			
	Supplementary health and long-term care			

		Monthly	Quarterly	Annually
Interest payments	Bank interest			
	Credit cards			
	Other loans			
Medical	Co-payments			
	Dentist/Orthodontist			
	Glasses, hearing aids, other equipment			
	Kupat holim (national health insurance)			
	Medicine			
	Other medical doctors			
	Physical therapies and other treatments			
	Therapy			
	Other			
Personal	Cosmetics			
	Dry cleaning			
	Hairdresser/haircuts			
	Other			
Pet	Food			
	Kennel			
	Veterinarian			
	Other			
Postage				
Professional fees	Accountant			
	Financial planner			
	Lawyer			
Restaurants	Dining out for business (not reimbursed)			
	Dining out with friends			
	Family dining			

		Monthly	Quarterly	Annually
	Take-out (coffee, candy, cigarettes, etc.)			
Savings	Retirement			
	Set aside for other goals			
Security	Bulletproofing (vest, car)			
	Migun (plastic car windows)			
	Neshek (ammunition, practice, license fees)			
	Shmirah (guard duty)			
Taxes	*Arnona* (property tax)			
	Foreign tax			
	Israeli tax			
	TV tax			
	U.S. tax			
	Other			
Telephone	Bezek			
	Cell phones			
	Phone card			
	Overseas carrier			
Transportation	Bus			
	Taxi			
	Train			
	Other			
Utilities	Electric			
	Gas/heating fuel			
	Water/sewage			
Vacation	Airfare/travel expenses			
	Dining			
	Hotels			
	Souvenirs			

		Monthly	Quarterly	Annually
	Other			
Other 1				
Other 2				
Other 3				
TOTAL				

Chapter 9
Planning for Your Future

It is not in the stars to hold our destiny but in ourselves.

– Shakespeare

The words of the great English writer are perhaps more relevant today than they were in the seventeenth century because in our modern world many of us actually do have the power to shape our financial futures. We know that certain events are beyond our control. But with forethought and proper planning we are, in general, able to prepare a more comfortable future for our families and ourselves than any of old William's confederates could.

Stop to consider: Do you have a financial plan? Does it enable you to record and integrate the various aspects of your financial life? Does it coordinate your short-term needs with your long-term goals? Does it balance withdrawals against anticipated streams of income? And, if an unfortunate incident should alter your flow of incoming funds, can your plan serve as a tool to help you restore balance to your economic life?

A good financial plan is analogous to a set of blueprints for a house. It is highly unlikely that a builder would begin construction without a master plan. He would not stockpile bricks, concrete, and electrical wiring without first studying his inventory requirements. The same holds true for financial planning. When you make your plan, begin with an overview of your personal situation. Set up a budget and track it carefully (see the suggestions in the previous chapter). Study your current economic situation. What are your concerns? What are your needs, goals, and hopes for the future? What is your tolerance for risk? How long is your investing time frame?

Who Should Have a Financial Plan?

If you ask the average person whether his finances are in order, chances are that before he replies, his thoughts will center on whether his checkbook is balanced and his bills are paid. If they both are, he'll probably answer in the affirmative. But these questions are only the tip of the iceberg when thinking about financial planning. A good plan involves a total review of your lifestyle, a reasonable listing of your aspirations, an honest understanding of your earning potential, and a complete accounting of your assets. A plan done too casually – for example, making a promise to yourself that you will save more in the future, or spend less tomorrow – tends to lose urgency and is easily forgotten. Committing figures to paper after careful consideration, however, will help consolidate your thinking and enable you to integrate the various aspects of your financial life.

Begin with a Financial "Snapshot"

Start with listing all family-owned financial assets. These might include a business, your home, other real estate, a car, collectibles, jewelry, stocks, bonds, cash, trust funds, and bank accounts. Add to this list your salary and any other sources of money coming into the family.

Continue your financial portrait by recording a summary of general expenses, mortgages, and other liabilities. Take note of any imminent decreases in family income (such as an upcoming retirement, a family member about to leave a job) or soon-to-oc-

Shmuel Ihungdim

"Four more days 'til retirement and I don't have any savings. Here's your chance to get into the Financial Planners Hall of Fame!"

cur major family expenses (such as needing to buy a larger house, a new car, or pay for a wedding).

Complete the assessment by directing your attention to money that will be coming in after the breadwinners are no longer employed. Look at retirement funds and pension plans – American social security, IRAS, 401(k) plans, and your Israeli plans, such as *bituach leumi, bituach minahalim, keren hishtalmut,* and *kupot gemel.* Note any personal insurance policies you have that will provide income in the future.

A questionnaire designed to help you focus on your financial picture is located on the Profile website, www.profile-financial. com, at the "Financial Planning" tab.

Set Your Goals

There's a good reason why financial advisors spend a great deal of time helping their clients express their objectives as explicitly as possible. They know that if the plan can't help the client to actually achieve his goals, it will be of little value to him. When you begin your plan, note down your short-, medium-, and long-term aspirations (such as buying a car, paying for a wedding, taking early retirement) and estimate the amount of money you will need at those times. Consider your financial options (take a second job, buy a less expensive car or use the bus, work an extra few years, assume greater risk in your investments) and determine which financial route you will take.

Differentiate between realistic goals and impractical wishes. Keep in mind that goals must be relevant and clearly stated if they are to be achieved, and that wishes, as uplifting as they may be, must remain in the realm of dreams. When putting pen to paper to begin your plan, therefore, it's a good idea to keep the following points in mind:

- *Realism*. Good financial planning can work well; it cannot work miracles.
- *Flexibility*. Plans should be user friendly. If goals are reachable, you will exert the effort to attain them.
- *Resilience*. A plan must survive changes in the economy as well as in your personal life. Build in some leeway but don't be too vague, as that will make the plan potentially ineffective.
- *Simplicity*. Make your goals concrete. If goals are too fluid, you never know when you have reached them. Instead of saying, "I want to have enough money to buy a car in three years," state, "I need $40,000 to buy a car on July 1, 20xx

Take Time to Determine Your Risk Tolerance

Many people avoid thinking about risk and hope that by putting the subject out of their minds, it will go away. But it won't. In fact, those people who shy away from investing because of the word "risk" and instead hide their money at home or deposit it in low- or non-interest-bearing bank accounts that purport to be "risk-free" may be subjecting themselves to inflation risk – which often engenders a greater loss than they would encounter if they were actual investors. (See Chapter 4 for an explanation about how inflation can diminish your money's value.)

As you set the parameters for your financial plan, be honest with yourself as to how much risk you can comfortably live with. Keep in mind that if your general cash inflow is not enough to cover your current budget as well as upcoming major expenses, you will have to acquire the extra funding elsewhere. Many people in these situations choose to invest and let their money work for them. Their selections (ranging from volatile high-flyers to ultra-conservative short-term CDs) reflect their willingness to absorb risk. Generally, the riskier the product, the greater the potential for gain – and loss. Every investor needs to balance the chance of losing money against the possibility of a profitable investment.

Establishing and monitoring your plan is an ongoing process that requires you to focus on risk. When you first get started, your tolerance for risk will help shape your investment choices. It will make you ask: What would I do if one of my investments dramatically declined in price? What if my portfolio dropped 20% in value? Would I wait for recovery? Would I sell out? What would be my time frame for making these decisions?

It helps if you avoid euphemisms. In fact, "risk" is sometimes considered a more palatable way of saying, "you might lose money." All sorts of terms are heard on Wall Street when people don't want to say "lose." For example, you might hear about a market "correction" or "adjustment," or perhaps an analyst will talk about hitting a "short-term trough," or "reaching a support level," or a "cyclical variation." All of these terms, and many more, are expressions to make losing money not seem too bad. When you want to understand your own tolerance for risk, don't ask yourself if you could survive a 20% drop in your account. Try using more specific figures: "How would I react if my account lost $30,000 in a week?" That's what risk really feels like.

Be Aware of Potential Problems
Always hope for the best, but prepare for potential problems. In

designing a successful financial plan, it is definitely a good idea to include a risk-management contingency component. Start your thinking with a "What if ..." scenario. What if your daughter was about to get married? Your son had an opportunity to enter into a business? What if the price of the truck you were considering for your company went way up? What if your house burned down? What if you lost your job, or became disabled? What if you died?

Let Someone Else Share Your Risks

While stocks, bonds, and cash may comprise a considerable portion of your portfolio, and you could sell them if you needed money, this wouldn't address all the possible worst-case scenarios. If the price of a new truck was higher than you had anticipated, you could wait on the purchase until you had more money, or dip into your savings accounts. But other occurrences would probably prove difficult for you to handle unless you could count on an inflow of cash. That's where insurance comes in handy. Having proper insurance coverage could mean that you and your family would suffer much less and sustain far fewer hardships in the event of a catastrophe.

If you, as a breadwinner, venture to leave your bed in the morning, conceivably something unfortunate could happen to you. Don't wait to see what that might be. The best time to think about insurance is before you actually need it. (How about now? Take a break from reading this book and call your insurance agent to schedule an appointment.) Regard insurance as a critical part of your overall financial plan, since it provides backup financing for you and your family in times of need. For the majority of workers, their greatest assets aren't their bank accounts or investment portfolios. It's themselves. It's their ability to generate reliable income. And if they can't do it because of a disability or an unfortunate event, then a well-designed insurance policy can provide the backup.

Check with the representative in the human resources department at your place of employment or with your insurance agent to get details on your *bituach minahalim* package and see the extent of the coverage you actually have. Evaluate if it is sufficient or if you need additional private insurance. You can easily track your different policies using the free insurance tracker that is downloadable at the "financial planning" tab of www.profile-financial.com.

SAMPLE ASSET ALLOCATION CHART

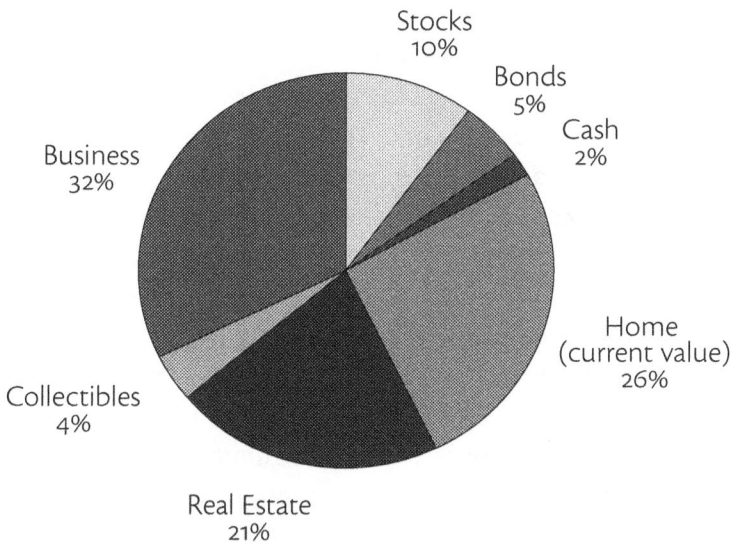

Set up an Asset Allocation Model

Your asset allocation model should show you what percentage of your portfolio is invested in the various asset classes. Begin by recording your current resources. Consider everything: your home, business, collectibles, stocks, bonds, and cash.

Look at your portfolio in the form of a pie chart, with the different investment categories you own depicted as slices of the pie. Often, seeing a pictorial representation of assets enables a viewer to understand where he is over- or under-represented. Above is a sample illustration that you can adjust to your situation. For a customizable worksheet, use the "Assets and Liabilities" page at the "Financial Planning" tab of www.profile-financial.com.

Now that you have an accounting of your current assets, are aware of your incoming cash flow and your debts, have established your goals, understand your insurance policies, and have considered your tolerance for risk, it is time to actually get started creating an appropriate asset allocation model. Whether you work with a professional financial advisor or sit down at the kitchen table with family members, it is important to put your pen to paper and get moving.

Rule of 72: Are We There Yet?

That depends on where you want to go. In monitoring an asset allocation plan some investors set goals for themselves. Then they try to see if they are on track by using formulas to calculate their chances of success. One popular technique is the "Rule of 72." By selecting a yield figure, they get a fairly accurate estimate that shows how long it would take for a fixed-income investment to double in value, assuming the interest was left to compound. Here is an example of how it works: If you owned a fixed-income holding yielding 4% and wanted to know about how long you would have to hold it to double your investment, divide 4 into 72 and your answer, 18, will indicate the number of years you must wait. If rates go up and you buy an 8% fixed-income investement, then you would only have to wait nine years (72 divided by 8). And, if rates approach those in the early 1980s and you receive a 10% return, then you can double your money in only 7.2 years.

Different Strokes for Different Folks

General guidelines for different age brackets are often cited to give readers a broad idea of what asset allocations are appropriate for different stages in life. As you read about the age groups below, see how you fit into the categories.

In many ways, asset allocation is a fine art as well as an economic exercise. It is the art of balancing the different holdings in your portfolio to enable you to meet your changing financial needs while keeping in mind your personal tolerance for risk. And so, when you actually sit down to do your periodic reviews, keep in mind the very important variable in the situation: *You!*

Twenty-Something: Developing a Foundation

Young investors may lack experience, and they may have limited financial resources, but what they do have is time. If you are an average investor in your twenties, chances are that you have finished with your national service, army, and university, and are now beginning your career. You may or may not have debts relating to credit card expenses, tuition bills, or car payments. And perhaps you've got the responsibilities of a new family. (If so, now is the time to prepare a will.) Even though retirement is decades away, start putting away a set sum of money on a periodic basis. Since time is on your side, gradually build a portfolio of growth-oriented stocks. At this stage in your life, income-producing investments aren't ideal since they usually have less potential for growth and you, being gainfully employed with an expectation of many more employable years ahead, are not in need of dividend or interest checks. While having a somewhat aggressive portfolio of stocks and mutual funds makes sense, keep in mind that wild investing schemes or fly-by-night penny-stock companies are rarely the economic superstars they claim to be.

Thirty-Something: A Time for Rapid Growth

As you pass through your thirties, you notice the world moves very fast around you. Things are always happening. You and your friends may be getting married, having children, buying a home, purchasing a larger car, and then even a second one, getting a promotion at work, etc. If you are a parent, you may worry about school tuition, the cost of extracurricular activities, and camp. Remember to stick to the budget you worked hard to devise. While college tuition and wedding bills may be far away, you've got to ensure that there will be money available when they come. You still want to focus on growth, since with many income-earning years still ahead to insulate you from occasional losses, you can afford to continue to take on a moderately aggressive risk profile. It's appropriate to continue to add to the growth section of your portfolio with high-quality growth corporations and perhaps some global and domestic mutual funds. At the same time, some of your resources should be put into intermediate-term bonds and CDs to save for "big ticket" items that will be needed from time to time – especially if you have a growing family.

Forty-Something: Growth and Income

As you enter your forties, you make an unsettling observation. Everything seems to be getting more expensive. It costs twice as much now to go to the movies as it did when you were a teenager. And when did the price of an ice cream cone get so high? If you have children, you'll see that teenagers are no longer content to wear hand-me-downs, and new sneakers are no longer NIS 150. Around the same time, you may be approaching college tuition payments and bills for wedding bells. In addition, your parents, who have always been self-sufficient, might need a bit of extra financial support and help in getting around. While reviewing your asset allocation, you realize that although the holdings seem to be doing well, your personal priorities are changing. You could use some extra monthly cash. It's time to start shifting the balance in your portfolio to include more dividend-paying stocks and a selection of bonds and CDs. Consider setting up a bond ladder to capture the higher interest rates available on longer-term instruments. Check with your employment benefits representative to be sure you are fully funding your retirement programs. Although you want to add current income to your household budget, you do not want to shortchange your retirement nest egg in the process.

Fifty-Something: Safety First

In your fifties, some of life's pressures may have eased. You are hopefully at an acceptable level on the employment scene and can stop putting in so many late hours. Your children may be in college, or married and beginning families of their own. Your account size may be diminishing as you pay the tuition and wedding bills for which you've been saving over the past couple of decades.

Find time to review the will you wrote when you were younger. It may not reflect your current situation, so consult with a lawyer to revise it. Also, set up an appropriate trust and draw up some powers of attorney, just in case.

Your portfolio may have grown nicely during the years, but now as retirement draws closer, it's time to become a bit more conservative with your assets to ensure that they'll be there when you need them most. Safety is now a major concern. If the stock market crashes, it would be very difficult to make up the shortfall. Try to keep some growth in your portfolio to stay even with inflation as well as to enlarge your retirement savings, but without as much risk as before. Shift to more dividend-paying stocks along with additional bonds. Follow the rule-of-thumb allotment formula: Deduct your age from 100, and keep the answer amount in growth investments, while the balance of your portfolio can go in fixed income. In other words, as a 54-year-old you should allot about 46% to growth investments and 54% to income investments. Don't forget, this is just a rule of thumb, not a financial planning panacea.

Sixty-Something: On to Retirement

As you enter your sixties, you look around and wonder if you are getting old. But you feel fine. You just got a good grade in an internet course you're taking. You're filled with funny stories to tell your grandchildren. You've become a pretty good tennis player, and you're considering a hiking adventure in the Galapagos. No, you aren't getting older; you're getting better.

You may have decided to work a few more years or maybe cut down to three or four days a week. But as long as you remain employed, you keep making contributions to your portfolio. You definitely plan to make the break and retire during this decade, but aren't sure exactly when. In reviewing your portfolio, check that you have the critical amount of capital saved up to afford a relaxing future. While you should be concerned about growth to combat inflation, you should begin to lean more toward safety. At this point in life, you can't afford the risk of gambling on a big investment that may turn sour. Re-evaluate your diversification among different sectors, checking that you are not too heavily invested in any one industry. If you have a number of insurance policies whose premiums have jumped in price, consider if they are all still of value to you. Again, review your will, trust documents, and powers of attorney. Are they still representative of your wishes, or are changes needed?

Retirement has finally arrived! Now there are even more decisions to make: Do you wish to live in a smaller home, a larger one, or stay put? In your same town or in a new locale? Think about which activities you wish to engage in – volunteer work? travel? a new business? Maybe you might begin to write a book or sort through your mountain of photographs. You have anticipated this time for many years and at last it is here. Don't waste this very important part of your life by accomplishing nothing. Keep busy. Now's your opportunity to help others, to have fun, to catch up on all the things you've always wanted to do.

Seventy-Something ... to One Hundred and Twenty

You've worked. You've saved. You've invested. And now you're retired. With discipline and determination you've managed to monitor your resources and have your assets accumulate. Your nest egg has grown just as you hoped it would through all the decades. Congratulations! Now it's time to enjoy yourself. Keep the majority of your money secure in a variety of income-oriented investments. But keep your guard up against the dangers of inflation.

The main issues that you need to think about include paying for health care and maintaining your lifestyle. Hopefully, you can also focus on charity, vacations, and family. And though it may be uncomfortable to think about, it's your responsibility to organize your affairs so that someone can handle them for you in the event of serious illness or death.

Let Your Financial Plan Be Your Guide

The keys to successful financial planning include knowing what your resources are, understanding what you'd like to accomplish, designing a reasonable plan, and then persevering to accomplish your objectives. Financial plans may run well, but they don't always run smoothly. Sometimes small changes have to be made; sometimes big ones. It is important for you to be flexible when it becomes necessary, but it is just as important for you to be disciplined and to work hard to follow the paths you so painstakingly designed.

Once your financial plan has been established, it will require ongoing maintenance on your part. Set up a portfolio review schedule. Whether it is quarterly, semiannually, or only once a year, be sure to gather your related materials and sit down to do a thorough analysis. As the years pass, two things will surely change: your life situation and the world of investments. As these happen, your ability to adapt and logically rework your portfolio will become crucial if you and your family are to continue leading the lifestyle you have been anticipating.

Follow Your Plan

> *If I had eight hours to chop down a tree, I'd*
> *spend six sharpening my ax.*
> – Abraham Lincoln

Although many people carefully design plans, either alone or with an advisor, not everyone follows them. Sometimes they don't quite appreciate the relevance of certain choices, are lax about keeping to a time schedule, or veer from the path they themselves chose in order to pursue a hot tip. Very often the deviation does no harm, and during the next review session any problems that occurred can be set straight. But sometimes the trouble is much greater, and the financial losses that result from the mistaken action do bring on considerable damage. Here are some of the most important points in creating and maintaining your financial plan:

1. *Avoid unrealistic expectations.* Don't think you can increase the value of your investments in one year by 20% by "taking a chance." Don't get "suckered in" by a fast-talking salesperson with a "get-rich-quick" scheme. Remember, if it sounds too good to be true, it probably is.

2. *Don't confuse your financial plan with your actual investments.* The plan is the blueprint for your financial program. Changes you make to the plan are based on different needs and happenings in your life. The investments, on the other hand, are the specific stocks, mutual funds, and other assets in your portfolio. The changes you make here depend on such things as your evaluation of a corporation's prospects, your wish to have higher-yielding bonds, your interest in owning some European companies, or shares in a gold-mining firm, or in the automobile sector, etc.

3. *Don't forget your goals.* A financial plan enables you to measure your actual success against your planned returns. Although the two may not be identical, they should move in tandem. Use specific numbers so that the exercise is not subjective. "It seems to be OK," is not an ideal answer to the question, "Is your financial plan on track?"

4. *Avoid putting your plan on the shelf and forgetting about it.* A financial plan is a dynamic document. It changes as your life progresses, and as the economy shifts. Keep it close at hand and in your thoughts when decisions have to be made.

5. *Don't think that financial planning is only for the wealthy.* Though a well-designed plan is essential for people with means, it's just as important for a family much lower on the income scale. Having a concrete plan can often serve as a guideline toward greater financial freedom and opportunity.

6. *It's a mistake to wait until a crisis arises before beginning your financial plan.* If you prepare in advance for unfortunate eventualities, you will have certain solutions already in place to help you deal with the situation. For example, you might have a disability insurance policy in effect that provides much-needed benefits, should an accident occur.

7. *Remember that working with a professional advisor does not mean giving away control of your assets.* An advisor is there to help you interpret your own financial situation, your own needs, and your own aspirations. He will help serve as your coach and guide as you follow the path toward financial independence. He will assist you in seeing different sides of the issues and present you with varying choices, but ultimately you are the one to make the decisions.

8. *Don't forget that your biggest problem – the one that could cause the most damage to your current and future security – would be not making a plan at all.* As it's often said, "If you fail to plan, you're planning to fail."

Summary

- A financial plan provides an organized structure for your portfolio, and a comprehensive way for you to correlate your income and expenses.
- A well-designed plan enables you to coordinate your short-term needs with your long-term goals.
- In designing and executing your plan, take the following steps:
    1. Compile a complete financial snapshot of your current assets and liabilities.
    2. Set goals that are realistic, flexible, resilient, and easy to understand.
    3. Consider your tolerance for risk.
    4. Anticipate potential problems.
    5. Set up an asset allocation model that will reflect where you are in life and where you hope to be in the future. Modify

your allocations as you grow older and your needs and aspirations change.

6. Buy specific assets that will enable you to reach your personal goals.

7. Periodically review your investments and make any necessary adjustments.

8. Be aware of pitfalls that can adversely affect your plan. Forewarned is forearmed.

Chapter 10

The Importance of Estate Planning

The trick is to stop thinking of it as "your" money.

– IRS auditor

You Can't Take it with You

Through the years, you diligently worked to build the assets and save the funds that now represent your net worth. But, when the inevitable occurs, will your money and property be passed on in the manner that you would want? Might the *wrong* person inherit your assets? What will happen to your children? Your spouse? Your business?

Will Your Heirs Have Problems?

When a loved one passes away, many challenges suddenly confront the surviving heirs, no matter the size of the deceased's estate. Who will inherit what? Who will have the authority to continue to run the family business? Is there documentation to prevent an incompetent relative from being put in that position? Who will care for family members with disabilities? How can assets in the deceased's name be made available for the family's immediate use? Who will pay the bills? If young children are suddenly left without parents, who will care for them? Who will handle the money being left for them? Will the funds be immediately turned over to them when they are no longer minors? If your children are already young adults, consider whether they would be ready for this monetary responsibility at their current age. Or would they be better off if you had set up a trust for them so that assets would be distributed as needed over a period of time? What if your spouse remarries a person with children and those children wind up becoming your benefactors instead of your own kids? Answers to all these questions have to be carefully considered and legally stated.

Surprisingly, many people don't have up-to-date wills and trusts that spell out their wishes, and this often leads to adverse consequences. For example, in the autumn of 2004, a judge in Brooklyn, New York, was charged with awarding excessive fees to his lawyer friend whom he had appointed to handle cases of local people who died without wills or executors. Ordinarily, court-appointed lawyers received 6% of an estate's value for their services, but in the cases under question, the lawyer was permitted to receive 8%. If you don't have adequately drawn-up succession documents, a court-appointed attorney may be delegated to process your estate. Will he provide for your heirs as you would have wished? How much will it cost?

Though Israel does not have an estate tax (yet), keep in mind that the United States imposes a graduated "death tax" on its citizens, regardless of whether they live – or die – on American soil or abroad. This tax is often quite significant. In the last few years, the exemption (the allowable sum on which estate taxes do *not* have to be paid) has continued to increase, and will do so until the year 2010, when the estate tax will temporarily vanish. However, the tax will be reinstated in 2011 and no one yet knows what it will look like.

Basically, the story of the U.S. estate tax is as follows: In 2001,

Congress passed rules that would gradually reduce estate taxes between the years 2001 and 2009. Then, in 2010, these taxes would be completely eliminated. Unfortunately, however, the reform wasn't made permanent. Unless Congress passes a new estate tax bill, in 2011 estate taxes will revert to the rules that were in place in 2001.

Estate Tax Exclusions

To get a better grasp on the topic, consider this: Let's say you have a $2.2 million estate and die in 2006, 2007, or 2008, and bequeath your assets to your children. You would have an exemption on the first $2 million, so $200,000 would be subject to estate tax. Die in 2009, and the exemption jumps to $3.5 million, so your whole estate would be estate tax-free. Dying in 2010 would mean no estate tax because the tax is eliminated for that year. But if the rules don't change, and you die in 2011, the exemption will only be $1 million; so your first million will transfer freely to your heirs, but the remaining $1.2 million will be taxed.

Unlimited Marital Deduction

The American estate tax does not apply to transfers at death from one spouse to another (as long as the recipient is a U.S. citizen). If an American dies and leaves $50 million to his wife, the money will not be subject to an estate tax. However, when she dies, bequeathing the assets to a non-spouse, the prevailing estate tax will apply.

If you have already done your estate planning, or are still in the "considering it" stage, keep these points in mind. Whether your assets could be subject to a U.S. tax, or to an estate tax Israel might one day enact, you may be able to lessen the blow by establishing proper will and trust documentation now.

Before You Think of the Hereafter

Lest you get too concerned with asset management after you are gone, remember that it is just as important – if not more so – to address potential problems that may affect your own needs while you are alive. When meeting with your estate planners, discuss the manner in which you would like vital matters to be handled during your lifetime, should you be unable to do so yourself. What would happen if you were unable to adequately function because of mental or physical limitations? Who would make financial decisions for you? Who would make the medical decisions pertaining to your health?

A "power of attorney" is the written right that you (the "principal") give to another person to act on your behalf (to be your "attorney-in-fact" or "agent") in specific matters. Various types of clauses and documents may apply under differing circumstances (such as only being applicable if you are alive or only relating to your brokerage accounts). Other instruments, which are broader in scope, may allow discretion in handling all financial matters, including the making of distributions from your trust. Thus, formats can be "limited" (the agent can act only in certain areas) or "general" (the agent can act in all matters). In addition, the power of attorney can be considered "durable" (which means it will remain in effect when/if the principal becomes incapacitated) or "non-durable" (which limits the scope of the agent's powers and responsibilities).

When sitting down with your lawyer to implement estate-planning documents, it is also imperative to consider health-related proxies. You should select people to make important health-related decisions for you if you should become mentally or physically impaired. In addition to appointing an attorney-in-fact to be responsible for ongoing medical decisions on your behalf, it is also crucial to write a "living will" to address another important related matter: how and whether or not you want medical treatment to be administered or continued if your physical condition is considered terminal with no hope of improvement. If you were to wish to have a "Do not resuscitate" order entered on your medical chart, your agent could present your document to your physician with the request.

Why Do People Need Wills and Trusts?

The concept of setting up a trust started in England during the Middle Ages, when knights went off to battle. A departing warrior would entrust his money and property to a friend or to the local church. They agreed to oversee day-to-day affairs, use funds to care for the family, and return the assets to the knight when he came back (or to the knight's children if he didn't return).

Even if you are not about to embark on a crusade, there are nevertheless good reasons for you to write a will and give thought to setting up an appropriate trust. If your assets might be subject to American estate taxes, you might want to consider initiating a divesting program. In this way, you can give away money during your lifetime as you see fit. This method of disbursement allows you to have full control of where and to whom your money goes and, depending on current tax laws, it might even save on taxes before and after your demise.

Begin with Your Will

A will is a must-have legally enforceable document that states how you want your assets to be allocated after your death, how you want particular family members cared for, and how other matters relevant to you or to your business should be handled. Your will takes effect when you die. Until then, you can change your will at any time, as you see fit. But upon your demise, the last version, called your "final will and testament," will be legally executed to govern the disposition of your assets and the fulfillment of all your final wishes.

Before you sit down with your lawyer to write your will or to begin thinking about an appropriate trust, make sure you have done some preparation. Organize your paperwork. Review your balance sheets. Look over your assets and liabilities. In addition, consider two points of prime importance: If you have minor children, who should be named guardian? And, who will be the executor of your estate?

Who Will Love Your Children?

If your children are still minors, have a serious discussion with your spouse to consider what would happen to them if either one or both of you were to die or become incapacitated. If you are the main breadwinner and were suddenly no longer around, would your spouse have sufficient funding to carry on? What type of extra help might be needed? Would there be enough assets for tuition, weddings, and other expenses that are important to your family?

While death leaves an emotional void in family life, do what you can to eliminate the risk of a financial void. Then consider the almost unthinkable. What would happen if both of you were no longer around? Who would care for your children? Where would they live? Who would pay their expenses? Are there potential guardians you might consider suitable for the job of raising your kids? Are they in sufficiently good health to handle such responsibility? Would they bring up your youngsters with the same values you hold dear? Should the prospective guardians also have control of the children's assets that you plan to leave for their benefit? Alternatively, should someone else, perhaps a professional trustee, manage the funds? What if the logical blood relative choices do not seem genuinely interested in your children's welfare? Or are not fiscally competent? Or do not share your values? Should you look at non-relatives? And what if the couple you designate subsequently gets a divorce? What then would happen to the children? It may be wise to give custody to an individual rather than a couple to avoid any confusion. After finally reaching a decision, your next step would be to discuss the matter with the person or people you wish to name to find out if, in fact, they would agree to the responsibility. Difficult as these judgments are, they are even more complex for parents who are divorced. Legal intervention is often necessary in such cases to determine how the children's needs can best be met.

In Israel, the appointment of guardianship comes from the court. However, generally speaking, your will or letter of intention is taken into consideration. Be sure, therefore, that you have explicitly stated your wishes on this matter and supported your comments with appropriate documentation.

Who Should Be the Executor?

The executor will be responsible for determining and carrying out your wishes after your death in accordance with the law. When choosing an executor, take into account the person's honesty, decision-making ability, and common sense, as well as his grasp of the world of finance and his willingness to seek out professional help, when and if needed. He should feel comfortable using the services of an attorney, an accountant, a financial advisor, and other experts as he proceeds with the required legal steps. Commonly, spouses, relatives, friends, business associates, bank trustees, personal attorneys, accountants, or financial professionals are chosen to be executors. Alternatively, it can also be an appointee of the court. Whomever you finally settle upon, be sure he is trustworthy and competent enough to carry out a series of duties that must be attended to efficiently and in a timely fashion. Perhaps before you make your decision, you will want to look below at a sampling of the many responsibilities that he will encounter.

Executors' tasks:
1. Locating, assembling, and organizing the assets of the estate.
2. Evaluating the assets (often professional appraisals are required).
3. Identifying which assets will pass through probate and which will pass directly to beneficiaries (e.g., insurance policies and retirement accounts with listed beneficiaries avoid probate and pass directly).
4. Dealing with probate issues. If your assets are not already in a trust when you die, then your will must be probated in court. Probate enables a judge to ascertain that the will is valid, and allows him to formally appoint the executor. If you have assets in multiple jurisdictions, say a home in Israel, a rental property

in New York, and a Florida getaway, your estate may require "ancillary probate," which means that the executor will have to engage in probate proceedings in every state where property is owned. The probate procedure is not confidential (whereas a trust is *not* open to public perusal) and the will itself is available for scrutiny by anyone.

5. Collecting assets owed to the estate and paying off debts, expenses, estate and final personal income taxes, and court and administrative fees for which the estate is responsible.

6. Notifying employers, retirement fund administrators, social security, *bituach leumi*, and any other issuers of benefit payments. Also, informing issuers of home, car, and other insurance policies to cancel or update policies to reflect new ownership.

7. Temporarily managing the estate's property and liquidating assets when necessary.

8. Keeping a careful accounting of all administrative details.

9. Completing the probate process and then distributing the assets as specified.

If, after considering the above listing, you feel that your executor will need help, or that your estate matters are so complex that it will take more than one person to handle them, consider naming a co-executor – possibly a lawyer or bank trustee – to share the responsibilities. Choosing a professional to be primary or co-executor of your estate can be advantageous for many reasons. Professionals are knowledgeable in their field and may be able to save money for your estate by doing things right the first time around; they are apt to be impartial when making decisions about your children's welfare; they are up to date with the constantly changing estate laws; and, in the case of bank executors and trustees, they provide your estate with continuity (should the person you are working with leave or die, another official will take over). Professionals, of course, will charge a fee. This may be based on a percentage of the total estate, on an hourly fee schedule, or on an agreed-upon set amount. Non-professionals may charge a fee, too. It's reasonable to pay someone for the service of being your executor because he will have a great deal of work and responsibility. If payment isn't offered, burdening a family member or friend with the work may be considered unfair. This could lead to a long, drawn-out process as the executor may not make your estate his top priority.

Review and Update Documents Regularly

Once you have chosen the guardian for your children, the executor for your estate, and have met with appropriate legal advisors, your work is still not done. In fact, until the end of your days, you have some very important obligations: to pay attention to your assets, keep them organized, maintain accurate and current records, and make appropriate document changes when necessary. If you don't, you may inadvertently create nightmares for your heirs. Consider the unfortunate scenario of younger children being left out of receiving the proceeds from an insurance policy taken out before their births (only the older siblings, who had been born already, were listed as beneficiaries). Or, what if a second marriage had occurred and the beneficiary listing wasn't changed from the first spouse to the second? How about the case where the chosen executor has become old and frail, and the alternate you so carefully selected has passed away. Maybe the money you had planned to divide among your children has been invested in real estate that cannot, or should not, be sold. Or perhaps, twenty years ago, you wrote that your art collection should go to your older son, your coin collection to your younger son, and your jewelry collection to your daughter. You did this because they were all worth about the same amount. But now the jewelry is worth five times as much as each of the other two. Periodic review can help avoid situations like these and provide motivation to correct the inequities.

While there are many technicalities involved in preparing estate documents, don't be discouraged from getting started. Just the opposite. Remember that careful planning of wills not only eases the emotional angst for the family, but conscientious planning can truly make a long-lasting difference. For example, John Harvard set up the university that bears his name by bequeathing his personal library and half his money to build the college; Alfred Nobel established the Nobel Prize in his will; and Cecil Rhodes created the Rhodes Scholarship in his final testament. You could rightly argue that other famous people died intestate (without a will), but we still remember them. American Presidents Abraham Lincoln, Andrew Jackson, Ulysses Grant, and James Garfield all died without wills. Were their affairs settled the way they would have wanted? Who knows? Is that the fate you wish for your assets and your heirs?

Will or Trust?

If you have a will, do you also need a trust? That depends. For some people, especially those who are less affluent, have simple family structures, and don't have a business, a simple will may be quite adequate. For others, a will *and* trust may be the better solution. For these individuals, a "pour-over" will might be worth considering. It allows assets previously not assigned to a trust to be "poured" into the trust upon the estate owner's death. If you have set up a trust and placed most of your assets in it, those assets will avoid probate; however, assets that are dealt with through a pour-over will must be probated.

Keeping Your Assets in a Trust

While trusts are complicated legal documents that should be written by professionals, the vocabulary within them should be understood by everyone involved. In order for a trust to exist, there must be "trust property" (sometimes called the trust "principal" or "corpus"). The creator of the trust (the one who establishes it) is called the "grantor," "settlor," or "trustor." The person who has legal control of the trust's assets is called the "trustee." Anyone who stands to benefit from the trust is called a "beneficiary." Often one person plays more than one role. Thus, a grantor can also be a trustee (or co-trustee) and also a beneficiary. Upon creation of the trust, the grantor and the trustee must be legally competent.

Trusts are established in different ways, depending on the grantor's goals. When the grantor (settlor) is both the beneficiary and also the trustee, it is important for him to choose a co-trustee or to nominate a subsequent trustee to avoid a court appointment of a trustee upon his death. If the grantor has chosen another person (or institution) as trustee, rather than himself, the trustee will manage the assets and distribute funds in accordance with the trust's regulations. If the trust is a "revocable trust," the settlor retains ultimate control and can replace the trustee if he is dissatisfied. On the other hand, if he establishes an "irrevocable trust," the settlor will have no ongoing say in any matters of the trust, having irrevocably handed over power to someone else.

Revocable vs. Irrevocable

For tax purposes, one of the most important characteristics of a trust is whether it is revocable (which means the settlor can take back all the assets into his own name) or irrevocable (which means the settlor permanently and completely gives his assets to the trust). Generally, if a trust is revocable, the government will view it as just another account belonging to the settlor. That's fine if you, as the settlor, are trying to avoid having your assets go through probate. However, if you are attempting to lower your tax obligations by placing your assets in a revocable trust, you will not accomplish this goal. The government takes the position that since you have easy access to the funds, you should pay any applicable taxes on them.

On the opposite side of the spectrum is the person who irrevocably gives money to a trust with no strings attached. It's as if he gave a gift to someone else. Should the government be able to claim that the donor has to pay tax on money that he no longer has, nor controls, nor benefits from? Determining the exact tax status of an irrevocable trust is a complicated question, beyond the scope of this chapter. Many people believe that they've established irrevocable trusts and think the money therein has escaped the reach of the taxman; but sometimes they are wrong. Beware – if you have any incidence of ownership; if you have any decision-making power over the money; if you stand to benefit from the assets; if you can write a check or use a debit card from the trust's bank account; or even if you can exert influence over someone else who controls the trust – the irrevocable status of your trust might be disqualified by the tax authority of Israel, the United States, or both. Then, all the assets would be considered yours for tax purposes. This is especially detrimental when a U.S. citizen is trying to get assets out of his own name before he dies to avoid having them become subject to the estate tax. Due to the complexities involved in estate planning, when creating a trust, make sure you get experienced, qualified tax and legal advice. Your trust has to work right the first time around. You don't get a second chance.

Should You Set up a Trust?

Trusts vary in focus and intent. Couples with children often set up revocable living trusts (also known as *"inter vivos"* trusts) to protect and benefit their families in the future. They retain control of the trust property by being both the grantors and the trustees, and can therefore withdraw assets to use for current needs. While they're alive, the trust's earnings are taxed as if they were the earnings of the grantors. In effect, the tax code makes no differentiation between the individual's assets and those of the trust. When the grantors die, the assets in the trust will normally avoid probate (which can sometimes be a hassle) and will move smoothly along as per the document's instructions.

In order to determine if a trust might benefit you and your family, consider a few of the compelling reasons why people choose to create them:

- An income stream can be established for minor children and/ or other heirs.

- Adult children who are unprepared to manage a large sum of money can receive funds at specified intervals.
- Assets can be protected from creditors. (Since this is a tricky issue, make sure a qualified lawyer designs your trust.)
- Probate can be avoided.
- Family finances can be kept confidential.
- Certain tax benefits can be achieved.

Common Trust Concepts

Trusts should be personalized to meet specific needs. There are many options available as to how they may be designed. The specific format of a trust can be designed to protect the grantor, beneficiary, or both. Below are some varieties of trusts and provisions that are commonly used in the U.S. If you are unsure of your category or what your needs really are, speak with a professional. Also, note that Israeli trust concepts differ from the American legal viewpoint. After you have developed a plan to achieve your goals with a U.S. trust, go over it with an Israeli trust expert to make sure that you have not inadvertently created more problems than you're solving.

- *Discretionary* provisions in a trust allow the trustees, as they see fit, to distribute interest and/or principal to the beneficiaries. Sometimes a trust includes a term called a "sprinkling" or "spray" provision, which narrows the discretionary powers of the trustees so that they can only distribute income (not principal) as they deem reasonable.
- *Special needs* trusts deal with people whose situation is beyond the norm, especially in the case of a handicapped family member. For example, some disabled people receive government aid. However, their public assistance could be cut if they were to receive an inheritance, even a small one. To provide help for disabled children and other dependent beneficiaries, while not limiting the other income streams available to them, special needs trusts may be used.

- A *Generation Skipping Trust* (GST) is ideal for people who believe in thinking far ahead. Also known as a "dynasty trust," this vehicle allows wealthy individuals to pass their assets to their grandchildren in a tax-saving manner. Ordinarily, if the money passed to the children of the deceased, it would be subject to estate taxes. Then, when these individuals died, the money would be passed on to their children (the original donor's grandchildren) and the funds could be taxed again. This type of trust allows a specified amount of money to be set aside in order to avoid double taxation.

- *Spendthrift* provisions in a trust prohibit the transfer of the beneficiary's rights in the trust to anyone else. In principal, a beneficiary who is entitled to income from a trust could transfer his income interest to a third party. This means that a trust beneficiary who racks up excessive gambling debts, for example, might be able to sign over his future income from the trust to the loan shark to whom he owes money. If the trust has a spendthrift clause, however, the trustees could refuse to disseminate any funds that would go to settle that debt. Similarly, if an unfortunate trust beneficiary drives himself out of business and is stuck with a lot of debts, the trustees can refuse to pay off the creditors.

- An *incentive trust* can help to compel the beneficiaries to achieve certain goals before they can receive funds. Distributions may be tied to the beneficiary taking certain actions, such as achieving a certain grade point average in school, finishing university, entering a profession, starting a business, passing a drug test, getting married, having children, marrying within the religion, etc. Incentives must be legal in order to eliminate a court overturning them one day. They are usually used to make sure that trust beneficiaries don't become "trust brats." Billionaire Sam Walton (founder of Wal-Mart) spelled out the philosophy that many trust makers follow when he said that he would leave his children enough money so that they could do anything, but not so much that they could do nothing.

- *Charitable Remainder Trusts* (CRTS) provide assistance to qualified charities and simultaneously benefit the donors. A highly appreciated asset can be placed into this type of irrevocable trust. By doing so, you would not have to pay capital gains tax on the amount that this asset (stock, home, art collection, etc.) appreciated since you originally acquired it. And, you would receive an immediate income-tax deduction for the contribution (the amount of which depends on various factors that you should review with your accountant). In addition to these tax savings, the donation would no longer be considered as your asset and thus would not be included in your estate (and not subject to any applicable inheritance tax). It is possible to design the trust so that even though the assets do not belong to you, you could receive a certain lifetime income from the trust. When you die, the charity would get to keep the asset.

- A *Qualified Terminable Interest Property Trust* (QTIP) allows assets to eventually be distributed in accordance with the written wishes of the donor spouse. It stipulates that should this spouse die first, the surviving spouse will receive the on-going income and a percent of the principal, but upon his or her death, the *corpus* (i.e., principal) will pass on to the heirs chosen by the first spouse. Under the guidelines of the QTIP trust, taxes are deferred until the death of the surviving spouse. QTIP trusts are most often used when there are children from a previous marriage. Even if there are not, some people use this trust to prevent a future spouse of the survivor from having access to, or wasting the estate funds.

- A *Qualified Domestic Trust* (QDOT) addresses the problem of transferring assets to a non-citizen spouse who may not qualify for a marital deduction. For example, a U.S. citizen with a $3 million estate could marry another U.S. citizen and bequeath the whole sum to her upon his death with no estate (death) taxes. If he married an Israeli, though, there would be estate tax due as the money passes to his non-U.S. wife. QDOT rules require a U.S. trustee to ensure collection of the death tax upon the demise of the surviving spouse. Speak to a qualified estate attorney if this is applicable to your situation.

Not All Trusts Are Suitable

A common misconception is that one can avoid taxes by putting assets in a trust. In some ways this may be true, but be aware that trusts themselves are subject to taxes, and sometimes at higher tax rates than are individuals. While trusts can provide some tax savings and cut probate-related expenses, they do not necessarily offer savings when it comes to estate or income taxes. Various financial "experts" sometimes suggest certain new or impressive trust strategies that provide tax savings. Use caution when listening to their advice since there are no magic trust solutions. For example, offshore schemes aimed at hiding money may well lead to grief. (*Hiding* money is not a tax-planning technique. It is tax evasion and, needless to say, illegal.)

Do You Need Expert Advice?

Although you may be a jack-of-all-trades, it is generally not a good idea to handle your will- and trust-making activities by yourself. No matter the size of your estate, it's in your own interest to have highly competent advisors on your side, helping you to manage your assets appropriately. Choose professionals who are experts in their fields, keep up to date with the latest rules and information, are willing to take time to let you express your concerns and hopes, and are available to you when you need them. Ideally, your professional advisors – your "Dream Team" – will not only work with you on a one-to-one basis, but also will consult and work with each other on your behalf.

Who Will Be on Your Advisory Team?

Your goal is to find highly qualified people who are knowledgeable in their field, intelligent, diligent, honest, and truly interested in helping you to accomplish your objectives. Ask acquaintances whose judgment you respect for references. Arrange meetings with each candidate you are considering and see how the interaction is between the two of you. Do you clearly understand what he is talking about? Does he listen carefully to your responses and opinions? Do you have confidence in his knowledge? Ask him about his credentials and experience. When you feel comfortable with his answers, continue by asking him about his fees. Be wary of an advisor who tries to rush you into making a decision, who makes you a now-or-never offer, who is more interested in bragging about himself than in learning about you, and who forgets – or is too busy to return your calls.

Financial Advisor. A professional financial planner is skillful in helping people analyze their needs and aspirations. He can show clients how to coordinate their goals with the reality of their finances. Often financial planners work with multiple generations in the same family, and help heirs understand their new economic situation. If assets must be liquidated to pay estate-related taxes and debts, he can offer counsel on which holdings would be suitable choices for selling. Frequently, a financial planner is also a fully licensed stockbroker and can provide in-depth advice on various investments as well as help in expediting transference of holdings in the account to beneficiaries upon receipt of the required documentation. (If there are still stock certificates in someone's name when he passes on, the executor will have to deal with the various corporate transfer agents and send each of them the required forms and a copy of the death certificate in order to have the shares reassigned to the beneficiaries.)

In choosing a planner, ask some of these questions: Is he licensed in the countries where he does business? Is he a Certified Financial Planner™ (accredited by the CFP board, which affirms his high level of achievement in financial education, experience, and ethics)? Is he a Registered Investment Advisor (who has passed the required testing and is registered with the U.S. Securities and Exchange Commission [SEC] as an investment advisor)?

Is he a certified TEP (a member of the Society of Trust and Estate Practitioners [STEP], an organization of highly experienced experts in the field of taxes, trusts, and estates)?

A financial advisor can help families before, during, and after the estate-settling process. Because he is familiar with the overall financial picture, the financial advisor is often the central hub of an advisory team – the coordinator of the group of professionals.

Accountant. This professional contributes to the advisory team by recommending tax-efficient ways to help the client set up his estate-planning documents and process tax-related forms. When there are choices to make, he explains the consequences and potential ramifications of the various alternatives to the heirs. For example, the discussion might focus on tax implications with reference to beneficiary claims on retirement plan assets, or on the proceeds of a business about to change management or be sold. An accountant can answer questions pertaining to filing the current year's taxes on behalf of the deceased. Perhaps a comprehensive review might be required in preparing final documentation. Tax issues might also arise regarding assets and tax rules in different countries. What are the implications for Americans living in Israel? What happens when *olim* inherit money from abroad?

Estate-planning Attorney. This specialized lawyer uses proper legal form and tax-efficient methods to help clients draw up their will and trust documents to arrange for the transfer of assets from one generation to the next. When the time comes, if the executor requires ongoing help, the attorney can continue to assist and provide guidance in settling the estate. In America, families frequently turn to lawyers for this kind of help in handling their estates. However, in Israel, where probate usually entails only minimal costs, and where there is currently no inheritance tax to contend with, it is less common.

Trust Officer. If the deceased chose a bank or trust company to be the fiduciary/executor of his will and/or trust, the officer of the chosen institution would meet with the heirs and handle the estate settlement procedure for them in a manner that complies with the wishes of the grantor. And, if it was stated in the trust documents, the trust officer (and the institution) would continue the relationship with the heirs by serving as a trustee (or co-trustee).

Development Officer. Many people feel that in addition to providing for their heirs, they also wish to pass on assets to a favorite charitable institution. Others want to contribute even before they are gone so that their assets can help even sooner. And still others, knowing of the potential tax and income benefits that can accrue from a major donation in the form of a charitable remainder trust, decide to follow the path of philanthropy. When a contributor is considering a major gift, he should speak with the charity's development officer, who can provide appropriate information and help arrange the paperwork.

Insurance Agent. Experienced agents or planners can help people decide which types of coverage they should carry to supplement their work-related policies. Insurance agents can help clients determine how much insurance they should have in case they become ill, sustain a disability, or die. How much business insurance should a person carry? How about malpractice insurance? Homeowners insurance? Liability insurance? Life insurance? In whose names should the various policies be? Who should be the beneficiaries? Would it be wise to set up a separate trust (called an ILIT – "irrevocable life insurance trust" – in order to limit estate tax liability) to hold a life insurance policy on someone's life? Can the way in which individuals establish their policies affect their taxes? Which companies offer the best coverage at the best prices? These are questions that an insurance agent can help answer.

Summary
- The United States currently imposes an estate tax that will disappear in 2010, but reappear in 2011. Israel currently has no death tax.

- Set up appropriate powers of attorney to grant others the right to make decisions for you pertaining to your finances and to your health, should you become physically or mentally incapacitated.
- Everyone should have a will, and possibly a trust. If you have minor children, determine who should be named as their guardian. Also, select a person to be the executor of your estate.
- Trusts are established to help the grantor achieve his goals. They vary in focus and intent, such as a Generation Skipping Trust, a Charitable Remainder Trust, an Incentive Trust, and more.
- A team of experts to help you with your financial affairs might include a financial advisor, an accountant, an attorney, a bank trust representative, a development officer, and an insurance planner.

Chapter 11
Dealing with Financial Success (Part 1)

Through hard work, a keen understanding of how the business world runs, your own intelligence, the sale of a closely held company, perhaps even a welcome inheritance... and with a bit of luck, you've managed to amass a sizable nest egg. Now what?

If you are still in your accumulating stage, you probably rise early each morning, get a head start on the news as you down your coffee, have your finger on numerous hot spots of your business during the day, and race home to spend some precious time with your family before they're all asleep. Managing your assets is an activity that winds up getting less attention than it should. You are well aware of the adage, "You work hard for your money. Now let your money work hard for you." But how are you going to get your money to work hard for you when you just don't have enough time to monitor it?

Who Will Help You?
Perhaps you have a full-service broker who offers you first-class support, keeps you posted on security offerings, promptly sends

you information, and is available to help you in a variety of other ways. Even if he is responsive to your wishes, however, there are limitations to what he can do on your behalf. Most brokers do not have discretionary power over client accounts. Thus, if you are out of town and your broker hears unfavorable news about one of your holdings, he may try to reach you to discuss the matter. But if he can't contact you, he's not allowed to take it upon himself to sell your position. And, even if he reaches you, you may choose not to take his advice at the moment. Perhaps you feel hesitant about making a quick move without studying the issue; maybe you're out on the town and are not in the frame of mind to make financial decisions; maybe you feel emotionally attached to the holding; or perhaps, you just might not like to make rapid buy-sell decisions.

Perhaps your real hesitation in spending time managing your account is the fact that you really don't want to be a portfolio manager, even if it is your own account. Despite being happy with your sizable investments, you really do not want the responsibility of making the day-to-day decisions. If this is the case, you are not alone. Many people with substantial holdings do not want to, or just cannot spend time studying their own securities. They don't want to keep reading up on potential new investments. Nor do they necessarily have the analytic skills and patience to research, trade, balance, and monitor their portfolios. They know that on-going attention is crucial in having a well-organized account, and they would like to have a financial professional undertake this responsibility. Therefore, they turn to money managers.

What Is a "Managed Money" Account?

Your financial advisor/broker can help you with portfolio planning, maintenance, and many related investment decisions. He can suggest suitable purchases and keep you apprised of recent happenings in the markets. But he has many clients who depend on him for guidance, and each one has different goals and financial needs. He cannot follow each and every client's financial holdings on a daily basis. Therefore, your broker might suggest that it would be in your best interest to have a portion of your assets handled by a money-management team whose focus is entirely on monitoring the markets, keeping current on research, and buying and selling positions according to a carefully constructed strategy. Advisory firms, working on a fee basis, set up individual managed money accounts (sometimes called "Separately Managed Accounts" or "SMAS") for clients over which the managers have total discretion. They trade securities within these discretionary accounts without consulting the clients, and send periodic detailed reports of all transactions so clients can keep abreast of what's happening.

Often financial managers of large corporations, foundations, university trust funds, unions, and other public and private organizations hire one or more money-management firms to invest portions of their asset pools. Though their portfolios may be in the hundreds of millions of dollars, investors with just $100,000 can often access the same managers through special programs (described below). If you don't choose to work through a managed-money program, but rather go directly to a specific management firm, then depending on the particular investment company, a minimum account requirement might be $1 million or more.

Nowadays, many money-management firms have relationships with brokerage houses that allow smaller portfolios to benefit from the same service larger accounts enjoy. Through these arrangements, the topnotch money-management companies agree to accept new client accounts with only a $100,000–$250,000 minimum. This lower entry requirement is just one of the reasons that investors (even those starting with well over these amounts) choose to have their financial advisors involved.

Another reason to choose to enter a managed money program through your financial advisor is that he can help you find a firm whose style best matches your needs. Your advisor, being uniquely familiar with your financial situation and with management firms that share your philosophy, reviews with you your goals for the money to be placed in the new account. Together you decide on a reasonable amount to allocate. You also talk about the amount of risk you feel you can take with these funds, your time frame for maintaining the account, and your thoughts about the investing style utilized by the different management firms you and your advisor have singled out. Your advisor may arrange a conference call or a face-to-face meeting with a representative from the money-management firm. In making your final selection, your advisor helps you narrow down the choices by reviewing with you current reports as well as track records to see which firm (or firms) would be most likely to help you meet your objectives.

A special team of analysts prescreens the money managers that your financial advisor recommends to you. Monitoring the selected management teams is an ongoing process on the part of your advisor's firm, and one that they take very seriously. When, in the company's estimation, a management group no longer meets the high level of achievement and service on which their selection was based, or if the top managers leave and their replacements are less experienced or unknown, your advisor's firm may remove the management team from the recommended list. If this were to occur, your advisor would notify you, and together you would determine if you should transfer your account to another choice on the roster.

From the thousands of money managers putting up their shingles, your advisor's company narrows down the vast number of candidates to just a few dozen. In their due diligence process to find the "best of the best," they focus on such criteria as:

- **Investment process**. The manager and his team should have a definable investment strategy that is clearly stated and followed.
- **Meeting client diversification needs**. Investors sometimes have substantial holdings in one stock or one sector, often due to corporate retirement plans, inheritance of a family business, or stock option plans. Can the managed account professionals

tailor portfolios to avoid inappropriate concentration in these areas?

- **Manager's track record.** In profitable as well as turbulent times, management needs to add value to client portfolios. Has the manager been in the position a long time so that a sense of his capability is apparent? Have the existing investment strategies led to anticipated outcomes? Do these managers excel over competitors in their field?
- **Management team stability.** Excessive turnover in personnel may suggest a lack of focus in the way money is handled. Is the staff a group of experienced and dedicated professionals who have built good reputations over a long time period? Are they held in high regard by both their peers and their clients?
- **Tax-efficient management.** With a separately managed account, clients and their advisors have greater control over how and when taxable trades should occur. Can the managers accommodate client requests to sell in order to realize capital gains or losses at the right times?
- **Nuts and bolts.** Can the firm handle the administration of the accounts, and can they provide the high quality of service that the clients of the brokerage firm expect to receive?

Helping to match you with a suitable money-management firm and maintaining surveillance of its ongoing performance are only the first two steps that your financial advisor takes in helping you turn over the reins to a professional money-management company. There is a third step: A very important reason to involve your advisor in your management firm decision is that he can assist you in reviewing the details of your account statements and help you measure how your holdings are doing. Having access to results from competing firms, he can also offer input on how your management team is faring when compared with others having similar objectives. Your financial advisor can be a voice of comfort and reassurance in a rough market and a source of information and explanations that you might need as you monitor your account.

The traders at the management firm carefully follow every detail of your account. They watch every up and down movement that a security takes. They have a plan for every holding. They are not emotionally involved with their decisions. They have a strategy in mind. And they follow it. Your advisor, to complement the services of the traders, reviews your account's progress, addresses any questions, compares your results with those provided by alternate firms, and provides you with the personal service you want. He understands your total financial situation – knows where you are now, and works to get you to where you want to be in the future.

Are Managed Accounts for You?

Many folks make and carry out their own decisions. They manage their personal finances, their family's affairs, and their own small businesses. They arrange their own vacations, write their own wills, choose their own stocks, and fix their own cars. These people are well organized, multi-talented, tireless, and they can find extra time. Then there are others who also make their own decisions, manage their businesses, see to family matters, are well organized and multi-talented, and maybe even tireless – but they know how to delegate and hire others to do many routine and specialized chores for them. They let a travel agent book their vacation, a car mechanic fix their transmission, an attorney write their will, a financial advisor help them achieve their retirement goals, and when it comes to day-to-day management of their stock portfolios, they let a management team take charge of the research, analysis, trading, and constant monitoring that their account deserves. Smart and competent as they are, people in this latter group feel that perhaps a lawyer, travel agent, mechanic, or financial advisor can handle the specialized tasks better than they themselves could.

Whichever group you are in, or maybe you are somewhere in the middle, consider if a managed account would be suitable for you. These accounts are certainly not for everyone; their minimum requirements make them available to only certain clientele. But if you qualify and if you feel this type of account management fits in with your investing philosophy, your financial advisor can give you further information and a list of managers whose styles match your goals. You can learn more about managed money by clicking on the "Education" tab at www.profile-financial.com.

Fees

Normally, managed accounts are handled under a "wrap-fee" arrangement. Based on the size of the account, a fixed percentage is assessed. Clients often prefer this approach because it means everyone is sitting on the same side of the table. In other words, the only way the managers can increase their own income is by increasing the size of your account. The fees that are deducted from the managed accounts are used to pay for the skilled services and tools of the team's researchers, analysts, managers, and administrators. In addition, there is no entrance or exit fee when starting or stopping with a manager. The wrap-fee normally also covers expenses for record keeping, issuing statements, trading commissions, holding and transferring investments, as well as for due diligence, overseeing, and account monitoring by the brokerage firm and its personnel.

For Now and for the Future

Now that you've got a well-designed and well-managed financial system, it is still essential for you to remain diligent. Proper monitoring on your part – with or without professional guidance – is essential if your fortune is to remain intact. Money managers aren't the only professionals who can help you in dealing with the complexities and demands of life in the upper financial spheres. In fact, there are concerns, above and beyond preserving and increasing investment portfolios, which ultra-wealthy families constantly address. They want to carry on family traditions, pass on assets, and donate funds to those in need. But because of the magnitude of their fortunes and their obligations – financial and otherwise – they generally do not have the option to tend to their wealth unassisted. The second part of this chapter examines the solutions that these families have found for successfully dealing with their wealth in all aspects of their lives.

Dealing with Serious Financial Success (Part II)

If you can count your money, you don't have a billion dollars.
– J. Paul Getty

Consider yourself lucky, brilliant, blessed, or some combination of the three. There is no doubt about it. With a net worth counted in the millions, you are very rich. However, does your money buy happiness, and are your days stress free? Do you have ample time to relax? Will your current and future heirs be as financially well endowed as you are? Will their good fortune, and your own, be shared with those in need?

Who Are the Very Wealthy?
When your assets grow to the stage where they are counted in millions, it's time to develop an overall strategy to professionally handle your family's needs. It's not sufficient merely to hire an accountant to do your taxes, or a broker to execute your trades, or a banker to negotiate corporate loan deals for your firm. You need a team of fully qualified, highly skilled advisors who have extensive

Shmuel Khungdim

*"No, dear. I don't love you for your money. It's for all
the wonderful things your money can buy."*

experience in working with the wealthy and in interacting with
one another in helping their clients achieve their goals.

The Team Approach

The team approach is not a new idea. Back in the 1880s, John D.
Rockefeller was determined to manage and preserve his assets for
future generations and to help support worthwhile causes. He realized that he couldn't handle all of these lofty goals himself, so
he established what is nowadays called a family office. Together
with staff consultants, they devised and enacted suitable, long-
lasting strategies.

Family businesses often span many generations. Young de-
scendants enjoy periodic income and/or principal from trusts,
established perhaps before they were even born. Often these
trusts cover a group of heirs, such as all the grandchildren, and
so large numbers of relatives may be connected by interlocking

trust documents. Due to such overlapping, and also because of the overall desire of some families to maintain voting control in certain companies, trusts are sometimes drawn up in a way that prevents sales of large blocks of the family's shares. For example, some Getty family trusts allow beneficiaries to receive millions in dividend income but none of the principal. The trust stipulates that in the distant future, when the last listed income heir dies, the corpus, as per legal requirements, will finally be distributed.

Many in the ultra-rich category are not part of a corporate empire. Heirs of non-corporate fortunes, entrepreneurs, wise or lucky investors, leaders in show business, etc., are also included in the world of high net worth. They too need teams of consultants to help them track, grow, and preserve their wealth and manage their busy lives. Though not major players in industry, their successfully invested fortunes and aspirations match those of the corporate crowd. And like those in the corporate group, they also look for professional family office guidance.

The Family Office

The scope of the family office extends well beyond corporate, financial, and trust matters. Members of the ultra-rich category, regardless of the source of their wealth, contribute to society and welcome being assisted. On a daily basis, these well-to-do folks often find themselves in social circles that include scions of other wealthy families, politicians, and the social elite. They are petitioned to support domestic and worldwide worthy causes and often select several organizations to which they donate large amounts of their time, energy, and money. How do they decide what to do and how to act in these diverse situations? The answer, very often, is that they are getting high-level expert advice from professionals at their family office.

Family office consultants work behind the lines. They are constantly in tune with the family's needs. Whether their help is required for tax and estate matters, for handling grant distributions from the family foundation, for dealing with family and business legal decisions, or for addressing any number of personal happenings, they are available. Family office consultants work diligently and discreetly on behalf of their clients on a full-time basis. They are always there for them.

Family office consultants make suggestions, supply facts, and act as a sounding board. They ask pointed questions. What procedures do you want to follow to measure progress? What means should be considered to assess accountability? What would be a fair system for the family members to use to rectify conflicts that might arise among them? Family office consultants offer guidance, counsel, and support in both business and daily life situations, in good times and in times of trouble. They rise to each challenge and use their knowledge, experience, ingenuity, and good judgment to assist their clients and to help solve their problems. In other words, they see to it that what needs talking about gets discussed, and what needs doing gets done.

Family Offices Make Philanthropy More Efficient

Family office consultants can add great value to the philanthropic work of the wealthy. While some individuals are content with merely giving charity, other donors extend their business outlook to their philanthropic endeavors. They are not satisfied by just knowing that money has been sent; rather, they want to know that their donation is being used as efficiently as possible for the specific project for which it was intended. While some charities appear well run, they often don't function as well as a for-profit business. Their leaders normally have a heart of gold, but frequently lack sophisticated business sense. Therefore, a family office can represent the donor by working directly with the charities in such areas as:

- examining the organization's short-term and long-term strategic plan (often focusing on budgeting and accountability),
- making sure the services that the charity intends to provide have solid underlying systems and are actually achievable,

*"Best friends? Hah! **Money** is a man's best friend."*

- encouraging and helping to implement new programs inside the organization,
- reviewing the credentials of the leaders and their staffs to make sure the right people are handling the donor's money,
- following through with the organization to oversee and audit the ongoing results of the philanthropic investment.

The Multi-Family Office: A Sharing Solution

Though you may not have the hundreds of millions of dollars that would justify creating your own staff for a private family office, you may still be an ideal candidate to participate in a multi-family office. This solution allows you to share the costs as well the benefits of professional management with others who might have similar goals, interests, and needs.

Even if your bank account size does not match those of the Rockefellers, the Gates', the Waltons, the Arisons, and the Dells, you may be similar to them in many ways. You know, just as they do, that time is precious. If the hours you or they spend addressing complex issues were instead used to further business, to share more time with family, or to explore new avenues in life, you would all be better off. The ultra-wealthy, as well as those somewhat less affluent, need customized advice on developing overall strategies. Both groups need help in investing assets, managing finances, handling taxes, writing wills and trusts, purchasing real estate, acquiring new businesses, giving and monitoring donations to charity, and many other matters. And, when possible, both groups want to find this high-level of guidance, instruction, and encouragement all coordinated under one roof. The services of a private family office, so necessary to those at the top of the financial curve, are now available to many people through multi-family offices. And, although your millions may not be billions, when you use the services of a multi-family office, you can feel as rich as Rockefeller. (For more information, go to the "Family Office" tab at www.profile-financial.com.)

Summary
Part i

- You work hard for your money. Now's the time to consider how to make your money work for you.
- Managed money advisory firms handle large accounts on a discretionary basis for private and public organizations, as well as for individual investors.
- Your financial advisor and his firm monitor the advisory company you select to manage your money, and compare its results with those of other management organizations. They also help you examine and keep track of money managers by checking on company policy, management history, results, and fees.

Part ii

- There are varying definitions of the term "wealthy." Sometimes it refers to people with several million dollars in assets. At other times the reference pertains to those with hundreds of millions and more.
- Consultants working in a family office form a team of multi-talented skilled advisors who handle financial and related

matters, and instruct, guide, and encourage family members to maintain their wealth and carry on with their traditions.

- Family offices can help to coordinate philanthropic activities to ensure that the investments in the charities are used efficiently.
- Because many wealthy people require the same type of high-quality economic and personal services enjoyed by the ultra-wealthy, multi-family offices have evolved to meet their needs.

Chapter 12

An Overview: Two Countries – Two Tax Codes

[Upon preparing his tax return] *This is too difficult
for a mathematician. It takes a philosopher.*
                                                  – Albert Einstein

Every country has its own unique, complex, and often incomprehensible set of tax laws. Those who have spent time filling out tax return forms know how many difficulties they can present.

Tax issues become even more complex when income has to be reported in multiple countries. Issues, such as questions of citizenship, country of residence, and sources of income, all must be scrutinized under different, and sometimes conflicting, tax codes.

Keep in mind that the information within this chapter should be used for reference only. It has been designed as a general guide to help you develop questions that you should ask qualified professionals. Laws and interpretations get updated frequently, and it is certainly advisable that you consult with your accountant or attorney regarding your individual situation.

The U.S.-Israel Tax Treaty

Tax treaties exist between many nations and, in general, are carefully designed to stipulate what income will be taxable by which country. In 1976, Israeli Prime Minister Yitzhak Rabin signed a tax treaty with U.S. President Gerald Ford. Among other things, this agreement tried to ensure that neither country would "double tax" its inhabitants by causing individuals to be taxed twice on the same earnings.

Unfortunately, understanding all the ins and outs of the treaty requires a great deal of tax knowledge. Even though the treaty covers a broad spectrum of different types of earnings (work income, property income, business profits, interest payments and capital gains, royalties, etc.) and how they should be taxed, many questions still arise. In general, let's say you pay tax to the United States on your American stock dividends. You should be able to take a credit for the amount you paid when you file your Israeli tax return. In other words, if you earn $10,000 in dividends from your mutual funds and pay 15% tax to the United States, you would pay Uncle Sam $1500. To Israel, however, you might owe 20%. You would need to file an Israeli tax return and pay the remaining $500, which is the difference between the 15% ($1500) already paid to the U.S. and the 20% ($2000) owed to Israel. On the other hand, you might pay the full $2000 to Israel, which could claim the "first bite" on the tax bill, and nothing to the United States, since the $1500 owed on the U.S. side would be superseded by the $2000 owed to Israel. This is an overly simplified example that doesn't cover all the details. It certainly pays to get expert advice to make sure you're paying the correct amounts to each country.

One important aspect of the tax treaty relates to individuals receiving social security or *bituach leumi*. The U.S. and Israeli governments each agreed not to tax the government pensions supplied by the other country. Specifically, Article 21 of the treaty states, "Social security payments and other public pensions paid by one of the Contracting States to an individual who is a resident of the other Contracting State shall be exempt from tax in both Contracting States." This clause not only keeps Israel from taxing your social security checks, but as a resident of Israel, your *bituach leumi* pension and your social security are exempt from U.S. tax as well.

Israeli Income Tax

For most Israelis, the act of filing taxes requires no effort since the Israeli tax authority (*mas hachnasa*) collects most people's income tax through direct deductions from their paychecks and bank accounts. Thus, there's no annual filing requirement. The rates of taxation vary from 10% for those earning around NIS 4,000 per month, up to 49% for those people whose income tops NIS 34,450 on a monthly basis (2005 rates). That means that a person earning the equivalent of $80,000 per year has reached the highest marginal tax bracket. (As a result of Israeli tax reform, the income tax rates are scheduled to decrease in steps so the top marginal bracket will be 44% in 2010.) In addition to basic income tax, be aware that national insurance (*bituach leumi*) and mandatory health insurance (*mas briut*) also take a bite out of take-home pay to the approximate tune of 10% to 16% (of which the employer and employee each pay a part). Self-employed individuals, company owners, high-earners, and certain others must also file tax returns.

Filing Your U.S. Tax Return from Overseas

The IRS's (Internal Revenue Service) *Tax Guide* states, "Most U.S. citizens and resident aliens abroad must file U.S. income tax returns, even if they can exclude their earned income." This statement refers to the foreign earned income exclusion – that is, if you earn $80,000 or less while living outside the United States, you may not owe any taxes to the U.S. (See the section below about foreign earned income.) In general, however, you must file a tax return even if you don't owe any money, regardless of whether you live inside or outside the Fifty States. You probably have to file a tax return unless you have earned less than the following amounts in a fiscal year:

2005 U.S. FILING REQUIREMENTS
FOR MOST TAX PAYERS

If your filing status is...	AND at the end of 2005 you were...	THEN file a return if your gross income was at least ...*
Single	Under 65	$8,200
	65 or older	$9,450
Married filing jointly	Under 65 (both spouses)	$16,400
	65 or older (one spouse)	$17,400
	65 or older (both spouses)	$18,400
Married filing separately	Any age	$3,200
Head of household	Under 65	$10,500
	65 or older	$11,750
Qualifying widow(er) with dependent child	Under 65	$13,200
	65 or older	$14,200

*Gross income means all of the income you received in the form of money, goods, property, and services that is not exempt from tax, including any income from sources outside the United States (even if you may exclude part or all of it). **Do not** include social security benefits as gross income, unless you are married filing a separate return and you lived with your spouse at any time during 2005. (Source: IRS publication 17, *Your Federal Income Tax – For Individuals 2005*, pg.4, www.irs.gov/pub/irs-pdf/p17.pdf.)

Foreign Earned Income

The IRS defines foreign earned income as income you receive for services you perform in a foreign country when your tax home is in a foreign country. This income includes wages, salaries, and professional fees, but does not include non-cash benefits, such as reimbursements for lodging, meals, and education.

The source of earned income refers to the physical location in which you earn the income, not the place where you are paid. For example, payment for work done in Israel is foreign income even if your paycheck is deposited directly into a U.S. bank. Thus, if you are the Middle East representative for a Chicago-based cosmetics firm, and if you live in Israel but your paycheck gets deposited to your Chicago bank account, it is considered as foreign earned income. As such, you might not owe U.S. taxes on the money. You would, however, have to pay income taxes in Israel on the funds deposited into the Chicago account.

Foreign earned income under $80,000 may be excluded from your U.S. tax obligation. If you earn over that amount, the overage is subject to U.S. taxation. Even though it is "subject," that does not mean you will necessarily have to pay tax on it. In fact, if you've paid tax on your earnings to Israel, you can use a foreign tax credit. This means that you can tell the IRS that you've already paid Israeli tax on your money, and because the two countries have a treaty to avoid double-taxation, the IRS will not tax the same funds a second time. As mentioned earlier, it's advisable to have a tax attorney or accountant review your situation. These professionals can also advise you if there are other U.S. taxes, such as the alternative minimum tax (AMT), which may affect you.

Change Your Address on File with the IRS

When you make *aliya*, you should inform the IRS of your new address using form 8822. To download this form, go to the "Client Forms" tab at www.profile-financial.com. It is also available at the IRS' web site (www.irs.gov), or it can be ordered by calling (U.S.) 1-800-TAX-FORM.

Extensions

As an American citizen living abroad, you have the right to an automatic two-month extension to file your income tax return. With an adequate explanation, this can sometimes be stretched out to a four-month extension by filing form 4868, also available at the websites mentioned above. Filing late, however, does not allow you to pay late. If you owe money, you must pay it by April 15, otherwise you will be liable for interest and penalties. Oftentimes, people will send in checks along with their extension forms, and then when they eventually file the return, they pay the difference or apply for a refund if they overpaid. Be careful about underpaying if you choose this option, since you might be subject to interest and penalties if you pay too little.

Foreign Currency and Tax Returns

The U.S. government requires that you report income on your U.S. tax return in U.S. dollars. If you receive money, or pay some or all of your expenses in foreign currency, you must translate the foreign currency into U.S. dollars. When you receive any foreign funding, use the dollar value on the day you receive it to calculate your U.S. tax obligation. The Bank of Israel posts both current and historical shekel conversion rates on its website at www.bankisrael.gov.il/firsteng.htm.

Non-resident Alien Spouse

An interesting tax situation arises when an American citizen marries a non-American. Usually, when a husband and wife file a joint tax return, they can file for a standard deduction. A standard deduction is a dollar amount that reduces the portion of income on which you owe tax. (The amounts change each year. In 2006, someone single or married filing separately gets a standard deduction of $5150. Those who are married filing jointly get a standard deduction of $10,300.) What happens if you are an American citizen living in Israel, married to an Israeli, and paying taxes in America – can you claim your spouse as a dependant and enjoy the standard deduction?

The answer involves a trade-off. You can claim your non-American spouse (termed by the IRS as a "non-resident alien" or "NRA") as a joint filer on your return (i.e., "married, filing jointly"), which normally implies a lower overall tax obligation because you can use a higher standard deduction. However, if you choose to have your spouse file a joint return with you, his or her worldwide income becomes subject to U.S. income tax. This means that the cost of using the higher standard deduction for a married couple filing jointly could be more expensive than not doing so. On the other hand, if your NRA spouse does not work or has only excludable income, then you would have no additional income on which you would owe U.S. tax; so perhaps it would be a good idea to file jointly.

Installment Payments

If you cannot pay the full amount owed to the U.S. government, Uncle Sam frequently grants permission to pay in monthly installments. However, interest is charged, and you may be hit with an additional late payment fee for the taxes not paid before the original due date, even if your application for an extension is granted. There is also an application fee required to request a deferred payment allowance. If you choose to pay in installments, pay as much of the tax as possible when you submit your return. Alternatively, depending on interest rates, it may be a good idea to take out a bank loan to finance the money owed.

Tax Home in a Foreign Country (The U.S. Perspective)

The IRS recognizes three different types of residency definitions: tax home, *bona fide* residence, and physical presence; each one has a different tax ramification. The implication of each category determines eligibility for claiming the foreign earned income exclusion, foreign housing exclusion, and other possible deductions. In order to claim the exclusion, you must maintain your tax home abroad, *and* be one of the following:

1. a U.S. citizen or resident alien who is a *bona fide* resident of Israel for an uninterrupted period that includes an entire tax year, or
2. a U.S. citizen or resident alien who fulfills the physical presence test in Israel.

Tax Home: Regardless of where you maintain your family home, your tax home is the location of your main place of business, employment, or post of duty. Your tax home is the place where you are permanently or indefinitely working.

If your work does not have a "main place of business," your tax home may be the place where you regularly live. The place you live is determined by your social ties to the area, as well as other indications of your degree of settlement. For example, Efraim and his family are in Israel for eighteen months, having been sent by Efraim's American high-tech firm to observe a subsidiary company in Tel Aviv. While in Israel, he has bought a house, set up a bank account, leased a car, and bought a cell phone. In addition, he has joined a synagogue, a local professional organization, and enrolled his children in a school. Since he has developed a permanent-type living arrangement, the U.S. tax authorities would probably view Israel as his tax home.

Another example: Ayala is a doctor who lives in Jerusalem, and spends every other month in Jerusalem with her family and patient base. On alternate months, however, she sees patients in New York, and maintains a small apartment in Manhattan. Israel would be considered as Ayala's tax home. Since she spends equal amounts of time in both locations, the location of her tax home becomes the place she keeps her familial and social ties. If, however, Ayala lived eight months in Manhattan and only four in Jerusalem, the United States would most likely take precedence as her tax home, even though her family was living in Israel.

Bona fide Residence Test: The *bona fide* residence test is used for U.S. citizens and U.S. resident aliens who are citizens of a country with which the United States has an income tax treaty in effect.

The United States does not consider you to be a *bona fide* resident of a foreign country if you have told the authorities of that country that you are not a resident, and the authorities hold that you are not subject to their income tax laws as a resident.

Bona fide residence is not necessarily the same as your domicile. Your domicile is your permanent home, the place to which you always return or intend to return. For example, if Yosef lives and works in Manhattan, but takes a two-week trip to Israel, he obviously maintains his permanent residence in the United States. However, if he comes to Israel to set up a small company, and sets up a home and business here, he establishes himself as a *bona fide* resident of Israel.

To qualify for *bona fide* residence, you must reside in a foreign country for an uninterrupted period that includes an entire tax year. Such a period would go from January 1 through December 31.

During the period of *bona fide* residence in a foreign country, you can leave the country for brief or temporary trips back to the United States or elsewhere for a vacation or business. To keep your status as a *bona fide* resident of a foreign country, however, you must have a clear intention of returning from such trips without unreasonable delay.

For example, Chana is the Israeli representative of a U.S. employer. She arrives with her family in Israel on November 1, 2004 and immediately establishes residence there. Her assignment is indefinite, and she intends to live in Haifa with her husband and children until her company sends her to a new post. On April 1, 2005, she goes to the United States to meet with her employer, leaving her family in Israel. She returns to Israel on May 1, and continues living there. On January 1, 2006, she completes an uninterrupted period of residence for a full tax year, and thus qualifies as a *bona fide* resident of Israel.

You do not automatically acquire *bona fide* resident status merely by living in a foreign country for one year. The length of your stay and the nature of your job are only some of the many factors to consider in determining whether you meet the *bona fide* residence test.

Physical Presence Test: If you are located in a country for 330 full days over 12 consecutive months, you are considered as being

"I'm just amazed at how two bright guys like us could have such a different interpretation of the tax code."

physically present there. The 330 days do not have to be consecutive. The physical presence test applies to both U.S. citizens and resident aliens. This test is concerned only with how long you stay outside the United States. The type of residence you establish, your intentions of returning, or the nature and purpose of your stay abroad do not affect this test.

The 12-month period can begin with any day of the month, and ends the day before the same calendar day, 12 months later. You do not have to be in a foreign country only for employment purposes. If illness, family problems, a vacation, or your employer's orders cause you to be present for less than the required amount of time, you cannot meet the physical presence test.

Charity Tax Laws

Giving charity may fill you with a sensation of morality and make you feel good, but an added bonus of charitable giving is that it could possibly provide a tax break. Both the Israeli and American governments encourage charitable donations by giving tax breaks on monies donated to accredited charitable organizations.

In Israel:

Israel supports charitable donations by letting people file for a return on their income tax at the end of the year. While most Israelis are exempt from personally filing tax reports, if you file Form #0135 with the tax authorities (*mas hachnasa*), you could get back up to 35% of the amount you gave to officially authorized causes (*amutot*). (While there are many worthwhile charities, unless they are recognized by the tax authorities, donors to their causes cannot claim tax rebates. To learn the status of a particular organization, look to see that it is registered as a "*seif* 46," which is the section of the tax code that defines qualified charities.) Simply submit the #0135 form together with receipts from the charitable organizations to which you have contributed, and a few months later you should receive a refund directly deposited into your bank account. If you are self-employed (*atzma'i*), be sure to give charity receipts to your accountant to include in the preparation of your taxes.

In the United States:

If you pay taxes in the States, you can also write off charitable donations against current income if your contributions are made to charities recognized by the U.S. government. For example, if a person with taxable income of $100,000 donates $15,000, he would find himself liable for tax only on $85,000. In the higher tax brackets, the savings can be substantial.

A tax consideration Americans sometimes face arises when they want to sell highly appreciated securities on which they have long-term capital gains. Someone who bought a stock years ago for $10,000 and finds it is now worth $80,000 may owe up to 15% U.S.

tax on the $70,000 profit if he sells it. That would translate into the dollar sum of $10,500. Should he want to donate the $80,000 he received from the sale of the stock to charity, he would be unable to do so, since after taxes he would only have $69,500 left. Thus, the charity would receive a contribution of $69,500, and the donor could only claim a $69,500 write-off. However, if he donated his actual long-term holding to the charity, the charity would be able to sell the stock and use the full $80,000 for worthy causes, and he would get to write off up to the full $80,000 (depending on his adjusted gross income), and be exempt from capital gains tax on those shares. Since recognized charities don't pay capital gains taxes, the charity would enjoy greater benefits from receiving the appreciated stock than from getting an after-tax contribution from the donor. Consult with your accountant or tax attorney to see how giving charity would affect your situation.

In Both Countries:
There was a case here in Israel where a client had donated money to a charity he liked; however, when he filed for his refund, the Israeli tax authorities rejected his request. After he investigated the situation, it turned out that the charitable organization (*amuta*) was not properly filing its tax documents and had therefore lost its special tax-exempt status (*seif* 46). When you donate with a tax benefit in mind, check that the organization is a recognized and accredited charity in the country where you will claim the tax deduction. Donating to an Israeli yeshiva, for example, might not qualify for a tax deduction in America unless the school has a qualified associate organization there. Such an affiliation might be called, "The American Friends of xyz Yeshiva."

Leaving a Legacy
Often a person chooses to name a charity as one of the beneficiaries in his will. If you are thinking of doing this, consider that a more powerful use of your money might be to cite the charity as a beneficiary of your IRA. Depending on the size of the estate

you leave behind, assets in an IRA left to a family member could be taxed upwards of 70%, when you take into account both the estate and income taxes. That means your $1 million IRA could possibly net your heirs only about $300,000 (depending on your other assets and the current estate tax regulations). However, if you leave the IRA to a qualified charity, the recipient organization would benefit from the full million. Some people who do this also buy a life insurance policy to benefit their heirs who, even after paying estate taxes, may net as much as they would have from the highly taxed IRA inheritance. Careful planning of posthumous charitable giving can ensure that the preferred charity benefits while your family still receives its inheritance.

Summary

- Since every country has its distinctive set of tax laws, tax issues become complex when you file returns in two countries.
- The United States and Israel have a tax treaty to prevent double taxation being imposed on their citizens.
- When filing U.S. income tax forms, several factors have to be taken into account if one spouse is not an American citizen.
- To determine if a U.S. citizen living abroad is required to pay income taxes to the American government, certain criteria must be examined.
- Making a charitable contribution of securities or naming a charity as a beneficiary of an IRA may result in significant tax advantages.

Special Guest Chapter
The Tax Scene for Israeli Investors

Leon Harris, CPA (Israel), FCA (U.K.)
International Tax Partner at
Ernst & Young Israel (Kost Forer Gabbay & Kasierer)
Tel: 972-54-644-9398, E-mail: leonharr@gmail.com

With thanks to Ed Rieu of the Ernst & Young U.S. Desk, London

About the Author

Leon Harris is an International Tax Partner at Ernst & Young in Israel. He is an Israeli Certified Public Accountant and a U.K. Chartered Accountant (FCA). Born and educated in London, he moved to Israel in 1983. He is married with three children. Since 1987, he has specialized in advising Israeli and foreign investors and businesses on the guidelines for the establishment and conduct of international operations. This guidance includes help with international tax planning, setting up business operations in Israel and abroad, corporate structuring and reorganization, and understanding finance incentives. He has assisted clients in reviewing real estate deals, estate and succession planning, and expatriate/personal taxation. Mr. Harris is the Chairman of the International Tax Committee of the Institute of Certified Public

Accountants in Israel. He writes the international column in the Accounting Institute's monthly tax journal and contributes articles to *The Jerusalem Post* and to *Masfax*, a leading tax weekly. He is the Israel correspondent for various publications of the International Bureau of Fiscal Documentation (IBFD) in Amsterdam. Mr. Harris is also a founding member of the Israeli branch of the Society of Trust and Estate Practitioners and founder of an Ernst & Young International Thought Discussion Group on E-Commerce.

Introduction

When I was young, my parents took me to the theater more than once to see the play *Fiddler on the Roof.* In a wedding scene, some guests in convivial spirits ask the revered Rabbi if there is a blessing for the Czar of Russia. "Why sure," he replies, "May the Lord bless and keep the Czar… far away from us!"

Some people occasionally apply the same principle to tax matters – they keep all tax matters far away and out of mind indefinitely. This is a "head in the sand" approach, and it offers little comfort if (a) you get caught, or (b) you file your tax returns but pay more tax than strictly necessary.

When it comes to investing, your goal is to maximize the after-tax returns while deducting any losses and interest on leveraged investments. And since you cannot take your wealth with you into the next world, another long-term goal is to transfer – when you're ready – as much as possible of your investments and other wealth to your family or other designated persons. This is because there are taxes on death and on gifts to contend with in a number of countries – the United States, Canada, the United Kingdom, and most European countries – even if you live in Israel. And Israel now imposes capital gains tax on gifts of assets to non-residents – such as your family abroad.

So what is needed is a general understanding of the tax basics, a review of any legitimate tax planning techniques, and advice from competent tax advisors in each country.

You can judge whether they're competent if they are qualified accountants or lawyers with worldly experience (in a tax sense) and are prepared to work in coordination with your other advisors, especially when it comes to tax solutions. Nobody has a monopoly on knowledge in the modern world. It may well be advisable to hire a financial or tax advisor to coordinate your financial affairs – more on that later. The remarks below relate to investments by Israeli residents and immigrants in securities – stocks, bonds, and mutual funds – but not in other investments, such as real estate or derivatives, as these are specialist areas deserving separate consideration. The remarks are general and subject to the specific comments of your own tax and other advisors.

Because of the frequent changes in Israeli tax laws, certain sections of this chapter may be outdated by the time the book is published. Therefore, we are making updates to these sections available via the internet to people who have bought the book. To receive timely updates, please complete the form at www.profile-financial.com.

Tax Basics

Who Is Taxable And On What?
Prior to the Israeli tax reform of 2003, Israeli residents were taxed under a "territorial" system, by which Israeli and foreign residents were subject to tax in Israel on Israeli source income. Therefore, foreign-source passive investment income, such as dividends, interest, and rent, was not taxable in Israel provided such income was first received abroad.

Following the tax reform, an Israeli resident is now subject to tax on a personal worldwide basis of income, regardless of whether it was accrued, derived, or received in Israel.

By contrast, a non-Israeli resident is taxable only on Israeli source income and gains.

So there is something to be said for a perpetual traveler who visits Israel and stays in a hotel or vacation home he owns in Israel without establishing Israeli residency status. Such persons used to be called "180-day commandos," but the tax reform now deems such persons to be Israeli residents, and they should now consider reducing their stay in Israel to below 425 days over every three-year period commencing in 2001 ("140-day commandos" perhaps) – see below.

New immigrants and returning Israeli residents enjoy certain transitional Israeli tax exemptions for five to 10 years after their arrival, but only on their pre-arrival assets abroad, not subsequent investments.

Most other countries apply similar rules regarding residents and non-residents of their country, but usually no transitional benefits – after all, which other country encourages immigration?

Who Is a Resident for Israeli Tax Purposes?

Subject to any applicable tax treaty, individuals will be considered as Israeli residents if their center of living, with regard to their overall personal, family, economic, and social circumstances, is in Israel.

Individuals will generally be presumed resident if they are present in Israel 183 days or more in a tax year, or 30 days in a tax year and 425 days in Israel in a particular tax year, plus the previous two years. A tax year is the year that ends each December 31. The definition of a "day" includes a part of a day. These "number of days" presumptions can be challenged by the taxpayer or the tax authorities.

Aside from the number of days present in Israel, the "center of living" circumstances listed in the Israeli Income Tax Ordinance ("ITO") are:

- location of a permanent home,
- place of residence of the individual and his/her family,
- place where the individual regularly works or is employed,

- location of active and material economic interests,
- place where the individual is active in various organizations, associations, or institutions,
- employment by official bodies.

Residency problems commonly occur if an Israeli businessman travels abroad most of the time but leaves his wife and kids at home in Israel. Is his "center of living" in Israel, even if his absence is greater than his presence? A recent Israeli court case ruled that for tax purposes, each spouse may indeed be considered a resident in a different city if that is how they really live.

These tests are for Israeli tax purposes and – in practice – for Israeli national insurance (social security) purposes. A person's tax status is unconnected to the person's immigration status. Unlike some countries, such as the United Kingdom, Ireland, and Australia, Israel does not have the tax concepts of "domicile" or "ordinary residence."

Dual Residency and Tax Treaty Tie-Breakers

Is it possible for someone to be resident in more than one country? Yes it is. For example, dual residence is established if someone is domiciled in Australia and present in Israel for 183 or more days in a tax year.

Such a person may face double tax reporting obligations in the two countries and must check his eligibility for foreign tax credits in both countries. This is a balancing act with no easy way out sometimes, because there is no tax treaty between Israel and some countries, such as Australia.

Israel currently has tax treaties with 38 countries,* and a few

---

*   Israel currently has tax treaties with: Austria, Belarus, Belgium, Brazil, Bulgaria, Canada, China, the Czech Republic, Denmark, Finland, France, Germany, Greece, Hungary, India, Ireland, Italy, Jamaica, Japan, Korea, Mexico, Netherlands, Norway, Philippines, Poland, Romania, Russia, Singapore, Slovak Republic, South Africa, Spain, Sweden, Switzerland, Thailand, Turkey, United Kingdom, United States, and Uzbekistan.

more are on the way. If an individual is considered resident according to domestic law in both Israel and another country that has a tax treaty with Israel, he or she can apply the "tie breaker" test in that treaty to allocate residency to one country only. This can certainly reduce exposure to double taxation (but U.S. persons – see below).

U.S. Persons

It should be noted that "U.S. persons" must file federal U.S. income tax returns on their worldwide income and gains, not forgetting U.S. gift and estate tax on their worldwide assets. A U.S. person includes U.S. citizens, U.S. green card holders, and U.S. residents (generally individuals resident in the United States for a period of time) according to detailed U.S. tax rules. All this is without regard to the fact that they may also be Israeli residents.

Therefore, people who are U.S. persons resident in Israel must report to the tax authorities of both countries and divide their foreign tax credits and resulting tax payments according to special rules in the tax laws and in Article 26(2) of the U.S.-Israel tax treaty. In our experience, Article 26(2) requirements are not always correctly applied, or the affairs of a person are not properly addressed, and too much tax is sometimes paid to the wrong government – therefore, specialist advice is recommended.

Here is an example: Suppose a U.S. person, resident in Israel for 20 years, buys publicly traded IBM stock in January 2006, sells it in February 2007, and makes a capital gain along the way. The tax rate in the U.S. is 15%, and in Israel, the rate is 20%. Is a tax check payable to: (a) the U.S. government, or (b) the Israeli government, or (c) both governments – double taxation?

The answer is (b), as the tax in the above example is payable to the Israeli government with no double taxation, applying Article 26(2) of the U.S.-Israel tax treaty.

Another safe harbor from double taxation concerns U.S. persons who qualify for a "Section 911 exclusion" (exemption) in the United States for non-U.S. earned income of up to $80,000 per year. Earned income covers an individual's salary or business profits but not portfolio or passive income. The U.S. person must be a *bona fide* resident of Israel (or any other country outside the United States), or physically present over 330 days in a 12-month period and a taxpayer of Israel (or any other country outside the United States). Such excluded earned income may be exempt from U.S. federal tax, but still be taxable in Israel.

Israeli Tax Rates for Investment Income

Passive investment income (not business-related) derived by Israeli resident companies and individuals will generally be taxable at the rates shown in Table 1. This table is a summary, and there are exceptions.

Table 1: Investment Income of Israeli Resident Individuals – Summary of Israeli Tax Rates				
Type of Income	Transactions in 2003–4	Transactions in 2005	Transactions in 2006 onwards	
			Holds under 10% of payor	"Material Shareholder" holds 10+% of payor
Capital gains – Israeli publicly traded securities				
Post 2002 gain[1]	15%	15%[2]	20%[2]	25%[2]
Pre 2003 gain	–	–	–	–
Capital gains – foreign publicly traded securities[3]				
Post 2004 gain[4]	N/A	15%[2]	20%[2]	25%[2]
Pre 2005 gain[4]	35%	35%	35%	35%
Capital gains – other assets				
Post 2002 gain[4]	25%	25%	20%	25%
Pre 2003 gain[4]	Up to 49%	Up to 49%	Up to 49%	Up to 49%
Interest				
On instruments "linked" to the consumer price index or denominated in foreign currency	15%–49%	15%–49%	20%[5 & 6]	Up to 49%
On "unlinked" Israeli instruments	10%–49%	10%–49%	15%[5 & 6]	Up to 49%
Dividends				
Standard rate	25%	25%	20%	25%
From Israeli Privileged or Approved Enterprise	15%	0%–15%	0%–15%	0%–15%
Real Estate Investment Trust (REIT), if conditions met	N/A	N/A	Up to 49%	Up to 49%

Notes to table on next page.

Notes to table previous page:

1. Calculated applying higher of proven actual cost or market value on last three trading days of 2002
2. A notional sale and repurchase could be elected in December 2005, enabling a new cost basis to be established for Israeli tax purposes.
3. Does not include investments in 2005 in mutual funds or bonds issued or guaranteed by foreign governments, or securities traded on a stock exchange or orderly market (Bloomberg, Reuters, etc) in a country that does not have a tax treaty with Israel – these will be classified as other assets.
4. Calculated by splitting the total gain on a time pro rata basis
5. Pre-2006 interest, calculated on a time pro-rata basis, will be taxed at pre-2006 tax rates.
6. Regular tax rates up to 49% will apply if interest expense is deducted; or if the interest is business income; or if a special relationship exists (e.g., customer-supplier, employer-employee, related parties)

Capital losses derived by individuals in 2006 onwards from foreign securities may be offset against capital gains from Israeli securities (and vice versa), or against dividends and interest income from securities (if otherwise taxable at no more than 25%). However, pre-2006 losses from foreign securities may not be offset against gains from Israeli securities (and vice versa) before 2007.

Companies assessable under the regular tax system – applying the Income Tax Law (Inflation Adjustments) 1985 – continue to pay tax at the standard rate of companies tax on capital gains from publicly traded securities (31% in 2006), but this rate is reduced to 25% for other post-2002 capital gains; various new technical rules apply. Non-business companies continue to be taxed at 25% on capital gains if they do not deduct finance expenses nor apply the Income Tax Law (Inflationary Adjustments) 1985.

See below for additional tax benefits for foreign investors and certain investment vehicles.

Individuals who are U.S. citizens or green card holders residing in Israel are taxable in Israel and in the United States on their worldwide income. Foreign tax credit provisions in the domestic laws of the two countries and the Israel-U.S. tax treaty should prevent double taxation and effectively "round up" the combined tax burden to the higher of the tax rates prevailing in the two countries. Experienced tax advisors should be consulted in this regard.

Financial institutions in Israel and others that remit income or consideration from investment transactions or forward transactions are generally required to withhold tax at source at prescribed rates for each individual security, according to detailed rules.

A "forward transaction" for Israeli tax purposes is an obligation or a right to deliver or receive in the future: foreign currency exchange rate differences, index differences, differences regarding interest, assets or prices, and a short sale.

However, if you conduct more than 20–30 forward transactions a month, it appears that you may be taxed in Israel at rates of up to 49% (rather than 20%) on all income and gains from them.

Israeli mutual funds are classified as either "exempt" or "taxable." If the fund is exempt, the investor is instead taxed. Commencing in 2006, it appears that the combined tax burden at the fund and investor levels for income and gains will be as follows:

• Exempt fund: 20% Israeli tax all paid by the investor.
• Taxable fund: 20% Israeli tax all paid by the fund.

In addition to income tax and capital gains tax, there is national insurance (social security) to consider. Fortunately, commencing January 1, 2004, no national insurance contributions are generally payable by investors (except major shareholders) with respect to: dividends on "foreign securities," other dividends of smaller (under 10%) shareholders, interest and gains from provident funds and further education funds, interest and discount premiums on bonds traded on the Tel Aviv Stock Exchange, interest and gains on non-work related savings plans and deposits, interest and discount premiums on short-term government bonds or "foreign securities," and residential rental income in Israel.

In other cases, national insurance contributions may be due on investment income (not capital gains) at various rates ranging from 0% to 16.05% depending on an individual's personal circumstances. However, 52% of national insurance paid on non-employment income is deductible for income tax purposes, resulting in a maximum effective rate of approximately 12%. Currently, an upper income limit for national insurance contribution purposes is applicable (NIS 35,760 = ~$7,800 per month).

New Immigrants and Returning Residents

An exemption is granted to new residents for the first 10 years after becoming an Israeli resident for capital gains derived from overseas assets held upon becoming a resident. If such an asset is sold after 10 years, a pro-rata exemption will apply according to a special formula.

Additionally, a new resident's exemption for passive (non-business) income from dividends, interest, rent, royalties, or pensions is granted for the first five years after becoming an Israeli resident, if such income is of a non-business nature and derived from overseas assets held upon becoming a resident.

The above exemptions are also available to returning Israeli residents who resided abroad for more than three years.

If no exemption applies, the following beneficial Israeli tax rates may nevertheless be applied to the income from publicly traded foreign securities of someone who is a "privileged individual" (see Table 2) in the years 2003–2005 only: interest and capital gains – 15%, dividends – 25%.

Securities Dealers

People who deal regularly in securities will be taxable at full rates (companies 31% in 2006, individuals up to 49%, plus national insurance liability – see above). This could conceivably include anyone conducting frequent securities transactions, rather than occasional transactions for investment purposes. The dividing line is not clear in practice, but the Israeli tax authority has indicated that no more than a "few tens" (20–30 apparently) of securities transactions a month may not be regarded as trading. In practice, the Israeli tax authority rarely catches internet day traders and

TABLE 2 — PRIVILEGED INDIVIDUALS — TAX YEARS 2003–2005 ONLY

A "privileged individual" is defined according to complex rules as someone satisfying the following criteria:

- Israeli resident for the first time, not a returning resident.
- Fulfills one of the following:
  1. Not more than 10 years have passed from the time the individual first became an Israeli resident.
  2. On January 1, 2003, not more than 20 years have passed since the individual first became a resident of Israel, and the individual declares before an income tax official that the source of the foreign security originated in assets outside of Israel, which the individual owned before he/she first became a resident of Israel.
  3. Was at least 60 years old on January 1, 2003, and fulfills one of the following:
     - No more than 20 years have passed from the time the individual first became an Israeli resident.
     - The individual was between 40–50 years of age when he/she first became an Israeli resident, and the individual declares before an income tax official that the source of the foreign security originated in assets outside of Israel, which he/she owned before he/she first became a resident of Israel.
     - The individual was at least 50 years of age on the date that he/she first became an Israeli resident.
  4. The individual turned 60 after January 1, 2003.

others unless it is clear that they are actively trading with a view to make a living from such activities. But if you personally dabble in more than a few dozen derivatives transactions per month, the

Israeli tax authorities have indicated you may have enough professional knowledge to be considered a securities dealer.

If you invest in U.S. securities from Israel in your own account
in the United States, you should not be taxable in the United States
unless you are a U.S. person (U.S. citizen, green card holder, or
U.S. resident – see above). However, if you are a non-U.S. person
there may be U.S. withholding tax on dividends and certain types
of interest; and U.S. real estate interests or securities will be taxable in the United States under the Foreign Investment in Real
Property Tax Act ("FIRPTA").

Finance Expenses

In principle, if you use leverage – borrow money to invest in securities – the interest paid should be deductible as an expense in Israel
against income from the investments concerned. However, if you
borrow money from a non-Israeli resident (e.g., a bank or a broker
in New York or London), you are expected to withhold Israeli tax
at source from the interest – generally up to 25% but reduced to
17.5% for a U.S. lender and 15% for a U.K. lender under Israel's tax
treaties with those countries – otherwise, no expense deduction
is permissible, and you may face possible penalties for failure to
withhold. In practice, enforcement in this area tends to be weak.

Furthermore, if you leverage your investments, the Israeli tax
authorities may use this to assert that you are a securities dealer
and therefore taxable at full rates.

Investment Losses

Investment losses are governed by detailed rules. Capital losses
derived by individuals in 2006 onwards from foreign securities
may be offset against capital gains from Israeli securities (and vice
versa), or against dividends and interest income from securities
(if otherwise taxable at no more than 25%). However, pre-2006
losses from foreign securities may not be offset against gains from
Israeli securities (and vice versa) before 2007.

Trusts

A trust is conceptually different from a company (corporation). A company is generally a separate person for legal purposes in most countries.

The Trust Law, 1979, in Israel recognizes a trust and defines it as a relationship, whereby a trustee is bound to hold trust property and to act in respect thereto in the interest of a beneficiary, or for some other purpose. This definition is similar to that found in the "common law" of most Anglo Saxon countries.

The parties to a trust are usually:

- the settlor (also known as the "grantor" in the U.S.), who contributes assets to a trust,
- the trustee, who formally owns the trust property, but for the benefit of the beneficiaries,
- the beneficiary or beneficiaries, who will ultimately receive income and/or assets from the trust,
- the protector (also known as the "appointor" in some countries) – found in some trusts only. The protector typically vets important decisions of the trustee and has powers to replace the trustee.

The principal rules of the trust will be contained in a formal document – the "trust deed." This is put into effect at the commencement of the trust. A trust is not usually registered with any governmental registrar, unlike companies. However, in any criminal investigation and/or any money laundering investigation, trustees and other professionals may be required to disclose any information that they have.

Israeli trusts face a significant impediment – it appears they cannot be used to transfer assets after the death of the settlor unless the trust is probated like a will (although alternative views exist). Trusts established and managed abroad by non-Israeli trustees typically do not face this impediment. Foreign trusts became more popular with Israelis after Israeli exchange control restrictions were repealed in 1998. Immigrants and foreign residents visiting Israel often need no introduction to trusts.

Until recently, Israeli tax laws contained only a few provisions relating to trusts. In certain cases, an irrevocable discretionary foreign trust holding overseas assets and administered by foreign resident trustees was arguably outside the Israeli tax net.

However, a comprehensive new trust tax regime is effective in Israel commencing January 1, 2006. It applies to common law trusts and civil law foundations, among others.

The aim of the new regime is to prevent tax avoidance by the Israeli resident settlors of an Israeli Residents' Trust by attributing annual worldwide trust income and gains to the settlor or the beneficiaries, and requiring the trustee to report and pay the Israeli tax on their behalf. This will apply irrespective of where the trustee is located.

In the case of a Foreign Resident Settlor Trust formed entirely by non-resident settlors, an exemption may apply to trust income and gains. Originally, this was meant to encourage inward flows of capital from families abroad to relatives in Israel. However, the exemption is conditional on the Israeli resident beneficiaries having no ability to control or influence the conduct of the trust. In practice, this may be difficult to prove, and various other conditions must also be met.

A separate exemption may also apply to income and gains of an irrevocable Foreign Resident Beneficiary Trust formed by an Israeli settlor exclusively for foreign resident beneficiaries, provided various conditions are met.

In the case of a Testamentary Trust, formed under the will of a person who was an Israeli resident upon his death, the Israeli tax outcome will depend on the tax status of each beneficiary.

Detailed rules govern migrations, the contribution of assets to each type of trust, and the distribution of income and assets from them. In addition, reporting and enforcement provisions are prescribed regarding trustees, settlors, and beneficiaries, irrespective of their location. In particular, unpaid final (non-appealable) tax debts may be collected from the settlor(s) and/or from the beneficiaries up to the amounts distributed to them (which could potentially mean up to 100% taxation).

With regard to reporting to the Israeli tax authority, Table 3 summarizes the situation.

Table 3: Annual Trust Reporting		
By:	**Tax years 2003–2005**	**Tax year 2006 on**
Trustee	N/A	Trust income and details are reportable and tax payable thereon by the trustee
Settlor	Details of trust settled in the year (from 2002)	Details of trust settled or contributed in the year
Beneficiary	Trust details – if a person received NIS 100,000 from trust monies in the year, or is a beneficiary of the trust	If received distribution, details of distribution and trust

Transitional reporting requirements apply in 2005 to 2007, and other transitional rules exist.

In the United States, there are detailed tax rules aimed at preventing tax planning by using trusts. U.S. persons and anyone else who holds U.S. assets should consult U.S. tax and legal advisors in specific cases. Following is a brief summary of certain aspects:

- Trusts (and estates) are generally treated as separate taxpayers and, with some important qualifications, are taxed similarly to individuals.
- A "simple trust" is one that: (1) is required to distribute all its income to beneficiaries each year, (2) cannot make charitable

contributions, and (3) generally makes no distribution of trust "corpus" (capital) during the year.

- Other trusts are generally "complex trusts" – these permit the accumulation of income and/or charitable contributions, or distributions of principal. A trust may switch from simple to complex and vice versa.

- Charitable deductions are available for amounts donated to recognized U.S. charities out of gross income, but not out of trust corpus, of complex trusts.

- A deduction available for distributions to beneficiaries is determined by reference to Distributable Net Income (DNI). DNI is the maximum deduction for distributions and the maximum amount that beneficiaries will have to report as income, even if the income is not distributed in the tax year.

- Beneficiaries of "complex trusts" are taxed in two tiers. The first tier consists of income required to be distributed (up to DNI), and includes distributions that can be paid out of income or corpus, to the extent paid out of income, without charitable deductions. The second tier includes all other distributions actually paid, or required to be paid, with charitable deductions.

- "Grantor trusts" are trusts over which the grantor (settlor) or grantor's spouse retains a certain level of control or a current or certain reversionary interest in income or corpus of the trust. The income from a Grantor Trust is taxed to the grantor, rather than the trust or the beneficiaries. A grantor trust may exist if any of the following apply: (a) the grantor or a "nonadverse" (uninterested) party can revoke the trust, (b) the grantor or the grantor's spouse holds a 5% reversionary interest worth over 5% of the trust corpus, (c) the grantor, or the grantor's spouse, or a nonadverse party, controls the beneficial enjoyment of the trust, or (d) trust income may be distributed, at the discretion of the grantor or the nonadverse party, to the grantor or grantor's spouse, or used to pay life insurance premiums for either.

- If a U.S. person makes a transfer to a "foreign trust" with a U.S. beneficiary, the income of the trust will be taxed to the transferor, unless the transfer is: (a) by reason of death (but an estate tax liability may need to be considered), or (b) for fair market value, or (c) to a foreign employee benefit or charitable trust. (IRC Sec. 679)
- "Throwback rules" generally tax beneficiaries of "foreign complex trusts" on distributions of income accumulated by the trust in prior years as if the income had been distributed in the years received by the trust. The compound interest charge on such back tax can sometimes be large. (IRC Secs 643, 667)

Life Insurance

Various other investment vehicles may be considered in particular cases. Life insurance "wrapper" or "universal variable" policies or bonds are popular in the United States, Canada, France, United Kingdom, and elsewhere. The tax treatment varies from country to country. See additional discussion below.

Double Tax Relief

In the event that tax is imposed abroad, Israel will generally allow a credit for foreign federal and state taxes against Israeli tax on the income from the same source ("basket"). Foreign city taxes cannot be credited.

Some foreign countries do not tax investment income in certain cases. For example, the United Kingdom does not tax non-U.K. residents on U.K. source capital gains.

The United States generally does not tax non-U.S. investors on interest income and capital gains (except from U.S. real estate) if certain conditions are met. Dividends paid by U.S. corporations to Israeli residents will generally be subject to withholding tax, taxable at a rate of 25% under the U.S.-Israel tax treaty (or 12.5% for Israeli 10%-or-more corporate shareholders). The non-treaty rate of withholding tax in the United States is 30% for dividends, interest, rent, royalties, and certain other types of income.*

The aforementioned conditions in the United States include the filing of declarations of non-U.S. status, usually on Form W8-BEN. Israeli residents holding U.S. citizenship, residency, or "green card" status will be taxable in the United States and Israel, but special foreign tax credit provisions may apply to them under the U.S.-Israel tax treaty.

Reporting Rules

Israeli resident individuals must file annual tax returns in various cases by April 30 following each tax year (calendar year). For the 2004 tax year, the due date was April 30, 2005 for filing "short returns" in the case of persons who derived income from foreign securities, but no additional income other than a salary below NIS 520,000. Other detailed reporting rules are prescribed and professional advice may be necessary. Each year the Israeli rules are updated, so check for changes.

Tax Planning

Tax planning should be within the letter and the spirit of the law and adequately disclosed in tax returns. Consideration may also be given to requesting an advance Israeli tax ruling where appropriate – for example where the Israeli tax law is unclear, or where large amounts are involved. Tax planning falls into two main categories:

- Last-minute planning – more politely referred to as "short-term planning," can still be effective.
- Longer-term situation – for the thoughtful investor who plans

---

* There are limited instances in which a U.S. corporation can make dividend, interest, and other payments to non-U.S. persons free of withholding tax – these would generally be achieved through specific planning.

his finances by reference to his stage and status in life. Tax planning is one ingredient in this.

Short-Term Planning

Tax mitigation may typically take the form of reducing the overall tax rate and/or deferring the tax liability on re-invested income. Both Israeli and foreign taxes should be taken into account.

Individual Investment

It may be worthwhile investing as an individual if you consider the following:

- Five- to 10-year exemptions in Israel for new or returning residents.
- People thinking of moving to Israel may consider establishing an overseas investment vehicle before their arrival to help optimize such tax benefits.
- Low Israeli tax rates from 2006 (20%–25%) for income and gains from Israeli or foreign securities, whether publicly traded or not.

Long-Term Planning

When it comes to financial matters, every astute investor should plan ahead. This is the case whether you have means, or you just mean to have means! So what can be done to improve your chances and your personal tax planning?

In essence, there are seven typical scenarios that require planning, as discussed below. These are:

1. Yuppie
2. Middle-aged
3. Just sold a business or inherited a fortune
4. Retirement
5. Giving to the family
6. Giving to charity
7. Family office

In all cases, appropriate professional advice should be obtained in each country from legal, tax, and investment advisors.

Yuppie

A yuppie is someone young at heart and on the way up! He (or she) lives hand to mouth and should make every effort to save at least some part of his/her monthly income. For Israeli approved employment-related plans – retirement provident funds (*kupot gemel*) – employers' contributions are generally exempt and employee contributions may qualify for a 25% or 35% tax credit within prescribed limits.

Middle-aged

A careful middle-aged investor may not only save pennies but also invest more than a few dollars. This may be the time to consider wrapping securities investments in an appropriate life insurance policy or in an appropriate mutual "fund of funds," with sub-funds for different types of investments, among other things. Tax and insurance advisors should be consulted in each country concerned. Features to consider include:

- In Israel, commencing 2006, the tax rate on life policies and mutual funds may arguably be deferred and limited to 20% of income when eventually distributed to investors/beneficiaries.
- Regular or periodic life policy payouts may be taxed at regular rates of up to 49% (plus national insurance where applicable). However, for certain insurance annuity policies, people of pension age or surviving spouses may enjoy an exemption on 35% of such payouts.
- U.S. citizens residing in Israel may wish to consider a life policy that is compliant with Section 7702 of the U.S. Internal Revenue Code, held via an Irrevocable Life Insurance Trust (ILIT). Such a policy may confer exemptions from U.S. income tax, capital gains tax, and estate tax if applicable conditions

are met, but is subject to gift tax if the amounts deposited exceed various annual exemptions and the $1 million lifetime gift tax exemption ($2 million per couple). For Israeli purposes, a contribution of cash should not attract Israeli capital gains tax, but other assets may be taxable. The trust may be reportable to the Israeli tax authority if the settlor (grantor) or beneficiary is an Israeli resident, or any amount is distributed from trust funds in a tax year to a beneficiary.

In addition, an investor and his spouse should each have valid wills that specify how their estates should be handled upon their eventual demise. Otherwise, if either spouse dies "intestate" (without a will), his/her estate will have to be allocated as specified by law. This may be different from what they wanted, and may also take far more time than the court probate process for dealing with assets covered by a will. In order to validly draft or amend a will that works well in each country concerned, consult lawyers and tax advisors in each country where assets are located.

Just Sold a Business or Inherited a Fortune

At this point, an insightful person will no doubt see the wisdom of re-assessing:

- living requirements,
- investment requirements – in securities, in a business, in real estate, etc.,
- pension and life insurance arrangements,
- will and succession plans.

In addition, a smart investor may want to ensure that children and grandchildren can live well enough, but cannot recklessly waste all the assets. This is a classic non-tax reason for establishing a family trust.

From the tax perspective:

- The beneficiary, trustee, and settlor of a "foreign resident settlor trust" or an irrevocable "foreign resident beneficiary trust" with foreign assets may arguably not be taxable in Israel in certain cases. Specialist advice is essential.

- Nevertheless, trusts must be disclosed by the trustee in many cases, and by taxpayers who (a) settle or contribute assets to a trust, or (b) receive any amount from a trust in the tax year. This is the case, even if no Israeli tax liability arises.

- Residents or citizens of other countries should check the tax rules in those countries as well – the United States, United Kingdom, and Canada each have comprehensive trust anti-avoidance tax rules. In civil law countries – such as France, Belgium, and Germany – trusts are scarcely recognized and are often liable to be challenged by the tax authorities of those countries. Consequently, caution is advisable.

- In the United States, any trust structure must be carefully considered before and after implementation. Many different types of trust are possible under U.S. tax law, including:

  - Simple trusts and complex trusts – taxable in the United States unless the beneficiary is taxable (see above) even if an Israeli tax exemption might apply.

  - Grantor trusts – a U.S. grantor (settlor) remains taxable (see above) even if an Israeli tax exemption might apply.

  - Grantor-retained annuity trust – An investor (as grantor or settlor) transfers appreciated assets to a revocable trust in favor of his or her children, in return for a promise to pay the grantor a prescribed annuity for a prescribed number of years. Any excess passes to the children with little or no U.S. estate or gift tax. Arguably, there may also be no Israeli capital gains tax on the transfer if the trust is disregarded for Israeli tax purposes, but trust income and gains may be taxable to the grantor. Consideration may be given to obtaining an advance Israeli tax ruling.

Retirement

Retirement is relative of course – some successful people just can't let go, while others just can't wait to start taking it easy.

With regard to pensions received from abroad, an Israeli resident taxpayer may generally choose between two main Israeli tax approaches:

- If the taxpayer has reached retirement age (as defined in the legislation – up to 67 generally), he or she may claim an exemption for 35% of the pension payments and pay regular Israeli tax rates on the remaining portion of the payments – resulting in a net effective income tax rate of around 32% (before national insurance, where applicable). There is no upper limit for "unapproved" foreign pension payments – whereas tax benefits for pensions from "approved" Israeli pension and provident funds are subject to monetary and other limits.

- An immigrant to Israel, who receives a foreign pension for work done in a foreign country, may elect to pay the tax that would have been payable in the country where the pension is paid had they remained resident in that country. This rule leaves open a number of questions – how is the tax calculated if a person worked outside his/her country of residence, or receives a pension from a country outside his/her country of residence? Furthermore, how are Israeli and foreign personal deductions or credits allocated if the individual has other sources of income in addition to the foreign pension? At present, it appears that any reasonable approach may be considered, provided adequate disclosure is made in the tax return.

- Immigrants from the United States and some other countries should remember to claim an exemption from tax in those countries on pension payments to an Israeli resident. This applies to immigrants from a country that has a tax treaty with Israel, but check the terms of each treaty in each case. In the case of a U.S. person residing in Israel, the U.S.-Israel tax treaty exempts the individual from U.S. federal tax (leaving tax payable only in Israel) on a pension or annuity paid following services rendered, injuries, sickness, or self-employment. However, it has been ruled that the California State lottery

prize payments made in installments are NOT annuities exempt from U.S. tax under the U.S.-Israel tax treaty. You can't
win 'em all....

Giving to the Family

Gifts in good faith to relatives or others are exempt from Israeli
tax unless the recipient resides abroad, in which case the gift may
be subject to Israeli capital gains tax – if it is an appreciated asset
such as shares in a company. A gift of cash by definition cannot
give rise to a taxable capital gain in any event.

If the donor is a U.S. person, there may be a U.S. gift tax liability unless annual exemptions or the $1 million lifetime exemp-
tion are used. In addition, smaller gifts of $12,000 starting January
2006 (previously $11,000) per donor to each recipient per year are
exempt from U.S. gifts tax.

The receipt of a gift in good faith is neither reportable nor
taxable in Israel – but there may be tax consequences for a foreign donor in his home country, e.g., in the United States, United
Kingdom, France, Germany, Belgium.

A gift will not be in good faith if it is really a disguised business receipt.

A gift can be made informally, or formally recorded in a letter or even a deed of gift. Sometimes it is prudent to record large
gifts to avoid any suspicion that the gift is really a disguised business receipt. A gift can also be conditional, which can give rise to
interesting possibilities in some cases.

If the donor is a non-U.S. person but the assets are U.S. assets,
then U.S. estate tax can apply if that person passes away, at rates
ranging from 18% to 47% in 2005, 46% in 2006, 45% in 2007–9,
0% in 2010 and 55% in 2011 onwards. Gift tax is also possible for
certain U.S. assets (not securities) gifted by non-U.S. persons.

A U.S. person is entitled to give an unlimited amount free of
U.S. tax to a spouse who is also a U.S. person. There are limits if
the receiving spouse is not a U.S. citizen, but tax may be mitigated by using a QDOT (qualified domestic trust). For Israeli tax

purposes, this may be an "Israeli Residents Trust." Such a trust will be taxable at the maximum Israeli tax rate (49% at present), unless a special tax rate applies without limit – such as 20% for most dividends, interest, and capital gains. The trustee will be subject to an Israeli reporting requirement. Distributions to Israeli residents should be exempt. Distributions may only be subject to Israeli capital gains tax if they are to beneficiaries who are not Israeli residents. The Israeli tax effect may thus be little or none, and considerably outweighed by the U.S. tax savings (if a foreign tax credit is granted). Nevertheless, this should be checked with advisors in each country.

Note that some other countries may also impose a tax upon the death of Israeli investors on assets or property in those countries, such as inheritance tax in the United Kingdom. This may sometimes be mitigated or avoided entirely by structuring the investment appropriately at the outset, in conjunction with advisors in each country.

Giving to Charity

Few would argue that an investor would be advised to share at least a portion of his good fortune with a good cause. My dear wife will often give a donation to a doorstep caller if the cause is a charity ("public institution") approved under Section 46 of the Income Tax Ordinance. In this way, we can claim an Israeli tax credit for 35% of such donations, up to a little over NIS 2 million ($440,000 approximately) a year.

Alternatively, my wife can donate an appreciated asset to the Israeli state, an Israeli municipality, the JNF or the JIA, or to any other charity in Israel (it is unclear if the charity can be foreign), and avoid an Israeli capital gains tax liability. This could save us 20% to 49% in capital gains tax in Israel. The same strategy may, in certain circumstances, have a similar effect for U.S. tax purposes. Any such asset donation strategy should, however, be fully checked out with advisors in each country.

Each country has its own rules for approving supposedly

genuine charities. In the United States, a donor can get a U.S. tax deduction for a donation to a recognized U.S. "friends of" organization or foundation that can then make an onward donation to a good Israeli cause.

In addition, the U.S.-Israel tax treaty allows U.S. persons to claim a U.S. tax deduction for donations to Israeli charities of up to 25% of adjusted gross income from sources in Israel. And an Israeli resident can claim an Israeli tax credit for donations to a U.S. charity of up to 25% of taxable income from U.S. sources.

Family Office

It is vital for an intelligent investor to keep a good grip on his finances and investments so that he can efficiently plan ahead and arrange personal matters appropriately. In addition, other family members will need to be groomed to take over these important tasks.

You may prefer to run the family financial office yourself, or you may turn for advice and assistance to a number of interested parties – trust companies, banks, and so forth.

However, if your wealth exceeds $1 million to $3 million, you should also consider a virtual family office consisting of a trusted team – independent investment advisor, private accountant, and lawyer.

You would consult with your team regularly or periodically to arrive at a coherent long-term wealth strategy covering:

- your business and private expectations,
- your business and private requirements,
- your plans to groom younger family members,
- your plans to transfer wealth to others in your lifetime or via your estate,
- your tax minimization strategy covering income and estate/gift taxes in all relevant countries.

If your team is smart and proactive, their benefit to you should far outweigh their cost.

Life Insurance

Various special investment vehicles may be considered in particular cases. Life insurance "wrapper," or "universal variable," or "with profits" policies or bonds are popular in Israel, the United States, Canada, France, United Kingdom, and elsewhere. The tax treatment varies from country to country.

The general intention is to pay a lump sum immediately or over a few years that buys life insurance coverage to the minimum extent allowed under local tax legislation (so the maximum possible amount can go into investments). The remainder of the lump sum is invested in securities, and the payout upon death or upon earlier withdrawal, according to the terms of the policy, is partly or mainly dependent on the investment performance of these investments. The insurance company may appoint investment advisors who are acceptable and even known to the policyholders.

For example, many non-U.S. policies may provide for a death payout of 101% of the value of the investment portfolio upon the death of the insured party (or second spouse to die, under some policies). Thus, if a policyholder pays a premium to a U.K. or Isle of Man policy of 500 that grows to 1000 upon the policyholder's death, the policy may pay out under its terms 1010 (= 101% of 1000).

Such a policy would not be recognized for U.S. tax purposes. In particular, Section 7702 of the U.S. Internal Revenue Code specifies a number of actuarial and other criteria for "U.S. compliant life insurance policies." In addition, the premiums must be paid in over a number of years (typically four to seven years, depending on the actuary's determination).

Furthermore, investments must meet diversification requirements under U.S. tax laws and not be subject to "investor control" in any way by the policyholder. Where these criteria and requirements are all met, larger payouts relative to the premiums may be made free of U.S. federal income tax, capital gains tax, and estate tax on the "inside buildup" of the policy portfolio and distributions to beneficiaries. However, excise taxes will generally be due at the outset at a rate of 1% to 3% approximately, depending on the U.S. state concerned (if any – offshore insurance company policies may still be "U.S. compliant" under Section 7702).

The U.S. Internal Revenue Code (Section 2042) includes an insurance policy in the insured individual's estate for estate tax purposes if that person held any "incidents of ownership" within three years of the death of the insured. The most common way to avoid the three-year rule is for an irrevocable life insurance trust (ILIT) to own the policy from its inception. The insured may not be the trustee or a beneficiary of the ILIT.

To avoid jeopardizing the right to exclude the proceeds from the estate of the insured, the insured should not borrow the cash value of the policy indirectly from the ILIT. Loans can be made to the ILIT and its beneficiaries.

If the trust is foreign, the grantor must report all contributions to and distributions from the trust. The penalty for non-reporting is 35% of the amounts involved. In addition, upon the grantor's death, the excess of the cash value of the policy over the sum of premiums paid will be subject to U.S. tax.

If the trust is a U.S. trust, then contributions and distributions are not reportable except to the extent there are income tax consequences (typically, in an ILIT there is no taxable income).

The trust will not be considered a U.S. trust unless, among other things, U.S. persons control all substantial decisions of the trust and the trust is subject to the jurisdiction of a U.S. state court. There should be a U.S. trustee, and no foreign person may be given any significant powers. A deemed sale may occur if a trust becomes foreign, for example if a U.S. trustee is replaced by a foreign trustee.

So how much can a U.S. person contribute to a U.S. compliant life policy or an ILIT? Well, the contribution will generally be subject to U.S. gift tax, unless covered by the exemption of $12,000 per donor to each recipient, or the $1 million lifetime exemption for the contributor ($2 million for a married couple). Much may depend on the specific circumstances and techniques adopted.

In Israel, it appears that a foreign *bona fide* non-business-related life insurance policy may be classified as a savings plan. As such, Israeli tax may be deferred until a distribution is made. At present, it seems, arguably, that similar treatment may apply to *bona fide* foreign life policies. Moreover, it appears that distributions of the savings (i.e., the investment) element will be taxed in Israel at 20% from 2006 (15% previously), while the death benefit may be exempt from Israeli tax. There is little published guidance in this regard. It is nevertheless important that the policyholder not select investments, to avoid appearances that the policy is effectively his or her own brokerage account taxable each time a transaction takes place. It is also important that there be an insurable risk – for example, substantial life cover; a penalty if there is a policy redemption within the first few years; and terms that take into account health, age, and other actuarial factors and so forth. A contribution of cash to the trust by an individual should not attract Israeli capital gains tax, but other assets may be taxable.

Any trust in the arrangement (such as an ILIT) should be reported to the Israeli tax authority by an Israeli-resident settlor in the first year; subsequently, the trustee or beneficiary must report if any amounts are distributed to an Israeli-resident beneficiary. Various other detailed aspects will also need to be considered.

Conclusion

Taxes on your investments can be tamed by having an understanding of the basics and a long-term wealth strategy.

Aim to be a sensible investor who plans the family finances by reference to your stage and status in life. Tax planning is one ingredient in this. The key requirements are: have an organized family financial office; use a tax-efficient investment vehicle(s); beware of double taxation especially if you are a U.S. person resident in Israel; beware of gift and estate taxes in countries where you live or hold assets; and take advice in each country as appropriate.

Since frequent changes in the tax laws often make writing about taxes nearly impossible, please complete the form at www.profile-financial.com if you would like to be informed when updates become available.

Glossary

Adjusted Gross Income (AGI) – Derived from the calculation of gross income (see definition of "gross income") minus allowable losses, expenses, and deductions from trading and business operations, and from contributions to qualified retirement plans. (The U.S. and Israeli definitions are not exactly parallel, so use this explanation only as a general guideline.)

Advance/Decline Line – Used in technical analysis, this line tracks the up and down progression of a security's pricing. It is also employed as a monitor of sector movement or as an indicator of the overall market's trend.

Aliya – The move to Israel. The specific definition is "moving up," which describes how people view the move to Israel.

American Depository Receipt (ADR) – This certificate, negotiable in U.S. currency, represents shares of a company traded on a foreign market. ADRs trade on various American exchanges, and buyers are entitled to the same amount of dividends and capital gains as shareholders receive in the home countries. ADRs are normally used as a convenient method to buy foreign stocks.

AMEX (American Stock Exchange) – A major market located near the New York Stock Exchange in lower Manhattan. This exchange handles equities and options, and also plays a large role in the ETF (Exchange Traded Fund) and "structured product" markets.

Amuta – A charitable organization in Israel.

Annual Report – Lists the assets, liabilities, and earnings of a company or mutual fund and serves as a "snapshot" of its current financial status. This financial summary typically includes a letter from the president to the shareholders describing the corporate happenings of the past year and the plans for the future. The report goes on to describe the company and its operations and concludes with a financial section providing detailed information.

Annuity – A type of insurance contract between a company and an individual. The contract purchaser, for his part, agrees to pay specific periodic payments or a one-time lump sum amount to the company. The company, in accordance with the contract, provides an agreed upon stream of lifetime income to the purchaser (and sometimes to the surviving spouse, should the holder die).

Ask Price – Also called the *offering price*. This is the lowest price a seller is willing to accept for his shares. It's the price you would pay if you were to buy the stock at the market. (Opposite of "bid price.")

Asset – Any property that has monetary value, such as cash, stocks, bonds, home, car, business inventory, collectibles.

Asset Allocation – A determining process of apportioning investments within a portfolio. Asset allocation is normally shown in the form of a pie chart, with different categories of investments (stocks, bonds, real estate, cash, etc.) representing different percentages of the pie. Risk tolerance, investment time frame, and long-term goals are key factors in making reasonable allocation decisions.

Asset Class – A type of investment. In an investment portfolio, the holdings usually are divided into three major classes: stocks, bonds, and cash equivalents. Other asset classes include real estate and commodities.

Atzma'i – An independent worker. This person is someone who is self-employed and who files his own tax returns in Israel. Normally, an individual working for a company (a *"sachir"*) does not have to file his own tax return.

Back End Sales Charge – Also called a "back-end" load. This is a sales fee charged by some mutual fund companies for redeeming shares. The charge decreases on an annual basis until it disappears. Funds that charge back-end loads are referred to as "B shares." ("A shares" charge up front, and "C shares" charge an as-you-go asset-based fee.)

Balance of Payments – This is an international accounting system to reflect the amount of currency that flows from one nation to another. For example, currency flows out of a country when payment is made for imported goods.

Balance Sheet – This financial statement details what a company owns (assets), what it owes (liabilities), and the difference between the two (called "stockholder equity").

Balanced Fund – A mutual fund whose objective is to provide both an income flow and an opportunity for growth. It generally has within its portfolio a mix of stocks and bonds.

Basis Point – $\frac{1}{100}$ of 1%. This term is used when calculating yields. For example, a bond yielding 4.25% provides the holder with 5 basis points more than a 4.20% bond.

Bear Market – Colloquially, this refers to a market condition when prices tend to fall. Pessimists about the financial situation are referred to as "bears."

Beta Coefficient – A measure of how volatile the price of an individual security is compared with the general market (often using the S&P 500 as a guideline). The S&P 500 is assigned a beta of 1. A stock or fund with a beta higher than 1 is expected to fluctuate more rapidly than the market average. A holding with a beta below 1 will probably show below-average volatility.

Bid and Ask Prices – The buy and sell prices for securities. The price quotes show the supply/demand situation at the moment of trade. A large demand to buy a stock means that many people are bidding more and more money in an effort to purchase the shares being offered. The highest bidder will get the shares. On the other hand, if there is limited interest, the seller of shares may find few people anxious to buy his shares and thus may have to accept (ask for) a lower price in order to negotiate the sale.

Bid Price – The highest price a buyer is willing to pay to buy a security. If you sell a security at the market, you will normally get the bid price. (Opposite of "ask price.")

Bituach Leumi – Israel's national insurance fund (comparable to U.S. social security).

Bituach Minahalim – An Israeli worker's pension fund, comprised of a number of components, including an employee pension plan, insurance benefits, and *pitzuim*.

Blue-Chip Stock – Common stock of nationally known companies with long records of profit growth and quality reputations. These securities tend to be considered more conservative stocks, though they certainly come with risk.

Bond – Essentially an IOU. A bond is issued by a corporation or government (federal, state, or local) entity. The certificate declares that the buyer of the bond has loaned money to the issuer and is entitled to receive a specific amount of interest until the bond is redeemed. Most bonds pay interest semiannually.

Bond Maturity – The completion of the bond issuer's debt obligation. It is the date on which the lender (the holder of the certificate) gets back the face value of the bond along with the final interest payment.

Book Value Per Share – This is a summary of a company's total assets (minus its liabilities), divided by the number of shares outstanding. This includes cash, securities, inventory, equipment, furnishings, office buildings, and property. Book value does not generally indicate share price. If a stock has an $8 book value, but the share price is $20, it means that buyers are willing to pay this premium to own a piece of the company's future.

Breakout Point – In technical analysis this is the point where a security's price rises above a resistance level (its previous high price) or drops below its support level (the lowest recent price). A breakout can signify that the security may begin trading at a new level in line with the direction it was going when it broke out of its earlier range.

Broker – A licensed investment professional who is authorized to conduct trades for clients.

Brokerage Account – An account with a brokerage firm through which one can buy and sell securities. Often, other services are also available to holders of these accounts, such as check-writing privileges, debit cards, borrowing, and more.

Bull Market – A term commonly used to denote a sustained, general rise in the market. Optimists about prospects for the market are referred to as "bulls."

Business Cycle – The economy usually moves up and down in cycles. Although these business cycles are not the same, they generally follow a four-part pattern (of varying lengths). These parts are:
• Expansion (an upsurge, or boom in the economy),
• Peak (which is the highest level, or top of the expansion period),
• Recession (a downslide in the economy) and,
• Trough (the low point in the economic pattern).

Buy and Hold – A strategy promoting investing for the long term. Rather than moving in and out of positions to follow trends, proponents of this philosophy buy stocks and hold them for long periods.

Call – An option contract giving the holder the right to purchase a specified number of shares of stock at a stated price within a given time period.

Callable Bond – A bond with a provision allowing the issuer to redeem it prior to the maturity date at a given price. Such bonds usually offer higher returns than non-callable bonds.

Callable Preferred Stock – Preferred stock that the issuing corporation has the right to redeem at a certain price and then retire.

Capital Gain – The profit realized when an investment is sold for more than the price at which it was bought. Capital gains are generally taxable in both the U.S. and Israel.

Capital Growth – An increase in the market value of a security. Capital growth and income are two primary goals most investors have when setting up their investment programs.

Capital Loss – The amount of money lost when a security is sold for less than its purchase price. Capital losses may be deducted from similar-type capital gains and, in the U.S., some capital losses may be used to offset earned income up to a certain limit.

Capitalization – See Market Capitalization

CD (Certificate of Deposit) – Usually issued by a banking organization, a CD is an instrument representing the deposit of a specific amount of money for a specified period of time, at a fixed interest rate.

Commission – The fee paid to a broker or brokerage firm for executing a trade.

Commodities – Goods, such as agricultural products, precious metals, foreign currencies, and oil, which are publicly traded on worldwide commodities exchanges. These transactions, which may be based on future delivery or receipt of goods, are often speculative in nature.

Common Stock – Securities that represent partial ownership of a publicly traded corporation. Owners of the stock can vote, in proportion to the number of shares they own, on certain corporate decisions and for members of the board of directors.

Compounding – The growth that results from investment income being reinvested. On a continuing basis, interest is paid on the original investment amount and thereafter on the ever-increasing accumulated interest as well. This compounding growth causes a "snowball effect," since the original investment and the new income both generate additional income.

Consumer Price Index (CPI) – A periodic measure of change in the purchase price of a set group of consumer goods and services. CPI is used to track inflation.

Convertible Bond – A corporate bond that may be exchanged (at the option of the bond holder) for a preset number of shares of common or preferred stock. Convertible bonds normally pay lower interest rates than non-convertibles because the growth potential of the underlying stock makes the deal more attractive. Often, low quality borrowers issue convertible bonds because they can borrow money at a lower interest rate than if they didn't add the convertibility feature as a sweetener.

Corpus – The principal or capital of a trust (as contrasted with the income derived from it).

Custodial Account – An account set up in the name of a minor, and managed by an adult for the benefit of the minor. Assets put into the account become irrevocable gifts to the child, but are controlled by the parent or other trustee as custodian until the minor reaches legal age.

Day Order – An order that remains in effect during a trading day but is then automatically cancelled if the trade has not been executed.

Day Trader – An investor who trades stocks with the intent of holding them for brief periods, often less than a day. His goal is to capitalize on minor fluctuations in a stock's trading price.

Deflation – A fall in the general level of prices and a decrease in the amount of credit available or currency in circulation. Deflation often leads to an increase in unemployment, since the lack of demand in the economy leads to fewer jobs.

Discount – The difference between the price stated on the face of a security (face value) and the lower price at which it is trading.

Discount Bond – A bond selling below par. Such bonds usually have face-value interest rates that are lower than the market norm.

Discount Rate – The interest rate charged to American bank members that borrow from any of the Federal Reserve banks. The Fed sets this rate as part of its monetary policy.

Disposable Income (DI) – This is the amount of money individuals spend yearly.

Diversification – The allocation of investment money among multiple assets. This type of distribution helps cushion a portfolio against an unexpected price decline in one or more of the positions.

Dividend – A distribution of a portion of a corporation's earnings to shareholders in accordance with the number of shares they own.

Dividend Yield – The annual percent return an investor receives on either common or preferred stock. It is calculated by taking the annual dividend per share divided by the stock's market price. Thus, a payment of $4 per share when the share price is $80 yields a dividend of 5%.

Dollar Cost Averaging – A system of buying fixed dollar amounts of securities at regular intervals, regardless of the price of the shares on the purchase dates.

Dow Jones Industrial Average (DJIA) – One of the most commonly used market measurements. It tracks 30 major companies that are considered representative of the market as a whole.

Earnings Per Share (EPS) – A corporation's net earnings, divided by its number of shares outstanding. When calculated for the previous year, it's called the "trailing EPS." For the current year, the term "current EPS" is used. And the calculation for the next year is called "forward EPS." Only the trailing EPS is an actual number, whereas current and forward EPS are estimates.

Equity – The total ownership of common and preferred stock within a corporation. Another definition refers to excess value of real estate above the outstanding mortgage, or monetary value of a company above its debt level. "Equity," or "equity instrument," is also a term for stock.

Eurobond – Eurobonds are international bonds that are sold outside of the country in whose currency they are issued. The prefix "Euro" does not mean that the bond is issued in the currency Euros. For example, a Spanish company might issue U.S. dollar-denominated Eurobonds to investors in Europe. Normally, national governments and large multinational companies raise capital in the international marketplace with Eurobonds.

Eurodollar – U.S. currency held outside the United States, primarily in European banks.

Exchange Traded Fund (ETF) – A fund that tracks an index (e.g., S&P 500, Dow Jones Industrial Average, any of the sector or international indexes) but trades like a stock. Benefits may include tax efficiency, transparency, all day trading (unlike mutual funds), and diversification.

Ex-Dividend – When the board of directors declares a dividend, they set a date of record. Share owners as of that date will receive the dividends. New buyers, purchasing the stock after that record date (ex-dividend) will not be entitled to these payments.

Executor – The person authorized to manage the affairs of an estate, as delegated in the will or trust documents of the deceased, and ratified and/or appointed by a court of jurisdiction.

Expense Ratio – Fund expenses, such as management fees and operating costs, comprise the expense ratio. This ratio is deducted from the portfolio's earnings to determine an investor's return.

Face Value – The amount appearing on the face of a bond certificate. This figure indicates the principal amount that the issuer will pay to the lender (the bondholder) when the bond matures. The listed figure is also the amount on which the interest is calculated. Face value is not necessarily market value.

FDIC (**Federal Deposit Insurance Corporation**) – A U.S. government agency that insures up to $100,000 of cash deposits and CD holdings by depositors in member banks (see www.fdic.gov).

Federal Reserve System (Fed) – The central banking system of the United States. It regulates the flow of money and credit.

Fiduciary – The competent individual named in a will or trust to act on behalf of the person writing these documents, should the writer be unable to act for himself. The fiduciary may be asked to assume the responsibility of executor, trustee, and/or guardian. The term "fiduciary" more generally refers to an individual who is in the trusted position of handling money for someone else.

Fixed Income Investment – An investment yielding a consistent rate of interest based on the face value of the offering. Bonds typify this class of investment.

401(k) Plan – A type of income deferral retirement plan used in the United States that allows employees to make pretax contributions which reduce their yearly taxable income. Employers often match some or all of employee contributions up to a specified limit.

Fundamental Analysis – A method of stock analysis that looks at the intrinsic value of a company. Analysts study general economic conditions to get a grasp of the market as a whole, then review specific industries, and finally analyze the financial viability of individual corporations.

Futures – Exchange-traded contracts for the sale or purchase of a specific commodity at a future date. Futures trading is normally considered a highly speculative form of investing.

Good-Till-Cancelled Order (GTC) – An open order to buy or sell a security at a certain price. The order remains active until it is executed or cancelled. Some GTC orders have a set time limit (e.g., 120 days), at which point the brokerage firm automatically cancels them.

Government Bond – A bond issued and backed by a government that guarantees complete and timely payment of both principal and interest. U.S Government bonds, usually called "Treasuries," are regarded as the highest quality and safest type of bond investment. (See "Treasuries.")

Grantor – The person who establishes a trust. Also called a "Settlor" or "Trustor."

Gross Domestic Product (GDP) – The total output of a country's economy. It's a measure of the final output of goods and services produced within a nation, even if produced in factories owned by foreigners. It also includes the country's exports minus the imports. By analyzing the yearly scale of activity, one can measure the fluctuations in the economy.

Gross Income – Includes income from all sources such as salary, other wages, interest and dividends, pension payments, rent collected on properties owned, and profits on investments.

Gross National Product (GNP) – The total annual value of goods and services produced within a country or produced by its citizens in factories owned by them but located abroad. Goods produced in foreign-owned factories within the country are not included.

Gross – The value of an income, asset, or profit before taxes and other expenses are calculated.

Growth Fund – A mutual fund with capital appreciation as its primary goal. Growth fund managers look for companies that have significant earnings or revenue growth (as opposed to looking for companies that pay out dividends).

Growth Stock – A company that experiences rapid revenue growth and is expected to see similar growth in the long term. Growth stocks tend to pay low dividends and sell at relatively high prices compared with their earnings and book values.

Hedging – The act of taking an offsetting position in a second security in order to reduce the risk of adverse price movements in the first.

Histadrut – Israeli labor union.

Igrot Hov – Hebrew for "bonds."

Income Fund – A mutual fund designed to provide current income by investing in fixed-income securities, such as bonds.

Index – A measuring guide of market behavior that uses a few securities representative of a sector or of the market as a whole. Some of the most popular indexes are the Dow Jones Industrial Average, Standard & Poor's 500, the Russell 1000 and the NASDAQ 100.

Index Fund – A mutual fund designed to replicate the performance of an established index. Investing in an index fund provides portfolio diversification with relatively low management fees.

Inflation – A condition of rising prices for goods and services. This leads to the declining buying power of cash.

Initial Public Offering (IPO) – The first sale of a company's stock to the public. Owners of private companies in need of additional funding to continue or expand their businesses often decide to "go public" and allow investors to buy shares of their enterprises.

Interest – An amount of payment made to a lender by a borrower for the use of a certain sum of money for a specified period of time. For example, a bond buyer lends money to a corporation or to a government and receives an agreed-upon interest payment on a set payment schedule – usually semiannually. Another example would be that of a bank client who makes a deposit of cash which is used by the bank to issue loans and for other financial purposes. The bank pays the depositor an agreed-upon percentage of interest for the use of his money.

Intrinsic Value – The intrinsic value of a company is determined by analyzing its sales, earnings, and other balance sheet factors. It is what the market perceives as the actual value of a security, as opposed to its book value or market price. This term is also used to describe the value of an option when it is "in the money." (*Intrinsic value* denotes the value that can be obtained immediately upon exercising the option.)

Investment Banker – A financial professional or institution that helps a corporation or municipality issue securities. Investment bankers also advise corporations and other major clients in investment decisions, mergers and acquisitions, private placements, and corporate restructuring deals. Investment banks do not accept deposits from clients, nor do they provide loans (like traditional banks do).

IRA (Individual Retirement Account) – An American retirement plan that allows workers to put aside earned income and enjoy tax benefits. Holdings within an IRA may include mutual funds, CDs, stocks, bonds, and other securities. Within this retirement category one finds traditional IRAS, rollover IRAS, education IRAS (now called Coverdell Education Savings Accounts), and Roth IRAS.

Irrevocable Living Trust – A legal agreement to transfer funds from a donor to a beneficiary via a trust which can, if properly established, provide tax advantages both during the donor's lifetime and subsequent to his demise. The establishment of such a trust means that the grantor is making a completed gift and thus gives up ownership and control of the included assets.

Joint Tenants In Common (JTIC) – A form of ownership in which, upon the death of one tenant, the deceased's property is retained by his estate.

Joint Tenants With Right Of Survivorship (JTWROS) – A form of ownership in which, upon the death of one tenant, the deceased's property is retained by the surviving tenant.

Junk Bonds – Corporate bonds issued by companies with lower than investment-grade rating. These bonds, with a high risk of default, usually are offered at above average yields to attract buyers, and are sometimes called "high-yield bonds."

Keren Hishtalmut – Israeli tax-deferred educational fund. Generally, the employer and employee each put in a percentage of the employee's salary. The money can be withdrawn every six years and used as the recipient sees fit.

Keren Neemanut – Hebrew for "mutual fund."

LIBOR – The London Interbank Offered Rate Index is an average of the interest rates that major international banks charge each other to borrow U.S. dollars in the London market. This widely used benchmark often determines the interest rate you'll receive from your bank, or the mortgage rate you'll pay when you borrow dollars.

Liquidity – The degree of ease and rapidity with which an investment can be converted into cash.

Load – A one-time sales commission assessed by some mutual fund companies. The basic types of loads are front-end (charged when the fund is purchased) and back-end (paid when the fund is sold; for additional features, see "Back end sales charge.").

Long – The state of owning a security. One might say, "I am long 100 shares of ABC."

Management Fee – The money charged by mutual funds to cover operating expenses.

Margin Account – A type of brokerage account from which additional funds can be borrowed at a specified rate of interest, using existing positions as collateral for the loan. Margin accounts give investors leverage to buy, with a limited amount of money, an increased number of shares which may enable them to make a bigger profit – or loss.

Market Capitalization – The total value of a company's shares, as calculated by multiplying the entire quantity of shares outstanding by the current price per share.

Mas Hachnasa – The Israeli tax authority (equivalent to the U.S. Internal Revenue Service [IRS] or the U.K. Inland Revenue).

Maturity Date – The day on which the principal amount on a fixed-income investment must be paid by the issuer to the holder of the obligation.

Minayot – Hebrew for "stocks."

Monetary Policy – In order to promote national economic stability, both Israel and the United States rely on their monetary governing boards. The Bank of Israel and the U.S. Federal

Reserve Board both set policies to monitor and control the money supply and to modulate interest rates. These money-flow regulations can, and generally do, affect the direction of the stock market.

Money Market Fund – A dividend-producing open-ended mutual fund that rarely fluctuates in its basic one dollar-per-share price. This type of fund invests in commercial paper, banker acceptances, repurchase agreements, government securities, certificates of deposit, and other highly liquid, very conservative issues. U.S. brokerage firms may sweep free cash in a client's account into a money market fund in order to keep the client's free money working.

Mutual Fund – An investment management company through which investors pool their money in order to gain ownership of a wide selection of securities. Because mutual funds focus on different sectors of the market and provide a variety of selections within categories, they are useful tools in portfolio diversification.

National Association of Security Dealers (NASD) – A self-regulatory organization which monitors virtually all U.S. investment banking houses and investment firms.

NASDAQ – One of the major American stock trading markets. The NASDAQ (National Association of Securities Dealers Automated Quotations) is the largest U.S. electronic stock market, with an elaborate computerized network of broker-dealers who go to market makers to get the best prices for their clients. (See www.nasdaq.com.)

Net – The amount of salary, profit, or other assets remaining after taxes and all other expenses and charges have been deducted.

No-Load Fund – A mutual fund that allows investors to buy and sell shares without an added sales charge. As with other mutual funds, no-load funds charge ongoing management and various additional fees to cover expenses.

NYSE (New York Stock Exchange) – The NYSE is the trading venue of many large and established corporations. Sometimes referred to as the *Big Board*, this exchange is the oldest stock market in the United States, with a total global market value of $20 trillion. (See www.nyse.com.)

Odd Lot – Publicly traded stocks are usually bought and sold in round lots of 100 shares. Trades involving fewer than 100 shares are called "odd lots."

Oleh (**pl.** *Olim*) – Hebrew for "a person who has moved to Israel."

Option – A contract that an investor purchases that allows him to buy or sell a stock at a pre-set price during a specific period of time.

Original Issue Discount (OID) – The difference between a bond's par value and its lower offering price. OID bonds are issued at discounted prices from their face values. Investors don't receive full payment until a future time, although they may have to pay taxes on the phantom income of these holdings on a yearly basis.

Par Value – When referring to bonds, the face amount that will be repaid to the investor when the bond reaches maturity. When discussing common stock, it is the dollar value assigned to the stock when it is first issued. Stock companies use par for bookkeeping purposes rather than for calculating market value.

Patach – Free foreign currency accounts that *olim* are entitled to maintain in Israeli banks for 30 years after their dates of arrival.

Pink Sheets – A posting of lightly traded over-the-counter securities (usually very low priced stocks) that are handled by market makers.

Pitzuim – Israeli severance pay fund.

Point – A $1 increment in the value of a share of stock.

Portfolio – A selection of assets owned by an investor, mutual fund, or other investment group.

Portfolio Manager – The person in charge of making decisions and managing holdings for an individual, corporation, mutual fund, or other entity.

Preferred Stock – An equity that represents ownership in a corporation. Preferred stock pays fixed dividends and has asset preference over common stock in the case of bankruptcy. Shares usually do not come with voting rights.

Premium – The market price of an option. "Premium" also refers to a price paid for a security that is over its stated value. The term "premium" also is used to refer to the amount paid for insurance.

Price/Earnings Ratio (P/E Ratio) – Calculated by taking the current share price and dividing it by the annual earnings per share. Speculative stocks often sell at high P/ES (when the share price is overvalued with relation to low corporate earnings) or sometimes at very low P/ES (if there is concern that the company may be unable to sustain its earnings).

Prime Rate – The interest rate that commercial banks charge their best, most credit-worthy customers.

Principal – A sum of money; an amount of money that is deposited, borrowed, or invested. When referring to a bond, it is the face value, payable at maturity.

Probate – A court proceeding in which the deceased's will is examined, validated as genuine, and then executed. During the probate process, which can last months or years, the executor must satisfactorily carry out the wishes of the deceased and dispose of and account for the assets. Probate matters are open to public examination.

Prospectus – A legal document that discloses investment objectives, pertinent details, and financial data of an issuer, such as a corporation or mutual fund. Public companies are required to make these reports available to investors.

Proxy – A person designated to act on behalf of another, or a document allowing this. With regard to the stock market, a shareholder's written authorization (called a "proxy") can be mailed in to the company stating how he wishes to vote at an upcoming shareholder meeting. The designated recipient of the proxy casts the vote according to the shareholder's wishes.

Put – An option contract that allows the buyer of the Put to sell a specified number of shares of a stock at a certain price within a specified time period. If the stock drops in price he can sell the shares at the agreed upon higher price to the Put writer who wrote (sold) the option.

Rating – The safety level of a bond. A number of firms rank companies and municipalities in accordance with their abilities to repay bond obligations and keep up with interest payments. Ratings range from AAA or Aaa (safest) to C or D (unsafe).

Real Estate Investment Trust (REIT) – A publicly traded company that invests in such facilities as residential buildings, industrial complexes, and shopping malls. In addition to dealing in commercial properties, some REITs also focus on mortgage investments.

Real Return – The return on an investment after taking inflation into account.

Reinvestment – A plan in which many corporations and mutual funds allow shareholders the opportunity to have their dividend income used to buy additional shares rather than be distributed to them.

Resistance Level – In technical analysis, a high area in a stock's trading range. Some investors believe this is a good time to sell.

Reverse Stock Split – A method used to decrease the number of shares outstanding, thus raising the per share price. For example, during a one-for-four reverse split, 100 shares of XYZ selling for $1 per share would be exchanged for 25 shares valued at $4 per share. The total value of $100 would remain constant. So too would the percentage of corporate ownership.

Rollover – A movement of assets from a qualified retirement plan into an IRA or other qualified plan. The receiving IRA plan can be called an "IRA Rollover."

Roth IRA – Another U.S. type of individual retirement account that allows workers to set aside funds. Although similar to the traditional IRA in tax-deferred growth, contributions are not tax deductible, and retirement distributions are generally not subject to U.S. taxation.

S&P 500 (Standard and Poor's 500) – A well-known index listing 500 of the leading companies on the NYSE, as well as some AMEX and NASDAQ stocks.

Secondary Market – A market where previously issued securities are traded. Brokerage firm representatives go to the secondary markets to help negotiate trades for investors wanting to buy or sell securities.

Securities Investor Protection Corporation (SIPC) – A nonprofit corporation created by Congress to protect clients of a brokerage firm, should it be forced into bankruptcy. All U.S. brokers, dealers, and members of national securities exchanges, and most NASD members are members of the SIPC. The SIPC provides up to $500,000 coverage per customer for the cash and securities held by these firms. Many firms carry additional insurance to protect the larger accounts. (See www.sipc.org.)

Selling Short – Selling a security that one does not own. If a person believes a stock price will fall, he can have his broker borrow shares on his behalf and then sell them. When the price drops, he can ask the broker to buy back and return the shares and "close out the position." The difference in price (minus expenses) is the investor's profit. If the price goes up, however, he incurs a loss as the shares must still be bought back and returned.

Settlement Date – The date by which an executed transaction must be paid for or delivered. In the United States, this is usually three business days after the trade was executed (T+3), or one business day after the trade date for listed options and government securities. Trades on the Tel Aviv Stock Exchange settle in one business day.

Settlor – The person who establishes a trust. Also, a "Grantor" or "Trustor."

Share – A unit of ownership. Corporations and mutual funds sell ownership in their companies in the form of shares.

Short Selling – See "Selling Short."

Social Security – A U.S. government program that pays benefits to retirees and disabled persons. It also provides certain survivor benefits to qualified family members.

Stagflation – A slowdown in the economy, high unemployment, and a rise in prices.

Statement – An individual's monthly record of account activity with his brokerage firm or bank. This is usually the best source of information about one's account and its historical performance. Clients should hold on to these along with other financial records.

Stock Certificate – A certificate of ownership of a company's stock. It includes the company's name, the holder's name, the number of shares represented by the certificate, an identification number, whether the stock is common or preferred, and the stock's par value.

Stock Split – Dividing the number of shares without changing the total value. When corporate shares are high in price, the directors may choose to split the shares 2-for-1 or 3-for-2, or any similar combination. The actual value of the shareholders' ownership remains the same. The splitting of shares and subsequent lowering of the share price leads to wider trading and more interest in the company, which could lead to an overall increase in the stock value.

Street Name – Securities that are held by a brokerage firm but still belong to an individual and are listed on that client's statement. When a client wishes to sell the holding, he simply calls in his order. It is not necessary for him to properly endorse and return a certificate to the broker before settlement date, because the brokerage firm holds the certificate in street name.

Style Drift – A deviation in a mutual fund manager's expected investment pattern.

Support Level – In technical analysis, the bottom of a stock's trading range. Some investors feel this is a sign that it is time to buy.

Technical Analysis – Followers of this method try to guess how traders will think about and react to news events. These "technicians" monitor indexes and trading volume and rely heavily on charts and graphs.

Teudat Zehut – An Israeli identification card.

Tosefet Yoker – A salary adjustment agreement developed by the *Histadrut* that raises salaries based on a calculation that resembles the Consumer Price Index (CPI).

Treasuries of the U.S. Government – Negotiable and liquid debt obligations issued by the American government in varying amounts and maturities. These investments are secured by the government's full faith and credit (that is, they are backed by the government's ability to raise taxes, if necessary, to cover these debts). Treasuries fall into three basic categories: Treasury bills, treasury notes, and treasury bonds.

Trust – A legal creation to specify how ownership of assets can be transferred to another person or organization for the benefit of a third party or the trustor.

Trustee – The person or entity, as named by the trustor, in charge of administrating assets in a trust.

Trustor – The person who establishes a trust. Also, a "Settlor" or "Grantor."

12b-1 Asset-Based Fees – Named after an SEC rule, this fee is collected by mutual fund companies for promotion, sales, and other marketing activities.

Uniform Gifts To Minors Act (UGMA) – A regulation that permits gifts of money and securities to be made to minors. An adult acts as custodian for such an account until the child reaches legal adulthood.

Unit Investment Trust (UIT) – A registered investment company that buys and holds a relatively fixed portfolio of stocks, bonds, or other securities for a predetermined amount of time.

Investors can buy units of the trust and share in ongoing interest payments, as well as in the principal when the trust is liquidated. Note that in England, "unit trust" is often the term used for what would be called a "mutual fund" in America.

Warrant – This is a certificate issued by the company that allows the holder to purchase shares at a specific price during a predetermined time period.

Wash Sale – Purchase and sale of the same security either simultaneously or within a 30-day period of time for the purpose of accruing tax benefits. Sales taking place within 30 days of a parallel purchase do not qualify for capital losses under U.S. tax laws.

Will – A legal declaration assigning responsibility and giving direction on how to dispose of one's assets after death.

Yield – The annual percentage return on an investment. If basing the calculation on a percentage of a bond selling at 100, it is referred to as the coupon rate. If based on a higher or lower bond trading price it is called a current yield.

Zero-Coupon Bond – A bond, sold at a very deep discount, that grows at a fixed rate with interest compounded until the bond is worth its full face value at maturity. There are no periodic interest payments from this type of investment, and taxes may be due yearly, depending on the bond, who holds it, and in what type of account the bond is kept.

Index

www.ingramcontent.com/pod-product-compliance
Lightning Source LLC
Chambersburg PA
CBHW021045090426
42738CB00006B/185